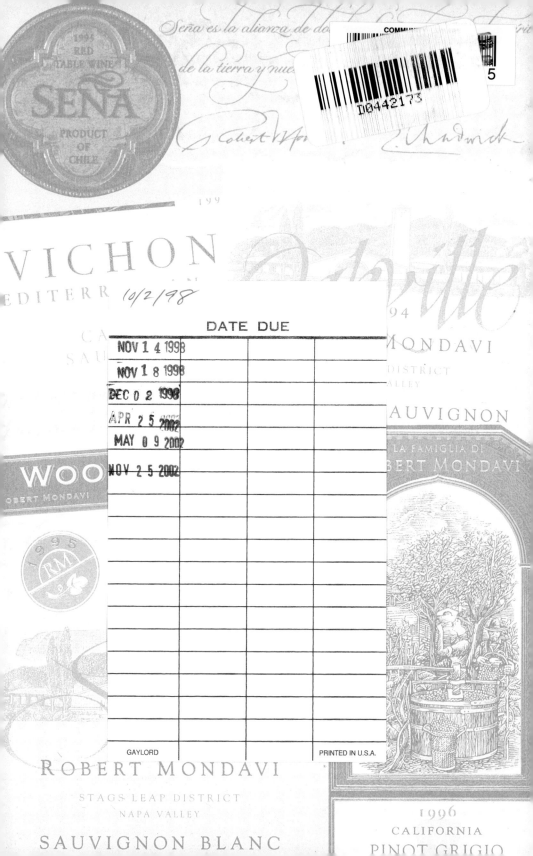

VICHON
EDITERR 10/2/98

DATE DUE

NOV 1 4 1998		
NOV 1 8 1998		
DEC 0 2 1998		
APR 2 5 2002		
MAY 0 9 2002		
NOV 2 5 2002		
GAYLORD		PRINTED IN U.S.A.

Harvests of Joy

Robert Mondavi

WITH PAUL CHUTKOW

Harvests of Joy

MY PASSION FOR EXCELLENCE

Harcourt Brace & Company

New York   San Diego   London

Requests for permission to make copies of any part of the work
should be mailed to: Permissions Department,
Harcourt Brace & Company, 6277 Sea Harbor Drive,
Orlando, Florida 32887-6777.

Library of Congress Cataloging-in-Publication Data
Mondavi, Robert, 1913–
Harvests of joy: my passion for excellence/Robert Mondavi
with Paul Chutkow. — 1st ed.
p.   cm.
Includes index.
ISBN 0-15-100346-7
1. Mondavi, Robert, 1913–   . 2. Robert Mondavi
Winery — History. 3. Vintners — United States — Biography.
I. Chutkow, Paul. II. Title.
TP547.M66A3   1998
641.2′2′092 — dc21   98-19170
[B]

Designed by Lydia D'moch
Printed in the United States of America
First edition
A B C D E

Contents

CONTENTS

Wine is Life.

— PETRONIUS

PART ONE

The Roots

CHAPTER 1

Heart and Soul

AT THE AGE of fifty-two, I should have been a happy man.

On the surface, life was good. The year was 1965, and America was prospering. I had a lovely, devoted wife, three delightful children—Michael, Marcia, and Tim—and we lived in what I knew was one of the most idyllic spots on the planet, the Napa Valley. For twenty-three years my brother, Peter, and I had been running a small family business, the Charles Krug Winery, and we were doing pretty well. While my wife Marge and I had to be very careful about what we spent, we were secure enough to live comfortably and provide for our children.

I also adored my work. For some people in the Napa Valley, wine was just a business, an agreeable way to earn a living. Not for me. Wine for me had always been something much larger and it still is. Wine to me is passion. It's family and friends. It's warmth of heart and generosity of spirit.

Wine is art. It's culture. It's the essence of civilization and the Art of Living. Wine has been with us for seven thousand years, almost since the dawn of civilization, and for centuries poets, painters, musicians, and philosophers have sung its praises. Even the Bible applauds its virtues. And wine to me is even more. When I pour a glass of truly fine wine, when I hold it up to the light and admire its color, when I raise it to my nose and savor its bouquet and essence, I know that wine is, above all else, a blessing, a gift of nature, a joy as pure and elemental as the soil and vines and sunshine from which it springs. "Wine is Life," Petronius said two thousand years ago, and I know exactly what he meant.

For most men and women, what I had would have been the makings of a wonderful, contented life. But not for me. In truth, I was feeling stifled at Krug. Like so many people who reach a critical juncture in their lives and careers, I felt I was not making the most of my business savvy and creativity. I was working hard, as always, but my enthusiasm was on the wane. Throughout the 1950s and early 1960s, we had been making good table wines at Krug. We were considered to be among the "Big Five" of the Napa Valley, along with Beaulieu Vineyard, Inglenook, Louis Martini, and Beringer Brothers. We had built our reputation on the strength of our white wines, and our cabernet sauvignon was considered among the best in the valley. Still, I felt our ambitions were just too tame. We in California had enormous potential; I knew we could become one of the great wine-producing regions of the world. But the American wine industry was still in its infancy, and no one seemed to have the knowledge, the vision, or the guts to reach for the gold, to make wines that could stand proudly next to the very best from France, Italy, Germany, and Spain.

I wanted to move Krug in a bold new direction. In 1962 I had traveled around Europe for the first time, visiting many of the great wine-producing regions of the world to see how they made their wines. In Bordeaux, Burgundy, Tuscany, and the Moselle region of Germany, I explored some of the most prestigious wineries in the world. I toured their vineyards and cellars, examined their equipment, talked with their wine makers, and, of course, tasted their wines. Above all, in these vineyards and cellars and tasting rooms, I imbibed the spirit, the passion, and the commitment that inspired the creation of truly great wines.

Much of what I saw was a revelation. At the great châteaus, the way of growing grapes and making wine was far different from what we had been doing for generations in California. While we had one basic approach for our red wines and another for our whites, their approach was far more subtle and sophisticated. They treated each variety of grape differently, and they had a distinct method and style for each type of wine they made. We made wines in bulk, using huge tanks; they kept their output small to maximize quality, and they aged their wines in small oak barrels to create gentleness, subtlety, and complex layers of flavor. The differences ran much deeper than method and equipment. We were a big, young country, oriented toward mass production and scientific research, and in our wine making we emphasized crop yields, sugar levels, and profit margins. The great European wineries, with centuries of tradition and craft behind them, put their emphasis on less tangible qualities such as style, character, and bouquet. To my mind, the contrast was stark: we were treating wine as a business; the great European châteaus were treating wine as high art.

This realization stirred something deep inside me, but I did not understand what until one day when Marge and I had lunch at La Pyramide, one of the great restaurants of France and the world. I still remember that day vividly. I had a meeting that morning in Lyons with a potential business associate, and Marge and I had a huge breakfast with him. Talking, discussing business, we lingered at the table until about eleven o'clock. "My god," I thought, "here we're going to have lunch in one of the best restaurants in the world, one with three stars in the *Michelin Guide*, and I'm already stuffed! What am I going to do?"

An hour and a half later, we drove into Vienne, a little village outside Lyons, and found our way to La Pyramide. The setting and atmosphere of the restaurant were tasteful and elegant, without being pretentious, and we sat down to a meal that was absolutely unbelievable. Each and every dish we tried was heavenly and distinctive, with flavors I had never tasted before. Nothing was heavy or too filling, and there were none of those rich cream or butter sauces you found in many French restaurants in those days. Every forkful was light and pure in the mouth; in every bite we could taste the passion and the artistry of the chef.

What really dazzled me was how each dish complemented and enhanced the other, the way the sounds of different instruments meld into a symphony. The wines we tasted during the meal were not big and bold like ours in California; they were gentle and complex, and they artfully accentuated the many sensations and feelings that the cuisine inspired. I'd go so far as to say that the food and the wine transported us into a world of gentleness and balance, of grace and harmony. La Pyramide to me epitomized the artistry and aesthetics we had been discovering all across Europe, and it inspired in me both a vision and a vow:

"This is the kind of wine I want to create," I told Marge. "Wines that have grace and style, harmony and balance."

During my travels in Europe, I was impressed with something else: an opportunity. I saw great extremes in wine making in Europe. The First Growth Bordeaux châteaus—Château Mouton-Rothschild, Château Lafite, Château Margaux, Château Haut-Brion, and Château Pétrus—made marvelous wine, subtle and complex, with flavors that were always crisp and clean. And I discovered the reason: these top châteaus were all using only new French oak barrels. Almost everyone else was producing wine the exact same way their forefathers had, and the results were not, to my taste, exceptional. I found many supposedly fine wines that proved to have off characters and bacterial defects. And I saw why: they were making their wine in oak barrels that were used, not new. This was one reason for those sorts of defects and "spent" flavors. To my critical eye, many of the European producers seemed to be asleep, content with the status quo; and so, frankly, I saw an opening. I felt certain that we in the Napa Valley could do just as well or better! It would take time, patience, money, and a full-blown education in how to make wine the way the great Bordeaux châteaus did, but I felt sure we could succeed. And what an exciting challenge it would be!

I left Europe elated. Some of the wines I had tasted there were exceptional, but I believed that we in California could do just as well and, in time, even better. Our soil, climate, and rootstocks were just as good as what I saw in Europe and in many ways better. We also had the right varieties of grapes to make great wine: cabernet, pinot noir, chardonnay, and sauvignon blanc. True, we did not have the Europeans' know-how or their craft and tradition. But I felt absolutely certain that we could learn quickly and make significant leaps in the quality of our wines. Over the following days, a great business and creative venture took shape before my eyes: I wanted to take American technology, management techniques, and marketing savvy and fuse them together with Old World tradition and elegance in the art of making fine wine. We would need passion, conviction, and courage, along with a willingness to invest in the necessary research, development, and new equipment. But with this combination, I felt confident that Napa Valley and California could ultimately create wines that would stand shoulder to shoulder with the great wines in the world.

I returned to the Napa Valley energized and ready to go. I wanted Krug to take up the challenge, jump in with both feet. I wanted us to shed our inhibitions, our complacency, our contentment with the status quo. I wanted my family and our company to commit ourselves to a true quest for excellence in our vineyards, in our wine making, and in our marketing and sales. The Napa Valley, in my view, was ready for just this sort of challenge. We were, in fact, a sleepy little farm community, with no sophistication, little economic vitality, and no fine restaurants. Our wine industry was by no means vibrant, either. At the time, we had only about twenty wineries in the whole valley, and only a half dozen were making quality wine. The situation around the state was not much better. The bulk of production in California at that time was jug wine, and the largest producers were Italian Swiss Colony in Asti, Roma Wine Company in Lodi and Fresno, and Ernest and Julio Gallo, located farther south in the Central Valley. But to me the potential was clear. We had magnificent climate and vineyards, a beautiful landscape, and proximity to cosmopolitan San Francisco. I was sure that we had what it took to become one of the great wine-producing regions of the world—provided someone would take the lead. I wanted that someone to be Krug.

I pushed my ideas hard inside Krug and with my family, and I did so in my usual ebullient, single-minded way. But the harder I pushed, the more resistance I encountered, especially after my father passed away. My father had always been open to my suggestions. To most of my family, what I was pushing sounded risky and pointless. We already had a respected business, and our extended family lived comfortably on the beautiful, historic grounds of the Krug Winery. So why rock the boat? Why tamper with our modest but stable success?

So I was stymied. We were a family business; I could not make decisions on my own. In our corporation, established in 1946, my parents controlled 40 percent of the stock. My brother, Peter, and I each had 20 percent, and my sisters, Helen and Mary, had the remaining 20 percent. When my father died in 1959, he left control of the corporation in the hands of my mother, who had no experience in business. We were a comfortable family business, but I felt we needed a great dream, a defining mission, a higher calling. I made my case again and again, but no one in the family, apart from Marge and my children, shared my larger vision. So in the months and years that followed, my frustrations only deepened.

I gave my younger brother, Peter, the most heat. Ever since childhood, our temperaments and ambitions had been very different, but we had followed parallel paths. In high school I played football, then he played football. I went to Stanford, then he went to Stanford. After graduation, I spent part of my summer vacation being tutored in wine making by Professor Vic Enriques of U.C. Berkeley. Peter later studied wine making at U.C. Berkeley. Then I did an apprenticeship in wine making in the Napa Valley; Peter did an apprenticeship at a winery down in California's Central Valley. In 1943, when I talked my father into buying the Charles Krug Winery, Dad had only one condition: that Peter and I run the business together. We agreed. Peter was serving in the U.S. Army, at the height of World War II, and so I set up all the wine-making operations at Krug. After the war, I took charge of marketing and sales and turned over the wine making to Peter. In the years that followed, we often clashed about wine making and other business matters, but whenever we failed to sort things through, my father would always step in and settle the dispute. After he died in 1959, we held an even keel for a while. But when I returned from Europe in 1962 and urged Peter to make dramatic changes to upgrade the quality of our wines, he really got his back up. I guess Peter felt I was encroaching on his turf. For my part, I felt Peter just did not share my ambition to commit Krug to the challenge and demands of making world-class wines. Peter, of course, might dispute that, but then again we always seemed to disagree and see things from very different perspectives. We still do!

At heart, I think it was a question of temperament. Peter was quiet, gentle, and self-effacing, a family man who loved to fish and adored spending time with his wife and children. When he was a small boy, the family affectionately nick-named him Babe, and more than forty years later everyone in the family still called him that. By contrast, I was always hard driving and ambitious, and no one ever accused me of being quiet or self-effacing. I never had enough time to fish; I was always too busy thinking of ways to improve our wines and grow our company. My business goals were clear and far-reaching: I wanted Krug to pioneer a whole new ap-proach to wine making in America. Through our work and that of like-minded wineries, I dreamed of putting the whole Napa Valley onto the map of world-class wines, right beside Bordeaux, Burgundy, and Tuscany. Peter, I imagine, thought I was an ego out of control.

My vision for the Napa Valley did turn out to be prophetic, of course, but Destiny did not play out quite as I had anticipated.

Looking back now, I guess the turning point came the year after I returned from Europe, on a fall afternoon when we were busy harvesting at Krug. In the mail that day, in an envelope with fancy lettering and a golden seal, I received a startling invitation. President John F. Kennedy was inviting me and Marge to attend a state dinner at the White House. The dinner was to honor the prime minister of Italy, and I was asked to attend as part of a group of prominent Italian Americans. I took the invitation as a tremendous honor and a golden opportunity for the Charles Krug Winery. President Kennedy and Jackie apparently wanted to show the Italian leader that our young country was starting to make some pretty good wines.

Flattered though we were, Marge and I were very nervous. After all, we came from what was then a small, struggling farm community. We had no wealth and next to no big-city sophistication. We were just small-town people running a small family business. So Marge and I were worried: How in the world would we fare at the Kennedy White House, with the charismatic president and his famous wife, surrounded by all the glamour of Camelot? Marge also had a more specific worry: What in the dickens should she wear to a White House dinner? What dress? What shoes? What bag? What jewelry? What coat?

Marge was particularly worried about a winter coat. She had a coat that was fine for the mild, damp winters in St. Helena, but it was not stylish, nothing suitable to meet a first lady who was always elegantly outfitted by the finest designers in Paris. In search of a solution, Marge went to the modest shops in St. Helena and the town of Napa, but she found nothing to her liking. So one day I took off from work and we drove into San Francisco to shop in the big department stores and fashionable boutiques around Union Square.

We both knew, though, that we had to be careful. The Charles Krug Winery was by no means booming and we had three children to feed, clothe, and put through school. As I recall, at that time I was earning only about $24,000 a year; hardly a princely sum. So after a thorough review of what we could afford, I had budgeted up to $1,500 for a coat for Marge. Even that was a stretch, but how many times in your life do you get invited to the White House? We went to I. Magnin and Marge tried on several different coats. None really caught her fancy and none seemed suitable for a dinner at the White House. Then the saleslady brought out something special: a mink coat. Mink! And it was gorgeous. Right away we both knew it would look perfect on Marge and it was just the thing to wear to the Kennedy White House. Alas, we also knew it would be way too expensive for our modest means. Prudence told us to stop right there and run out of the store. On a lark, though, Marge decided to try on the coat, just to see how she'd feel wrapped in mink. Well, the coat fit perfectly and Marge looked smashing. She loved the way it made her look and feel. Still, the price tag was a staggering $5,000, way beyond our means, and that was that. We left I. Magnin thinking, "Oh well, maybe one day, maybe one day . . ."

A few weeks later, though, Marge still had not found a coat, and when we went back to I. Magnin we found that same mink coat on sale for only $2,500. Now we faced a terrible temptation. Splurge? Or be prudent? Even on sale, the coat was a difficult stretch for us. And in a business where one bad crop or one bad storm can leave you bankrupt, who goes around buying mink coats? No one in my family, that was for sure. Still, we had to look our best on this proud occasion, and surely no one in the Mondavi family would want us to look like bumpkins next to the president and first lady, would they?

So, after long, agonizing deliberation, Marge and I made a pact. We would cut back on all nonessential spending over the next year. We would watch every nickel and dime, give up restaurants and movies, and even cut back on our food budget. This was a once-in-a-lifetime occasion, dinner at the White House. So Marge and I decided to cast prudence to the winds and buy that beautiful mink coat. Alas, this soon proved to be a fateful decision, for reasons I was too blind to foresee.

When he heard about that mink, my brother, Peter, couldn't understand it. I think he already believed I had developed an irresponsible taste for the high life — who, after all, needed to have lunch at La Pyramide? — and in his eyes the mink was just further proof of my lavish, irresponsible ways. I think his wife, Blanche, was probably annoyed as well. I imagine she was thinking, "Why does Marge get a mink and not me? For that matter, why are *they* going to the White House and not us?" There was no open conflict at that time, but I believe that mink coat ignited what proved to be a long, slow-burning fuse.

For all that, we never did get to go to the Kennedy White House for our taste of Camelot. The president was assassinated on November 22, 1963, before the dinner was to take place. The visit of the Italian premier was later rescheduled and it became President Lyndon Johnson's first state dinner; we were on hand at the White House for what turned out to be a rather subdued but elegant affair.

That fuse kept burning though, through the next two years of simmering tensions and sometimes open conflict. Then one day in November 1965, all the Mondavis assembled at one of our big family gatherings at the winery for what was supposed to be a happy, festive occasion. It turned out to be anything but. I don't remember exactly how it started, but at some point, Peter and I started to squabble. Tempers flared and Peter accused me of spending too much company money on travel and promotion. Then he really lost his temper and accused me of taking money from the winery. How else could I afford to buy that mink coat? In essence, I felt my own brother was accusing me of being a thief and a swindler.

"Say that again and I'll hit you," I warned him.

He said it again.

Then I gave him a third chance: "Take it back."

"No."

So I smacked him, hard. Twice.

Growing up, Peter and I rarely fought. I do recall going at it once as teenagers, in one of our bedrooms, and we really tore the place up. But after that, never. So here we were, two men in our early fifties, acting like kids in a school yard—with terrible consequences. When it was all over, there were no apologies and no handshake. Quite the contrary. Like a

cleaver, the fight split our family in two, and there was no re-
pairing the damage. It broke my mother's heart, divided our
sisters, and left our children hurt and confused. The Mondavis, up to then a close-knit Italian family, were now
deeply — and very publicly — split.

The fight and its aftermath soon became notorious
across the Napa Valley and throughout the American wine
industry. Some evil-tongued gossips spoke of it as a modern-
day version of Cain and Abel. My father might have been
able to impose a peace in the family, but by then he had
been dead for several years and it was just too much for my
mother to handle. Lawyers and mediators were brought in.

One of those mediators was Joe Alioto, a prominent San
Francisco attorney who would later become the city's mayor.
At this stage, Joe had already been on our board for a year or
two and had become a trusted adviser to the family. Later, he
would serve as Peter's chief lawyer when Peter and I squared
off in court. Immediately after the fight, it was Joe who came
in to mediate, along with Fred Ferroggiaro, chairman of the
Finance Committee of the Bank of America and also a member of our board of directors. After the family met, it was Fred
who delivered the verdict: I was to be put on six months' paid
leave. Then Joe Alioto took me aside. This was a turbulent,
confusing moment in my life, and I remember it to this day.
We were walking under the orange trees at Krug, between
my mother's house and my house, and Alioto and I had a
heart-to-heart chat. He said something I'll never forget:

"Bob, let me give you a piece of advice. As a friend. Hire the smartest attorney you can, so that *we* don't steal *you* blind." Needless to say, I followed his advice.

That leave was supposed to be a cooling-off period, for all sides, but the attempt proved futile. My son Michael was about to graduate from Santa Clara University, and the family and its advisers for some reason—I think it was probably because Peter wanted to keep Krug for his own children—decided to bar Michael from working at Krug. To me, that just added insult to injury. So the rift deepened. I held on to my Krug stock, though, and Peter and I later headed into an ugly and very costly legal battle, one that would take years to settle. It was a gruesome experience, and even now, more than thirty years later, though Peter and I have managed to reconcile, some of those wounds have yet to heal.

Out of our terrible fight, though, came my liberation. Once I was put on leave at Krug, I was forced to rethink my entire direction in life. In 1965, at the age of fifty-two, I was at a decisive crossroads and I knew it. If I was ever going to make a dramatic change in my life, if I was ever going to summon the courage to follow my own star, now was the time to do it. That winter I took Marge to Hawaii so that we could rest and reflect on what to do next. When we returned home to our house on the grounds at Krug, I continued to ponder. I'd take a card table and chair and set them up out in the vineyards. To think, to reassess, and to evaluate my options.

What I needed now was a fresh start, an exciting new challenge. But what? And where? Despite my love of the wine business, all the upheavals at Krug had left me dispirited, and I wanted to consider fresh options. I still had significant financial obligations; Michael, I knew, could find work, but Marcia and Tim were still in school and that was costly. So I wanted to find a direction that would be both prudent and stimulating, not just for tomorrow and the day after, but for the rest of my life. Still, the question remained: What to do? What would ignite my passion and my imagination and creative energies? To what great challenge could I dedicate myself now, sweat and blood, heart and soul?

During my reflections, I considered several different businesses. But my heart kept leading me back to wine. It was my life, it was my way of life, and it had been that ever since I was a boy. When my parents, Rosa and Cesare Mondavi, came here as immigrants from Italy at the start of the century, they were dirt poor, with next to no education. But they brought with them warmth and optimism, strength of character, and a rock-solid belief in both family and the value of hard work. When I was growing up, the center of our existence was always the kitchen. Mother would work at the kitchen table, making pasta or polenta from scratch, and my brother and sisters and I would gather round her and talk and laugh and sing songs and help in any way we could. Meals were a sacred time for us, the gathering of the family, and wine always enjoyed a prominent place on our table.

Throughout my childhood, good food and festive meals were not something we went out to restaurants for; they were the bedrock of our daily lives at home. They were — and they remain — the very heart and soul of our family and the Italian way of life.

So in my years at Krug, when I traveled around America doing promotion and sales, I was not just selling wine. I was a man on a mission, a man with a calling. When I talked wine, I was not peddling my wares — I was preaching the gospel. And I was trying to plant deep into the soil of our young country the same values, traditions, and daily pleasures that my mother and father had brought with them from the hills and valleys of central Italy: good food, good wine, and love of family.

The more I pondered this, at my card table out in the vineyards, the more clearly a new path began to emerge. In Europe three years before, I had formulated a vision and a vow: to do whatever it took to make great wines and to put the Napa Valley on the map right alongside the great wine-making centers of Europe. I had envisioned doing all this via Krug, but it was not to be. So what if I went out on my own? If I wanted to start a winery from scratch, with the sole intention of making world-class wines, what would it take?

I'd need capital. I'd need prime vineyard land. I'd need to build my own winery. I'd need to enlist experts in the arts of growing grapes and making fine wine the European way. Everything we did would have to be of the absolute highest quality, even if it cost top dollar. After three decades in the wine business, I knew a great deal, but I also knew I had much more to learn. To succeed would demand hard work and team effort in the vineyards, in the cellars, and in sales and marketing. The performance of each person would be crucial to our overall success. One common goal and one common ethic would have to unite us: the unwavering quest for excellence.

I also had to plan this business for the long term. There was just no way we could dramatically improve the quality of our wines overnight; the process would take years, perhaps even a generation or more. This was not a venture for anyone looking for a quick return on capital or for anyone who didn't understand how capricious the weather could be — or how damaging one frost could be for an entire grape crop. With so much to build and to learn, mistakes would be inevitable; this was not an adventure for the faint of heart. I'd have to choose my partners wisely, and I'd have to keep looking ahead, five years, ten years, even twenty and beyond.

I knew the risks were incalculable; we were entering uncharted waters. No winery in California had ever launched a full-blown campaign to make world-class wines, at least not successfully. In terms of image, the Napa Valley did not give us much to build on, either. St. Helena, where Krug was located, was a delightful little town and in many ways typified the entire valley: it was quintessential small-town

America. But it was hardly the obvious platform for a national marketing campaign or the birth of a brand name.

I faced another formidable obstacle: there was simply no significant market in America for fine wine at that time. While Italian families like ours ate and drank as our parents and ancestors had for centuries, we were the exception. For the vast majority, America was still a steak, potatoes, and beer kind of country. To millions of consumers, cheese meant Velveeta and bread meant Wonder or Roman Meal. In big-city restaurants, where there was a demand for quality and elegance, fine wine meant French, Italian, or German; in most of America's finest restaurants you could not even find one California wine on the wine list. As a result, the prevailing wisdom in the Napa Valley back in 1966 was that if you wanted to make truly fine wines to compete with the French and Italians in that very narrow niche in the marketplace, good luck. In fact, while Marge and my children were supportive of my ambitions, most of the friends I consulted believed that creating a winery to make truly fine wines would be a one-way ticket to financial disaster. "Start a new winery from scratch?" some of my friends said, shaking their heads. "Bob, be serious." A few even said, or intimated, "Swallow your pride, Bob. Go back to Krug."

But I was not about to back down, and as I pondered moving forward, I clung to my conviction. I was convinced that we could create a substantial market in America for fine wines. The key was education. We had to teach people how to appreciate fine food and wine and the crafts and artistry behind them. In our home, with Marge and the kids, and in the homes of our Italian friends, we didn't eat fried chicken and hamburgers. We ate pasta made from scratch and fresh greens from our gardens. Our mothers and wives cooked with olive oil, baked their own bread and rolls, made their own soups and preserves. We didn't grow up eating Velveeta; we ate *parmigiano*, pecorino, and Gorgonzola. When I was a boy, everyone who came to our house loved my mother's cooking; I dreamed of inviting all of America into her kitchen to see her cook, taste her food, and sample some fine Italian wines. With one Sunday lunch at her house, I felt sure we could convert the entire country to the joys of fine food and wine!

With this conviction, and with a deep reservoir of confidence in myself and my family, I finally made the leap of faith. I decided to create a winery with several interlocking layers of ambition. One, to make great world-class wines. Two, to combine European craft and tradition with the latest in American technology and management and marketing know-how. Three, I wanted the winery to be stunningly beautiful, so that it would become a magnet for tourists and wine lovers from all over the globe. Four, every day we would invite visitors in to taste our wines, and via tours and educational events, we would help them learn how to appreciate fine food and wine. Maybe there was no market yet for fine wine in America, but so what? I was determined to create the market we needed, even if we had to do it one visitor at a time! I knew that if we made an outstanding wine, the market would follow.

Everyone thought I was crazy, of course. As soon as word spread of my plan to build my own winery—the first new winery in the Napa Valley since the late 1930s—I began to get skeptical looks and comments. Start a new winery? Make wine that would stand beside the greatest wines in the world? Set out to transform the eating and drinking habits of an entire nation? What arrogance! What folly! Bob Mondavi has a screw loose. He's spent too much time with his head in his barrels.

I could hear the guffaws up and down the Napa Valley, but I paid no attention; I had too much to prove and too much to do. Let others be naysayers, let them shy away from risk and seek shelter in the status quo. I knew I was embarking on a great adventure and a colossal gamble, loaded with risks and obstacles. But I was not going to retreat or stay on the sidelines. I was going to roll up my sleeves and plunge in. I might fail, but it would not be for fear of trying. And this was for sure: I would not one day go to my grave wondering what I might have achieved with my life if only I had had the courage to follow my passions and reach for the stars.

Making bold decisions can be so energizing. Once I decided to set out on my own, I felt totally reborn. I had left an unhappy, confining situation at Krug and now I felt free. Now I had a clearly charted direction to follow and a path to blaze. Now I would rise or fall on the strength of my own talents, my own resources, my own gumption and wit. I was like a little kid again, bursting with energy, ready to climb the mountain, conquer the world, go for the gold. Yes, at the unlikely age of fifty-two, the great adventure of my life had finally begun.

But could I really pull it off?

CHAPTER TWO

A Passion
for Perfection

I FEEL BLESSED.

So many men and women search and search but never find their passion, their calling, the sense of mission that would ignite their hearts and fill their lives with meaning and joy. And so many men and women dream of one day starting their own business, but they lack the necessary skills and resources, and they lack a guiding vision of how to create a business and make it successful.

I'm among the lucky ones. I discovered my passion early in life, and then I spent three decades pursuing it, learning the intricacies of wine making and business. So when I finally decided to go out on my own, I had the necessary skills and I knew where to find financial backing. But what about that guiding vision of how to succeed in business? Here, too, I was lucky. When I decided to create the Robert Mondavi Winery, I was able to draw inspiration and guidance from two people near and dear to me: Rosa and Cesare Mondavi.

My parents were amazing. And so is the story of how they came to America. My father and mother both came from families of poor Italian peasants. And they grew up in farmhouses just a few hillsides apart. For several generations, their families had lived and worked the land in a part of Italy that few Americans know: the province of Le Marche, a region of farming and mining deep in the interior of Italy. When you come from as far away as California, the province of Le Marche looks and feels like the middle of nowhere. It's a long drive east of Florence and a long drive south of Venice. The nearest big city is the port of Ancona, on the Adriatic coast and that, too, is a long drive away. Imagine West Virginia and that will give you an idea of the look and feel of Le Marche and its comparable location on the map of Italy.

My father was born on January 20, 1883, in the environs of the rustic little town of Sassoferrato. I say the "environs" of Sassoferrato because my father was probably not born in the town proper. He was probably born at home in the family farmhouse, with the help of family and local midwives. That was the tradition at the time among both the rich and the poor. My father had two brothers, Rico and Giovanni, and one sister, Rosa. My mother, whose maiden name was Rosa Grassi, was born a few hillsides away seven years later, on March 28, 1890. She had one brother, Nazzareno, whom everyone called Neno. When I was growing up, my parents rarely talked to us about their lives back in Italy. That was the past, a closed story, and like so many other immigrants, they focused almost exclusively on their new lives in America. But Mother's childhood home outside Sassoferrato is still standing, and from it you can piece together, through facts and intuition, what my parents' early years were like and why they chose to come to America.

Sassoferrato is a pleasant place, with a medieval feel, a multitude of small churches, and a commanding view of the surrounding hills and valleys. To get to the tiny hamlet where my mother was born and raised, you take the main road out of town and turn off onto a narrow country road that leads up through fields and pastures that I bet have not changed one iota in a hundred years. Toward the top of one hill, there is a mud path leading into a group of now rundown farm buildings. The place is pretty much abandoned now, apart from a shepherd or two. But this is where my mother was born and grew up, more than a century ago. The hamlet is now called Colmeroni; people say that back then it was known as Caboccolino. Both names are built around an Italian word for *hill*.

Everything in Colmeroni is quite primitive, even today. On one side of the enclave is an old two-story barn made of stone. The ground floor is nothing more than a big open space with a dirt bottom. This part of the barn must have housed animals and farm tools. Now it's cluttered with the hulks of rusted plows and other farm machinery. Upstairs is just one large room. It's empty now, but this used to be the local schoolhouse. The room is bare and gloomy, and perhaps this helps explain why Mother barely learned to read and write.

Opposite the barn is an old farmhouse, also built of rough-hewn stone. The heavy timbers of the doors and window frames are now deeply scarred, victims of time and the harsh winters in Le Marche, but the thick stone walls stand firm, facing the wind and rain with a certain stubborn pride. The interior of the farmhouse is spacious enough for two or three peasant families, provided they live cheek by jowl, as they did in my mother's day. The place is a shambles now, but there is still the brickwork of the fireplaces, and you can tell where the families probably cooked and slept. A nephew of my mother's, Giovanni Grassi, still lives in Sassoferrato, and he says my mother was probably born right in this house. And certainly it was here that she spent the first eighteen years of her life.

Her life was anything but easy. I've heard some astonishing stories from Giovanni and friends in California who lived near this hamlet until the 1950s. It is hard for us to even imagine a poor sharecropper's daily life. Up before dawn, feed the animals, light the fire, cook breakfast for the family, then out to the fields—men and women—for a long day's work. Needless to say, there was no electricity or plumbing back then; there's very little in the hamlet now. In my mother's day, the peasants had to hike a half mile or so to an underground spring to fetch their daily water supply for drinking and cooking. Then they'd carry it home in large terra-cotta urns, slung over their shoulders with heavy leather yokes. Quite a load for a woman to carry.

I'm sure the landlord-peasant relationship was no picnic, either. My mother's parents, Giovanni and Lucia Grassi, came from many generations of Italian peasants and share-croppers, meaning they were among the poorest of the poor. As was usual at the time, all the land where my mother's family worked and lived was owned by *il padróne*, the boss and landlord. His house, spacious and well-to-do, still stands today, commanding the top of the hill, a short hike up from my mother's farmhouse. Under the quasi-feudal system of the time, *il padróne* rented land and living quarters to peasant families for a small monthly fee. In exchange, the peasants could use some of the land for their own animals and gardens, but they also had to plant and tend whatever crops *il padróne* ordered. On top of that, they would also have to give him 50 percent of whatever they harvested. The peasants pay rent, do all the work, and give away half the profits, too. Imagine! Under this system, families like my mother's had next to no real freedom. They were totally at the mercy of *il padróne*, the weather, and whatever price their crops would fetch in the local market. This was no life for the faint of heart; only the strong survived.

My mother, at a very early age, went to work beside her mother. She learned to cook, sew, mend, wash clothes, tend the fire, and keep house, while her brother, Neno, helped his father in the fields and with animals and other heavy chores. I'm sure my mother had barely a moment free to go to the little school in the barn. No one seems sure, but by most accounts, she was taught to write her name and other basics by a woman who employed her for a while as a domestic, possibly the wife of *il padróne*. My mother was very smart, though, and she had an iron will. Even as a young girl, she was known in her family as what we Italians call a *tèsta dura*, literally a "hard head." People often say the same of me!

Living under these conditions, Mother was forced to learn valuable lessons. The Grassi family lived off the land. Their meals came from their gardens and followed the rhythms of the seasons. They made their own bread and pasta from flour and grains. Their meat and eggs came from animals on their own farms or those of their neighbors. They probably made their own olive oil and wine; most peasant families in Italy did and still do. These culinary skills and values my mother held dear all her life, to our constant delight. Millions of Americans are only discovering them now.

Seeing my mother's farmhouse and its setting helps explain why my parents always felt so at home in the Napa Valley. Looking out from her doorstep, even today you see almost no hint of industry or urban clutter. The hillsides are green and fertile, and the slopes are terraced in a very clever way to facilitate planting, tilling, and harvest without spoiling the beauty of the landscape. From behind my mother's house, you can look out across an unspoiled stretch of valley and see Sassoferrato, its medieval walls curling around the town and making it into a minifortress. In the Napa Valley, we have no medieval walled villages, of course, but in terms of topography and landscape you can see the similarities.

Sassoferrato in those days was hardly a land of opportunity. Most peasant families like theirs barely scratched out a living from the land, and many of the men were forced to leave their wives and children and go to work every day in the nearby sulfur mines. Other men left home entirely, in search of better-paying jobs. Some went to work in the docks and shipyards of Ancona; others made their way north to the big factories in Milan and Turin. Still others chose to do long stints in the Italian army and shipped out to Italian colonial outposts in Libya, Ethiopia, and other parts of Africa.

America also beckoned. Today, if you stand and have an espresso in the cafés of Sassoferrato, almost everyone you meet had a grandfather or a father or an uncle or a brother who, at some stage, made their way to America — to find work and a better life for themselves and their families. There seems to have been an informal pipeline that developed between the towns of Le Marche and the heart of America, especially to a number of mining towns in Pennsylvania and Minnesota. There also seems to have been a clear pattern: Men would go work in the mines in America for a period of two years. During that time, they would live cheaply, save as much as they could, and send part of their earnings back home. After two years, they would return to their hometowns to see their families and wives or sweethearts. Some then chose to stay home; others packed up their families, kissed their parents good-bye, and formally emigrated to America.

My father was part of the exodus. Though he rarely talked about his youth, relatives have told us that my father was a very serious and intelligent boy, and for a while my grandparents pushed him toward the priesthood. My father had other ideas. Dad did get in a few years of schooling, and he learned to read and write, but then he had to go to work full-time to help feed the family. His older brother, Giovanni, was the first to leave Italy and come to America. He somehow found his way to a job in the iron ore mines of Minnesota, just after the turn of the century. In 1906 my father followed suit. Perhaps he was encouraged by his brother or by letters from friends already working in America, or he was just pushed by the idea of securing a better life. I don't know; Dad never talked about it. In any case, my father got himself into that emigrant pipeline and landed in Ely, Minnesota. He worked there for two years in the iron ore mines, saving his money and dreaming, no doubt, about that dark-eyed sweetheart he had left back in Sassoferrato.

In 1908 my father returned to Italy. And to my mother. By then she was eighteen, and along with her "hard head" she had a pretty face, beautiful eyes, and a strong constitution. Her manner was quiet but cheerful and forceful, and everyone could see that Rosa Grassi had a warm, generous heart. When my father asked her to marry him and go back to America with him, my mother eagerly agreed. They were married in a small church in Sassoferrato and they honeymooned in a little house outside town, just over the hill from my mother's family's farmhouse. Then, by ship, they crossed the Atlantic and made their way back to Minnesota.

They settled in Hibbing, another iron ore town filled with immigrants, and my father returned to the mines. He hated being cooped up down in those holes, which I guess is only natural for someone raised on a farm in Italy, with all the greenery and open air. He also hated the work; it was backbreaking and poorly paid. It was also dangerous. In fact, his older brother, Giovanni, was killed in a mine accident, leaving behind a widow and two small children. When that happened, Dad began looking for a way out of the mines.

Soon thereafter my father moved the family to Virginia, Minnesota, another mining town. There he teamed up with an Italian family named Brunetti and opened a grocery store. The store was located on First Street, one of the main shopping streets of Virginia. They stocked fresh pasta, tomatoes, olive oil, Italian sausages, and prosciutto, plus Italian cheeses, sweets, and a variety of wines. They did a good business, mostly among the Italian community, but they had a larger clientele as well. Being in business suited my father. Reading books always gave my parents trouble, but they had no problem understanding people. Like many Italian peasants, they were also resourceful about money; they had to be. So business was a good fit for him. And my father soon began to make decent money.

During these early years in Minnesota, Cesare and Rosa started a family. Mary, the oldest of the four of us, was born in Hibbing in 1910. In 1912 my sister Helen arrived. I appeared on June 18, 1913: Robert Gerald Mondavi. Peter arrived the following year, fourteen months after I was born. So within a space of about four years, they had four children. And four more mouths to feed.

Mother worked like a slave. Four young kids were already a handful. But to generate additional income we took in boarders, most of them miners from Italy. We had a large house, and on the average we had at least a half dozen boarders at any given time. Sometimes we had as many as fifteen or eighteen. Mother cooked for all of them. Two big, hot meals a day, and always it was the essentials of the Italian way of cooking: pasta, tomatoes, olive oil, and strong homemade red wine. Every day she would also make something cold for the miners to take down into the shafts. Apart from the cooking, Mother also washed our boarders' clothes and sheets, mended their socks and coveralls, and tidied up their quarters. I have no idea how she managed it all. The mines functioned twenty-four hours a day and our boarders worked in shifts. Some worked days; some worked during the night. Almost every day my mother worked till midnight and then she'd be up again at 5 A.M., making breakfast for the miners. Amazing woman!

Mother had a special gift: she knew how to make hard work fun. Ours was a traditional Italian family. My father was the provider. My mother was in charge of the house, the cooking, the children, and the boarders. The kitchen was her fiefdom, and she always enlisted us kids and some of our boarders to come in and give her a hand. She'd spread fresh eggs and flour across the kitchen table and we'd make pasta from scratch, with Mother showing us every step in the process so we could learn how to do it ourselves. We'd sing songs as we worked, and when we had a break, we'd play hide-and-seek. Our favorite place to hide was always under Mother's large, billowing skirts. Family; hard work; high spirits; healthy, hearty meals—my childhood was a daily infusion of all four.

My father was small in height, sturdy in build, and quiet in manner. With us kids, he brooked no nonsense. His word was law, but his words were few. A nod of the head, a shrug of the shoulder—that was his idea of a conversation. Still, he conveyed to us children very clear lessons about right and wrong. And one of his lessons was always enough. One day, for instance, I saw some money on his dresser and decided to help myself to a small loan. When my father discovered what I had done, boy, did he get angry! I'd never seen him so angry. I got a good walloping and, of course, I learned the lesson, then and there, once and for all.

My father had his core commandments: honesty, integrity, hard work, self-reliance, and one more that was set in stone: A man's word should be his sacred bond. In our family, these were not empty notions from a Sunday sermon. They were living, breathing rules to guide our thoughts and actions. They were also the bedrock of my father's business creed. Always treat your colleagues, your staff, and your customers exactly the way you want to be treated—that was his golden rule of doing business the Mondavi way.

I also learned other lessons, of a darker nature. Virginia, Minnesota, was governed by a strict caste system and we Italians were considered the bottom of the barrel. The Swedes, along with immigrants from other Scandinavian countries, ruled the roost. The word was that Italian families were not even allowed to buy property in certain parts of town. I did not see this firsthand, of course, but I still felt the sting of prejudice. At school and in the play yard, we were often teased and called "wops" and "dagos." Those insults burned deep. My parents spoke Italian at home, among themselves and to us. But I refused to speak Italian. At least in public. The reason was simple: I did not want to invite being called a wop or a dago. Like most kids, I just wanted to be like everyone else. And that meant speaking English— and only English.

The Brunetti grocery store did well, so well that Dad was able to sell his portion and go into business for himself. This time he bought a saloon, and soon it was filled with Italian immigrants looking for a home away from home. Dad worked like the devil and the saloon did pretty well. But then came Prohibition. The law was called the National Prohibition Act of 1919, but everybody referred to it as the Volstead Act. The *hated* Volstead Act. The law banned the sale of liquor and beer. But wine was a slightly different story. The law allowed people to make two hundred gallons of wine a year, as long as it was for family consumption. The law also permitted the sale of sacramental wine for religious purposes. Still, the law was bad news for my father and his saloon. And it was bad news for all the Italian families in Virginia, Minnesota.

To them, Prohibition was incomprehensible. Wine was food, a staple of our daily lives. Outlawing hard liquor might be understandable, but wine? Many Italians doubted the government would actually enforce such a ban, and many secretly vowed to find ways to skirt it. Others concentrated on making their two hundred gallons of legal wine for their families. But they needed grapes. By this time, my father was a respected businessman and a man known for his integrity. He was also secretary of the local Italian Club. So to procure grapes and maintain their Italian ways of life and wine, the Italian Club selected my father for an important mission: he was to go out to California, buy grapes, and then ship them back to Minnesota for local families to make wine.

So in 1919 my father boarded a train and went out to California. Almost as soon as he arrived, he fell in love with the young frontier state. And why not? There were no bitter cold winters. No mines. The caste system existed, but it was not as rigid, and there were fewer ethnic prejudices, rivalries, and restrictions. Enchanted, my father traveled up and down the state, inspecting grapes, buying lots, and then arranging for shipment back to Minnesota. Mission accomplished, he returned home. Two years later, though, he and Mother made a momentous decision. They decided to sell the saloon, uproot the family again, and move us all to California. My father was going to go into the grape and produce business.

I was all of ten, but I remember the train ride out. We went via Chicago, and at some point in the journey—I think it was in Chicago—our train stopped and split off some cars. I don't know how it happened, but one of my sisters and I wound up in one part of the train, while the rest of the family was pulling out of the station in the other—on their way to California and going without us! Well, I screamed bloody murder until the railroad people came to the rescue. They halted both trains and got us reunited. I can just imagine my parents saying to each other, "That Bobby, always going off in his own direction!"

For his headquarters my father chose Lodi, California, a quiet farming community south of Sacramento. Lodi at the time was the grape capital of the United States, and my father planned to go into business buying grapes wholesale and then shipping them back east to our Italian friends in Minnesota and to customers in the Midwest and up and down the East Coast. Lodi, he also figured, was a small, peaceful town that would be a fine place for them to settle in, raise the children, and grow the business.

In both places, I had a happy childhood. I was raised with the values of the old country: love, discipline, and hard work. In our household, there was always plenty of love. And with four kids in the family, we always had playmates. In Minnesota, in winter, we'd play in one of the icehouses. We'd jump from the rafters into the thick beds of sawdust below. In the summer, we'd fly kites over the quarries, using balls of string we got from my father's grocery store. We'd spend our summer afternoons at the swimming hole, and on Sundays several Italian families would get together and have huge picnics at nearby parks and lakes. All the kids would swim and play together; marbles, hide-and-seek, kick the can. I loved marbles, and even back then I was a ferocious competitor. I simply hated to lose!

Sundays also meant church. I served as an altar boy and sang in the choir. Here, and later in Catholic school in Lodi, the prime motivator was fear. There was only one way, one path, and you had to follow it. Or else. In some ways — but certainly not all — this was fine training, especially for a headstrong young boy like me. I learned discipline, I learned the importance of faith, and I learned to fear God.

During my boyhood years, though, another quality came to the fore. I'm not exactly sure when or how it began, but early in life I set myself a goal: to excel. My goal was simple:

Whatever I chose to do, I wanted to be The Best. I also wanted recognition; I wanted everybody to know that in this endeavor or that, Bob Mondavi was the best. So I was a fierce competitor, and not just in marbles. In the classroom. On the playground. On the football field. In the swimming pool. During the summer, I used to work for my father nailing together the wooden crates he used for shipping grapes and other produce. Here, too, I wanted to prove myself to be the best. My brother, Peter, and I, along with a group of workers, held lively competitions among ourselves to see who could nail together the most boxes in a single day. With the precision of a systems engineer, I studied the way most of the workers nailed boxes, and then I created for myself an efficient assembly line. Using a helper, whom we called a cleater, to prepare the slats, and streamlining the various hand movements required for nailing, I trained all summer. Then, on the big day of our final competition of the summer, I nailed together no less than two thousand boxes. No one we knew had ever come even close to that. So, with my usual modesty, I declared it a world record and declared myself champion of the world.

During these summers on the job, I earned more than just pride and the satisfaction of hard work done well. Peter and I got paid according to our output. For every one hundred boxes we nailed together, we got paid $1.25. So two thousand boxes was $25, for one day's work. That was good money in those days. My father put the money in a special account for us. Over the years, adding in other jobs we did for my father, together we saved close to $15,000!

Whatever the realm, I wanted to excel. I never felt I was very smart; in fact, I always had a bit of an inferiority complex in that regard. But even as a youth, I could see that brains were not enough. Becoming the best meant that you had to be willing to work harder than everyone else. It meant sacrifice. It meant setting clear goals and doing whatever it took to reach them. And whatever it was going to take for me to become the best, I was willing and determined to do. I also had something many people don't have: I had complete confidence and faith that I could and would succeed. I just had to work hard and have patience.

Hard work alone, though, is never enough; you have to have common sense. I realized that no one could excel in everything, so you had to carefully assess your strengths and weaknesses—and those of your competition. Then you had to be very realistic in evaluating where, with hard work, you could excel. At Lodi Union High School, for instance, I went out for football. I was not the biggest guy on the team; I had short legs and weighed only 140 pounds. But I was tough and I had explosive speed. Above all, I worked very hard. And it paid off. Senior year I helped lead our football team to the regional championship and I was chosen Most Valuable Player. "Nobody ever gets by Bob Mondavi"—that was my reputation. I was also on the swim team and one year I was president of my class.

My success in athletics, and even in box nailing, gave me the confidence to tackle challenges in other areas where I did not feel as strong. Though I was far from the best student in our class, for instance, during my high school years I set myself a big academic goal and managed to attain it: I got accepted at Stanford University. Why did I choose Stanford? Because everyone said that among all the universities in California, Stanford was the best. Simple as that. Peter applied and got into Stanford one year later. At the Farm, as we called it, I studied economics and business administration and I learned to drink beer and scotch. When I arrived, I thought for a while I might try out for football, but everyone on the Stanford team was a giant next to me! So I decided to play rugby instead. This was only common sense.

At Stanford I also had a larger awakening. Up until then, whatever my parents told me I took as gospel. Whatever the priest told us I took as gospel. In grammar school, what the nuns told me I never even questioned. Throughout my Catholic upbringing, I was taught the fear of God, but never the love of God. And I bought it all. So throughout my boyhood, I had always been motivated, first and foremost, by fear. I was always afraid of failing to win approval, afraid of falling short. I was convinced, too, that I was not as intelligent as many of my peers. My first year at Stanford, though, I had a wonderful professor of religion and philosophy who opened me up to another way of seeing and thinking. "Use your own damn head!" he would urge me. "You are just as intelligent as anyone, if you open your mind and heart." Jesus Christ, he taught us, was not God or even a superman; he was a human being, a human being who taught love. This to me was stunning; it opened my eyes and mind. If Jesus was just a human being, like the rest of us, I needn't feel so small and intellectually handicapped. Through this process of opening, I began to shed my fears and trust my own instincts and common sense. And I became convinced that if I really put my heart and soul into something, I could succeed. I also realized that to succeed you didn't have to believe in, or rely on, outside forces. Above all else, you had to believe in yourself. This was a powerful lesson and an inspiring message!

During my junior year, my father came to me and asked me what I was thinking about doing after graduation. I told him I was thinking about becoming either a lawyer or a businessman. My father was a man of great wisdom; when he spoke, I listened. He told me that he thought there was a great future in the wine business in California. Prohibition had been repealed a few years before, and many of the grape growers he did business with were now moving into wine. My father also thought the repeal of Prohibition would generate a growing market for table wine. At the time, about three-quarters of the wine being sold in the United States were sweet dessert wines: port, sherry, and muscatel. But he was convinced that was going to change, as more and more people discovered the Italian way!

I thought deeply about what he said and it made sense. Why not start in a young industry and grow with it? My father also added another crucial bit of guidance. He knew grapes; his business took him up and down the state buying various varieties of grapes, including zinfandel, muscat, carignane, and alicante bouschet. And the very best grapes in the whole of California, he told me, came from only one place: the Napa Valley. The Best—that was all I needed to hear.

So during my senior year, in addition to business, I studied chemistry to prepare for studying the chemistry of wine making. After graduation, I found myself a mentor for a summer crash course, Vic Enriques—a professor of enology at the University of California at Berkeley—and plunged in. I immersed myself in viticulture—the growing of grapes—and enology, the intricacies of making wine. Later, I was also exposed to the teachings of two very knowledgeable University of California professors, Maynard Amerine and Albert J. Winkler, both of whom had a profound impact on the evolution of the California wine industry. They brought real science to wine making, and I felt certain that if you followed their advice, you couldn't help but make decent wine. Many people came to agree with me. Amerine and a group of eminent enologists from U.C. Davis went on to write *The Technology of Wine Making,* which for the past several decades has been considered the bible of our industry. This first immersion into the craft of wine making was very stimulating for me; and wanting, as always, to excel, I worked day and night to turn my summer crash course into the prelude of a full-scale apprenticeship in the Napa Valley.

In the fall of 1936, when I first arrived in the valley, I found myself a room in St. Helena and went to work for Jack Riorda, a friend of my father's who ran a small bulk-wine business called the Sunnyhill Winery, later known as Sunny St. Helena. Jack was making pretty good bulk wine, but he was having trouble selling it. My father helped him sell and ended up becoming his partner shortly before I joined the business. As Jack's assistant, I worked the harvests and helped with the crush and wine making. I wasn't earning much money, but I loved the work. And I felt right at home among the many Italian families in St. Helena. Soon I was convinced: I had found my passion and the place where I wanted to put down my own roots.

Now that I had a place to call home, I returned to Lodi to see Marjorie Declusin, my high school sweetheart. We had met on a blind date in my senior year, and apart from one childhood crush, she was my first love. After I went off to Stanford, we dated from time to time when I came home for holidays, but her mother didn't approve of me. She was a teacher, with family roots tracing back to northern Europe, and she looked down on Italians. I had one devil of a time winning her over! Now, without further to-do, I asked Marge to marry me. She agreed, and in 1937 we got married in a lovely wedding ceremony. We then moved into a nice little house on Charter Oak in St. Helena, intent on settling into the Napa Valley and starting a family.

My dream was to one day make fine wine. At Sunny St. Helena, though, we were not making fine wines to be aged in oak; we were making clean, inexpensive bulk wine to be consumed young and fresh. We did not grow our own grapes, either. We bought grapes from various growers in the Napa Valley and then made wine in our facility on the outskirts of St. Helena, now the site of the Merryvale Vineyard. Then we'd sell it wholesale and ship it in railroad tank cars. Often we referred to our product as tank car wine. At various destinations back East, the wine would be off-loaded for bottling, distribution, and retail sale. At that time, there was no national network for wine sales and distribution. In the wake of Prohibition, the wine business was still just struggling to its feet. Within a few years, though, we boosted our production to 500,000 gallons and then 1 million gallons, and we became one of the valley's most important producers of bulk wine.

In 1940 Jack Riorda became ill and died. His daughter took over his ownership portion, and for the next three years I ran the day-to-day operation. One of my main priorities was to upgrade the quality of our wines. In fact, I set myself a goal: I wanted to make the best tank car wine in America. As it turned out, I didn't have the time to achieve that goal. When the United States entered World War II, we all shifted gears. I and many other people in the valley, in addition to growing grapes, helped expand the valley's production of vital food goods, both for the war effort and the home front. As such, I was exempted from military service. But I also kept on at Sunny St. Helena, learning my way around the wine cellar. Then in 1943 I heard from friends about a golden business opportunity.

The Charles Krug Winery had fallen on hard times and was going to be put up for sale. Louis Stralla, who had been leasing Krug and making wine there since 1933, and Paul Alexander, from the St. Helena branch of the Bank of America, both came to me on a Friday in March and urged me to have a look at Krug. They knew that my ambition was to go into the fine wine business one day and they thought this was my chance. But I had to hurry. Paul Alexander said there was a man from Ohio who wanted Krug and was planning to call James K. Moffitt, who owned Krug, the following Monday morning.

I was interested in Krug. The winery had been founded in 1861 by Charles Krug, one of the early pioneers who recognized the true potential of the Napa Valley. The location was ideal, five hundred acres just north of St. Helena, with Mount Helena rising in the distance. And Krug was rich in history and tradition. It was the oldest operating winery in the valley, and one of Charles Krug's first assistants was none other than Joseph Beringer, who later founded the famous Beringer Vineyard. As a result of all this, the name Krug had a rich resonance in the American wine industry. The name

Krug is famous in Europe, too—there's a prominent champagne house in Reims by that name. There was no relation to Charles Krug as far as I knew, but the name still had the right ring.

I did not have the money or the necessary line of credit to buy Krug. If I wanted the winery, I had to convince my father to buy it. I had to go to Lodi immediately, and as my father was very conservative, I knew I had to go with a good idea of how to finance the deal. And I had the idea. At Sunny St. Helena, we were selling our bulk wine at twenty-eight cents a gallon. I wanted to put in a bottling line and sell the bottled wine to distributors at a dollar a gallon, but Jack Riorda's daughter did not want to expand the business. I figured that if we bought Krug, we could buy all of Sunny St. Helena's bulk wine, bottle and label it at Krug, and then sell it at that same dollar a gallon and make a handsome profit.

So the next day I rushed down to Lodi to convince my father to buy Krug. We sat down in the kitchen and I laid out my plan. The price was right, I told him. I now knew how to make wine, and instead of selling it in bulk as we did at Sunny St. Helena, we could cut out some of the middlemen and bottle and sell our own wine. To my way of thinking, that was the way to make real money. My father listened carefully, and my mother listened, too, as she worked in the kitchen. But then Dad gave me a steadfast no. He liked the wholesale end of the grape and wine business and did not want to get involved with bottling and setting up a sales force and network. I pressed, but Dad just would not budge.

I was disappointed, but I wasn't finished yet. Before I went to bed in Lodi that night, I told Mother it was absolutely essential that we buy the Charles Krug Winery. It would be a dream come true for the family. Still, when I went to bed, I thought the idea of buying Krug was dead in the water. Somehow, though, during the night my mother worked a bit of magic. The next morning, as I was trying to figure out a way to tell my father he should change his mind, he came downstairs and before I could get a word out he said, "Bobby, when do you want to go up to St. Helena to see the Charles Krug Winery?"

"Immediately!" I said, and off we went that Sunday morning. We went up to the Napa Valley, I showed him Krug, and that did it. Krug was a small paradise of a property, with lovely vineyards and a distinguished pedigree as the oldest winery in California. Once he saw it, my father agreed to buy Krug—provided my brother and I would work together and build the business. Done and done. So I called Paul Alexander and he agreed to set up a meeting with James K. Moffitt in San Francisco the following morning. We closed the deal the very same day.

So now the Mondavi family had its own winery, and in the beginning I ran it alone. At the end of the war, though, when he was discharged from the U.S. Army, Peter joined me at Krug and for the next twenty-three years we ran the business together. There were two lovely homes on the property. Marge and I occupied one, and the other we kept available for our parents when they came up to visit from Lodi. After my father died in 1959, Mother came to live at Krug. Later, my sister Helen also built a house at Krug for herself and her two children, Peter and Serena. So Krug was more than a winery; it was a large, idyllic, happy family compound.

Until it all fell apart.

As I explained before, my twenty-three years at Krug were often frustrating—in part because I was always driven by that same lifelong ambition: to be The Best. While I was at Krug, when I drove by Beaulieu or Inglenook, I would bow my head in reverence, as a mark of respect, as if I were in church. They were the best; my unwavering dream was to join their ranks. And I knew there was only one ticket in: make wines as good as theirs—or better. I also knew that we had to work harder at Krug and undertake a true quest for excellence. So for years I clashed with Peter over the quality of our wines and finally, to chase that elusive goal of being The Best, I decided to set out on my own.

To dream is easy; turning your dreams into reality is anything but. And few people have the ability and means to realize their vision. So when I left Krug, I knew my road would not be easy. But I felt sure of my direction and I was confident that in time I would be successful. To learn how to become the best in a given field, some people read how-to business books or study how other entrepreneurs began with nothing and built their empires. Not me. I looked back into my own life experience. I looked at the lessons and values I had learned from Cesare and Rosa and at what I had learned from my own unrelenting campaigns to become The Best.

Out of these I defined and set forth the guiding ethic of my new winery: the pursuit of excellence. Excellence, no matter what the cost. No matter how hard the work. No matter how great the personal sacrifice. Yes, I was going to work like a fanatic, and I'd probably drive everyone around me like a fanatic. But great artists are always fanatics. The painting or the poem or the symphony is not finished until every brushstroke, every syllable, every note, is finally perfect. And in perfect harmony with the rest of the creation. If we wanted to enter the ranks of The Best, if we wanted our wines to stand beside the great wines of Bordeaux and Burgundy, we had to hold ourselves to just as rigorous a standard. If we wanted to enter the kingdom of high art, I knew we had to go beyond the pursuit of excellence and cultivate a passion for perfection.

Nothing less would do.

CHAPTER 3

To Kalon

THERE IS NO SECRET: great wine begins in the vineyard. The better the grapes, the better the potential to create wines that can compete with the best in the world. So once I had formulated a clear vision and guiding philosophy, I set out to find myself a jewel. I wanted to build my winery on the finest stretch of vineyard to be found in the Napa Valley and, in fact, the whole of California.

From my thirty years of growing and buying grapes in the valley, I knew most of the vineyards that produced high-quality grapes. But I had other considerations as well. The winery I envisioned was to be a showcase for the most advanced wine-making techniques and equipment in America, if not the world. Aesthetics would be key. In France, the great châteaus were temples of style, tradition, and refinement. This was the lead I wanted to follow. I wanted my winery to have elegance and style, to be a place that would properly highlight our talents and the work going on inside. I also wanted it to be a place that would attract streams of visitors. So did I want to be up in the hills? Or down on the floor of the valley? Did I want to be near St. Helena or farther north in Calistoga? Or in the center of the valley, near Rutherford, Oakville, and Yountville? With these questions in mind, I looked at several vineyard sites, but none really sparked my imagination. None felt like home.

The longer I looked, the more I began zeroing in on one particular section of the Napa Valley: Oakville. This little town was nothing more than a tiny crossroads surrounded by a wealth of beautiful vineyards. Today, with its population of four hundred, it's still not much more than that. For what I wanted, though, Oakville had glowing assets: location, climate, and grape quality.

As many of you know, the Napa Valley is situated about an hour's drive north of the Golden Gate Bridge, above the San Francisco Bay. We are located significantly inland, meaning we are well protected from the fickle weather and temperatures you find closer to the Pacific coast. The valley itself stretches north-south over a distance of about thirty miles. When you drive in from the south, from San Francisco, the valley looks like a long bowl or a giant canoe, with a majestic bow of hills rising up in the north, above the town of Calistoga. The valley is enclosed to the west by the terraced slopes of the Mayacamas Mountains and to the east by the rugged hills of the Vaca Range, which we call the Sil-

verado Range. Thanks to these mountain ranges and our inland location, the Napa Valley has a climate that is almost
ideal for growing grapes and bringing them to full maturity.
During much of the growing season, the days are sunny and
warm while the nights are cool. Even during the summer,
heavy mists and fogs slip in over the mountains during the
night, providing cool temperatures and vital moisture for our
vines and grapes.

Oakville sits at the geographic and agricultural heart of
all this. The town is situated between the town of Napa to
the south and St. Helena to the north. The surrounding
vineyards fan out across a plain that is flat, fertile, and during the summer, drenched with sunshine—ideal for growing cabernet sauvignon and several other top varietals. As a
site for a winery, too, I knew this location would be perfect;
it would facilitate our trucking and deliveries and the com-
muting of our staff. Oakville's location—right on Highway
29, the main road through the valley—would also be a natural asset for attracting tourists.

As I narrowed my search, I considered three different
properties in and around Oakville. There was one, though,
that stood head and shoulders above the others. It was a vineyard with a distinguished history and a magical name: To
Kalon. I had first encountered To Kalon during one of our
early expansion phases at Krug. We needed more grapes to
boost production, and we were looking for a good vineyard to
buy or lease. Old Louis M. Martini Sr., one of the most

knowledgeable and hardheaded vintners in the Napa Valley, urged me to take a look at the To Kalon Vineyard in Oakville. "Bob," he said, "that darn place at To Kalon is one of the finest places in California for cabernet sauvignon." I went to see To Kalon and Louis was right: it was a fine property, producing first-rate grapes. So at my urging we began buying grapes grown on the To Kalon property, and in 1958, I think it was, we went even further. We purchased a 325-acre parcel of To Kalon for Krug, in the name of the parent company my father had formed: C. Mondavi & Sons.

As a site for my own winery, To Kalon held out an array of good qualities. One was its remarkable history, which dates back almost to the beginning of grape growing in the Napa Valley. There is some disagreement as to the precise year when wine making began here, but historians do agree on this: in 1838 a tough, adventurous trapper and mountain man named George Calvert Yount came to the valley, pitched his tent, and began building himself a two-story log cabin home. According to Charles L. Sullivan, in his authoritative *Napa Wine: A History*, Yount also planted vegetables, built a corral, and began a herd of cattle. Most important, he decided to plant grapes. At that time, the Spanish missionaries, who did so much to settle the state of California through their unique system of regional missions, were known to be avid grape growers. So Yount went to the mission in what is now Vallejo and purchased a substantial quantity of mission vines. He brought them back to his property, above what is known today as the town of Yountville, and planted the Napa Valley's very first vineyard. Soon thereafter, George Calvert Yount began making wine.

By 1852 other settlers in the Napa Valley had planted high-quality European grape varietals and were also producing wine. Then in 1868 a pioneering viticulturalist named Hamilton W. Crabb purchased a 240-acre plot of land in Oakville and began growing grapes and making table wine and raisins. According to Sullivan, Crabb later decided to try his hand at making higher-quality wine. He obtained certified cuttings of "noble varietals" from Bordeaux and the Loire Valley and planted them in a large diversified vineyard, which he named Hermosa. The noble vines from France flourished under Crabb's care, and almost right away his vineyard was deemed by many experts to be the finest in all of California, especially for growing cabernet sauvignon. By the end of the 1870s Crabb had 160 acres in vines, a winery with a 300,000-gallon capacity, and a reputation as one of the leading wine makers in California. As his success grew, Crabb changed the name of his vineyard from Hermosa to an ancient Greek word: To Kalon.

A century later, when I came along, Crabb was long gone, of course, but To Kalon's sterling reputation remained intact. The vineyard also boasted a proven track record for producing almost the entire range of grapes I intended to use in my bid to make wines that would stand with the very best in the world. My plan was to build our reputation on wines made from four of the five noble varietals, namely: cabernet, pinot noir, chardonnay, and Johannisberg Riesling. These were the prestige varietals, the kings of the marketplace, the ones that fetched the highest prices per bottle—and carried the highest profit margins. To make money and grow our business, though, I planned to make some less expensive wines and sell them in very high volumes for the mass market. Specifically, I intended to make a chenin blanc and a light but flavorful gamay rosé. To my mind, To Kalon would give us a strong foundation to make a prestige cabernet. To fill our production targets, we would buy additional fine grape lots from other growers around the valley. That was my basic business plan.

Along with its reputation and grape quality, To Kalon's physical beauty fit perfectly into another key element of my strategy: tourists. As I said, back in 1966 there was little or no market for fine wine in most of the United States. And there was little tourism in the Napa Valley. As a start-up company, we would have little money for public relations and advertising or for the kind of extensive marketing necessary to build a brand name and a national market for fine wine. So what to do? I wanted my showcase winery to be so lovely and welcoming that it would attract hundreds of tourists daily and entice them to drive in and taste our unique style of wines. Visitors could then buy our wines right on the premises, by the bottle or the case—sales for which we would not have to pay a cent to any distributor or sales rep.

My real aim, though, was not sales; it was to spread the word about our wines and about our larger dreams for the Napa Valley and California wines. If we could create a tourist experience that was both delightful and educational, our visitors would leave happy, with their trunks full of wine. And they would come back another time, perhaps bringing friends. Through word of mouth — the most cost-effective form of advertising — we'd be able to sell our wines, promote our valley as a tourist destination, and build a much larger market for fine California wines, one visitor at a time. The more tourists we'd attract, the merrier we'd be.

Today, of course, this strategy seems almost self-evident; wineries up and down the state of California now work very hard to attract tourists. Back in 1966, though, no one was doing what I had in mind, at least not on the scale I was envisioning. At Krug, we had long led the parade in tourist events and promotion. In 1952, I believe it was, we took an old storage shed, emptied it out, slapped on a coat of whitewash, and put in some tables. This was our original visitors' tasting room. We served cheese and crackers along with our wines, and on big weekends we'd attract hundreds of people. To help get the word out, we also produced a witty and informative newsletter, *Bottles and Bins*, about Krug, of course, but also about the Napa Valley and its wines and wine makers.

A decade later, in the early 1960s before I left Krug, a young woman from Switzerland named Margrit Biever came to us with a fine idea. She suggested we hold a series

of outdoor concerts at Krug. We could create a festive cultural event, she said, invite lots of people, and serve a selection of our wines. With one event, we could simultaneously
support the arts and promote our wines. I loved the idea and
I could see this young woman had a definite flair for both art
and business. As Margrit suggested, we did put on what we
eventually called our August Moon Concerts, and the results made clear the potential of this kind of marketing and
synergy. Now, as I planned my own winery, I realized that
To Kalon and the other potential sites in Oakville along
busy Highway 29 would be ideal for tourists and tasting.
Imagine the concerts and other cultural events we could put
on in the center of the valley; imagine the number of visitors
we could attract!

With all these ideas percolating in my head, in early
1966 I returned to To Kalon for a fresh look and a thorough
evaluation. What I found was amazing. To my eye, the vineyard was a treasure, and I imagined that its beauty had not
changed one iota since the days when old Hamilton Crabb
had planted it back in the 1870s. The vineyard had changed
hands, though, several times. In 1943 a vintner named Martin Stelling Jr. bought a portion of the To Kalon property,
along with surrounding hillside acreage, and developed it
into about five hundred acres of first-class grape varieties. In
1950, though, Stelling was killed in a car accident. Three
years later, Ivan Shoch, Stelling's foreman, purchased part of
the estate. Ivan was one of our principal suppliers at Krug,

and he and his wife, Barbara, had become close friends of
ours. It was through Ivan that we had purchased our own
parcel for Krug in 1958. Now Ivan urged me to buy another.

The parcel I had my eye on was — and is — a magnificent
stretch of vineyard. It stretches from the edge of Highway 29
back to the foothills of the Mayacamas Mountains. As I
walked the property, I carefully examined the quality of the
vines and the soil. It was composed of rich alluvial loams,
with a more gravelly soil on the slopes. There appeared to be
very good drainage. I also liked the vineyard's exposure to
the sun. The annual rainfall in its microclimate also
promised to be well suited for the kind of top-quality wines I
wanted to develop. I examined these qualities of the site
with a very critical business and wine-making eye, and I
liked what I saw. But there was something more.

Walking through To Kalon, admiring its contours and
vines, smelling the richness of its soil, I knew this was a very
special place. It exuded an indefinable quality I could not
describe, a feeling that was almost mystical. The place just
seemed to radiate a sense of calm and harmony, of peace
and serenity. In its whole expanse of vines and greenery, I
could not see a single blemish or man-made intrusion. No
winery, no building, not even a shed or electrical pole to
spoil its natural beauty. As I walked, I felt a powerful, almost
inexpressible connection to this land. And some root intuition inside me seemed to say, "Yes, this is the place." As I
thought about it, even the name old Hamilton Crabb had

given to this vineyard a century ago seemed to me a remarkable fit. It perfectly captured my guiding ambition and spirit. In Greek, *To Kalon* means "highest quality" or "highest good." To me, that meant, simply, The Best.

I wish I could say that I ran out and immediately purchased this idyllic stretch of vineyard, but I did not. There were other pieces of the puzzle that had yet to fall into place, and the other Oakville sites had their attractions as well. I had two issues in particular that I needed to address before I could go forward: the architectural design of the winery I wanted to build and the financial backing I needed to put together the whole package.

The design issue proved to be one of the most stimulating aspects of the entire venture. In the early 1960s, as a member of the Wine Institute, I had been among a group invited to Menlo Park to see the new headquarters of *Sunset* magazine. When I saw that beautiful building, I said, "By gosh, if I ever build a winery, this is what I want! It has that warm feel." So I called Bill Lane, the owner of *Sunset* magazine, and asked him who had actually designed Sunset House. He told me it was not an architect, but a highly respected designer named Cliff May, who was considered one of the fathers of the distinctive California ranch house. Bill gave me May's phone number and left him a message in advance, explaining who I was and what I wanted. Bill called me later and said, "Bob, you know Cliff May was so excited by my message that he called me back at three o'clock in the morning!"

By this time, I had put together a small group of friends who wanted to back my venture. Bill and Ina Hart, very close friends of ours, had long been urging me to go out and start my own winery. They were more positive about it than I was; in fact, they even promised to loan me money just to make sure I'd take the plunge! I also received promises of support from two prominent grape growers in the valley: Fred Holmes and Ivan Shoch. Bill and Ina were offering me money out of friendship and their belief in what I was doing. Holmes and Shoch were friends, too, but they also saw my venture as a good business opportunity. In exchange for giving me some start-up capital, they wanted shares in the company and they wanted to become two of my kingpin suppliers of top-quality grapes. They stood to gain twice over. That was fine with me; I just wanted to get my venture off the ground. On the strength of these different promises of support, I went ahead and set up a meeting with Cliff May.

So one day that winter I rounded up Fred and Ivan and went to see Cliff at his offices down in West Los Angeles. When he heard my plans, Cliff said, "Bob, how big are you going to have this winery?" I wanted to avoid that question. Initially, we were thinking of building a small winery, producing only about twenty thousand cases of wine a year. But I was sure it would soon get much larger. I also knew Cliff May was very expensive, charging not 10 percent, like many architects, but 12 percent. So we sparred for twenty-five or thirty minutes and then I finally said to him, "You know, if you draw this up for what we want in the future, maybe

50,000 or 100,000 cases, all my money will be going toward your fee. We won't have any money left over!"

He said, "Bob, I'll make a deal with you. If you agree to go ahead and retain me, I'll design this for you to handle twenty-five thousand cases. But I'll also design it so that you can expand it." I agreed; I knew Cliff was the man for the job. Now he had to help us choose just the right site and find the right design. Soon after our meeting, Cliff flew up to Napa for a personal look at the three sites we were considering in and around Oakville. He flew up in a private plane and landed at John Daniel's tiny private airport beside Inglenook. With Fred, Ivan, and my son Michael, we picked Cliff up at the airport and drove him around the valley, to give him the feel of the place. Then we took him around to the potential sites. At one stage, Cliff asked me what qualities I wanted the architecture of my winery to convey. My answer was easy to say but difficult to achieve:

"I want the building to declare, 'Here is a heart and soul.' I want something that tells people this is not a factory; this is a home, a place with real character and feeling." Wine making is a very personalized endeavor. When I open a bottle of wine, I want to taste the pride and character of the wine maker. I wanted the building to declare something similar: "Here is a very personal venture; here we have great pride in what we're doing."

Wine to me is all about sharing. So I told Cliff that along with plenty of space for wine production, I wanted the winery to have a gathering place large enough and properly equipped to entertain our families and visitors, a joyous space where we could celebrate the joys of wine and food, of music and art. I also expressed the hope that the entire complex would harmonize well with the surrounding landscape. And with California history and our mission tradition. Some 160 years before, Spanish missionaries had come to Sonoma and the Napa region and they had left a very deep imprint. Also, I very much liked the style of the missions they had built up and down the state of California. These were now enduring landmarks, and I wanted my winery to be an enduring landmark as well. Cliff was quiet as I spoke, but I knew he understood.

When we arrived at To Kalon, Cliff and I walked along together, marveling at its beauty and serenity. Suddenly Cliff stopped me and said, "This is the site." In his mind, there was no question; To Kalon was far superior to the others. The aesthetics were perfect. Immediately he visualized the completed winery complex, set back against the foot of the Mayacamas Mountains. Then he took out an old nine-by-twelve-inch manila envelope and with a pencil he began sketching on the back. He first drew a large archway. "This will be the entrance," he said. "For a mission style, you'll need a tower, like a bell tower." And he drew a modest but distinctive tower to the right of the archway. Then he sketched a V spreading back from the archway, like the wings of a graceful bird in flight. "You can have your production on one side," he said, "and your hospitality and visitors on the other." After that, Cliff pulled out his camera and took photos of the grounds from various angles, so he could later elaborate a more formal architectural plan. But it was from that rough sketch on the back of an old manila envelope that the unique design and feel of the Robert Mondavi Winery was born.

Cliff returned to L.A. and soon came up with a finished architectural plan. It was stunning. The winery he envisioned was a rendition of the California mission style, with flavors of old Spanish monasteries and haciendas. The design exuded elegance and simplicity. The structure was light and airy in feel, by no means monumental in scale or industrial in look. The low, V-shaped building had a broad, open archway in the middle and two arms opening out to embrace the vineyards behind. The point of the V faced the highway, and through the graceful archway you would see the vineyards and the Mayacamas Mountains in the background. To the right of the archway, as you faced the winery, just as he had done in his sketch, Cliff had placed a lovely campanile, a bell tower like the ones you see beside medieval churches in Italy.

We all went for Cliff's design immediately; we felt the warmth. And I felt sure the design would accomplish exactly what we wanted, while accentuating the idyllic landscape and serene feeling of the To Kalon Vineyard. We eventually decided to place the winery close to Highway 29, instead of setting it back near the mountains, but otherwise we followed his plan to the letter. Frankly, though, I had no idea his design would become one of the landmark buildings of the Napa Valley, nor that it would eventually help us attract some 300,000 tourists a year!

Now it was time to act. I had the site I wanted, the design I wanted, and I had the backing I needed. But I had to move quickly. There were plans in the works to turn the entire Stelling Estate into a luxury housing and resort complex, complete with homes, shops, gas stations, and even a small model winery that would show tourists how wine was made in the Napa Valley. Under one option I considered, we would be that model winery. To me, though, the entire project sounded a bit like Palm Springs, or worse. Under the plan, more than two thousand acres of prime vineyard and hillside property would be broken down into parcels of five to ten acres as sites for homes surrounded not by fairways but by vineyards. We doubted the project would ever be approved by the county but we supported the plan publicly, in the hope that we could secure a parcel early on. I figured that no matter what the fate of the resort project, the price of property on the Stelling Estate was bound to escalate. Some of the big spirits companies, sniffing an opportunity, were already moving into the Napa Valley. In 1964 John Daniel had sold Inglenook to a large cooperative, United Vintners, and I felt other big buyouts were in the offing. So I wanted to make our deal before they moved in and drove up the price of land. Worse, once the big companies moved in, I knew it would be much more difficult for us to go into the marketplace and establish a niche for our wines.

So as soon as Cliff May put his seal of approval on To Kalon, I sent Ivan Shoch into action. As their vineyard manager and owner of part of the land, Ivan had become a trusted friend of the Stelling trustees and of Hardy Rapp, the San Francisco real estate developer who managed the Stelling Estate. Ivan set up a meeting for us with Hardy Rapp and we began putting together the deal.

At the same time, I had to settle my affairs with Krug. I was still on a formal leave of absence, though I think everyone in the family knew I was not intending to come back. Nonetheless, I went to Peter and my mother and told them my plans. Since Michael was barred from working at Krug, I told them I intended to build a small winery for the two of us to run, a winery producing only about twenty thousand cases of wine a year. I sought their approval to do so. No way, my brother, Peter, retorted; that would be direct competition for Krug. My mother heard me out, but despite my pleading she sided with Peter. "Bobby," she said, "don't do this."

But the die was cast.

I went ahead with my partners and purchased that lovely twelve-acre stretch of prime To Kalon Vineyard, to be the future home of the Robert Mondavi Winery. With Cliff May, we began planning the construction of the winery. And I began the necessary legal and bureaucratic moves for starting my own business. Peter and my mother, along with Joe Alioto and their other advisers, responded pretty much as I expected: they made it clear there was no healing the split. While I maintained my stock and vote in board meetings, my formal involvement with daily operations at Krug was over. And this rupture also set the stage for our later battle in court, brother against brother.

Now, though, my great adventure began in earnest. And thank god for good friends. To put bread on the table, I went to work as a wine consultant. The Guild Winery down in Lodi and the Mirassou brothers, friends of ours who ran a winery in Mission San Jose, each put me on retainers of $1,000 a month, to help them develop their wines and sales. Bill and Ina Hart, as promised, loaned us $50,000 to help buy the land from the Stelling Estate. To close the deal, I borrowed another $50,000 from the Bank of America, and the Mirassous were kind enough to cosign the loan. Fred Holmes and Ivan Shoch joined us as partners and put in another $100,000 so we could start building the winery. These friends believed in me and in my dream of making world-class wines. And they shared my larger dream of turning the Napa Valley into America's answer to Bordeaux, Burgundy, and Tuscany. Without their help and support, my great adventure might well have sputtered to an abrupt halt, right then and there.

We broke ground on July 16, 1966, my daughter Marcia's birthday, and soon our project was really humming. To

Kalon became a bustling construction site. We had a core staff of only three, as I recall, but we had crews tending the vineyards and, in some areas, ripping out weak vines and re-planting. And we began holding meetings to decide on such issues as the name of the winery, the look of our labels and bottles, and what kind of corporate structure to establish. Suddenly, we were all caught up in a swirl of hard work and high spirits. Even now I'm flooded with happy memories of those first days of creation. Memories of Marge cooking huge meals for our family and work crews. Of my son Michael working alongside me, and Tim and Marcia coming aboard during the summer.

Marge was vital to our start-up. She was always very supportive of my dreams and ambitions and, as I said, some of her closest friends helped me put together the initial financing. In the first hectic months, when money and manpower were tight, Marge anchored the kitchen, managed comings and goings on the site, and dealt with scores of problems every single day. She was also a good adviser. By the time I started my own winery, we had already been married twenty-nine years, and she knew all my strengths and weaknesses. In the beginning of our marriage, Marge couldn't boil water. Over the years, though, she had developed into a very good cook and she was always an excellent mother. The kids adored her and so did everyone else, including my parents. And in our start-up years at the winery, she anchored the household and kids and also helped at the winery.

As we were constructing the winery and tending the vines, I spent time reaching out to a number of grape growers across the Napa Valley. Like any start-up venture, I needed to generate revenue the first year in order to establish my credibility in the marketplace and to reassure my partners and creditors at the bank. I also needed to begin covering the heavy cost of building our showcase winery. So I sat down with a number of top-quality grape growers to discuss terms for buying all or part of their crops. Several of these growers had already worked profitably with me at Krug and were now eager to join my fledgling business. They also believed in my campaign to improve the quality of our grapes and our wines. Up to then, the grape industry in the valley had been static and closed; many of the growers welcomed me as a breath of fresh air. We did not plan to buy juice. We wanted to do all our own crushing in order to maintain tight quality control from beginning to end.

During the growing season in 1966, we were fortunate in a number of ways. We had no frost, our spring and summer were very warm, and by July and August we were seeing good, well-balanced fruit. In late September, we started to bring in the harvest, and I can tell you we worked like dogs. Family, partners, and friends all pitched in. I can still see Michael, Bill Hart, and Ivan Shoch working in a frenzy, feeding the grapes into our brand-new crusher. Since we were not at full capacity, the Krug Winery pitched in and crushed some of our grapes. In what was to become a harvest tradition at our winery, we held an outdoor celebration: a blessing of the grapes. We gathered beside our crusher, and as the grapes began pouring in, a local priest blessed the fruit and thanked God for his bounty. I felt so proud that day. Although we had been in existence for only a few short months, the Robert Mondavi Winery was up, running, and crushing grapes!

During this period, Michael was away part of the time doing a stint in the National Guard and I was busy with a thousand aspects of launching the winery. Fortunately, though, we had an excellent hand in the cellar: Warren Winiarski. Warren had come west from Chicago, determined to learn how to make wine, and he had spent time at Chateau Souverain before joining our frenzied start-up operation. "I have very fond memories of 1966," Warren recalls now. "I was there digging the holes, setting the ladders against unfinished walls. We were making wine with sawdust, pipe dope, and electrician's tape. I remember long, long hours of frustration trying to get everything properly set up. But the wines we made during this period have a constant endearment for me due to the circumstances of their making. It was a fabulous environment, a grand experience, and we had lots of inspiration and enthusiasm from Bob at the top."

While our main focus was on making top-quality cabernet sauvignon, pinot noir, chardonnay, and Johannisberg Riesling wines, we made other wines that first year and they provided us with some surprises. Rosé wines were popular in

America at the time, and we set out to make a cheerful, drinkable gamay rosé. We fermented the wine at a cool temperature and it turned out light, delicate, fruity, and very pleasant to drink, especially in warm weather. This is a wine to be sold and drunk young, and we put it on sale in March 1967, just six months after our first harvest. This was the very first wine we ever sold. The quality was a long way from where I ultimately wanted to be, and I knew we were still at the very beginning of what we needed to learn. But that little gamay got us off to a fine start, at $1.79 a bottle!

One of our growers also provided us with a fine crop of sauvignon blanc, and for a while we puzzled over what to do with it. At the time, much of the sauvignon blanc being made in America was of poor quality, and as a result, the reputation of the varietal was not very good. But I was undaunted. At Krug, we made a nice, light chenin blanc from a comparable grape, and it had been a prizewinner and a big commercial success. And I knew that in the Loire Valley they produce delightful white wines made from the sauvignon blanc grape, including Sancerre, Pouilly-Fumé, and blanc fumé. So, I wondered, why couldn't we find a way to reinvent sauvignon blanc and turn it into a success in America? Done and done.

We took that crop of sauvignon blanc and aged it in French barrels to produce a wine that was light and refined, yet with plenty of character and charm. In that first year we made both a sweet and a dry version. In a tasting session with Michael, Fred Holmes, and Ivan Shoch, we came up with a catchy, original name—a twist on the name of a wine from the Loire. We decided to Americanize blanc fumé and call our wine Fumé Blanc.

And what a success it turned out to be. It was a hit even in our first trial tastings. I have a vivid memory, for instance, of a tasting in Lodi. Marge's mother helped organize it. She got together a group of her fellow schoolteachers, all women, and we came down from Oakville with a selection of our new wines. I didn't think our Fumé Blanc would go over well at all, but it proved to be a tremendous success. We had the same reaction from all our preliminary tastings. When we formally brought out the wine in 1968, the name and the wine were enormous hits, and today Fumé Blanc remains one of our signature wines and one of our most popular.

The unexpected success of our sauvignon blanc crowned an amazing first year in operation. It was a year full of lessons for me, many of which I still hold dear today. One lesson, though, stands out above all the rest. When we started out the previous spring, everyone in the Napa Valley said we were crazy. Bring in a harvest in your first year in operation? Crush grapes your first year? Make good wine the first time out? No way! Impossible! Why even bother to try? When we brought that first harvest in, people across the valley were just amazed. And they were amazed at the quality of the wines we produced. I was not surprised in the least. From the beginning, I knew we could succeed. I had the confidence and the faith. And I was proven right. So to me the lesson was crystal clear:

If you want to succeed, you have to listen to yourself, to your own heart, and you have to have the courage to go your own way. If I had listened to all the skeptics and naysayers I've met along my chosen path, not just that first year but all along the way, you know where I'd be today?

Nowhere!

CHAPTER 4

The Innovators

I'M A GREAT BELIEVER in research and innovation.

From the outset, I wanted my winery to draw inspiration and methods from the traditional Old World châteaus of France and Italy, but I also wanted it to become a model of state-of-the-art technology, a pioneer in research, and a gathering place for the finest minds in our industry. I wanted our winery to be a haven of creativity, innovation, excitement, and that unbelievable energy you find in start-up ventures when everyone is committed, heart and soul, to a common cause and a common quest.

I had always found enormous excitement in doing my own research and pursuing new ideas. As soon as I started out at Sunny St. Helena, back in 1937, I set up my own personal wine lab in a room under Jack Riorda's house. At the end of the working day, I'd draw off some samples of the wine and run tests on them during the evening and late into the night. I'd become totally immersed and I loved every minute of it. Later, when I moved into my own place with Marge on Charter Oak in St. Helena, there was a small tower out back that housed our water tank. I had running water and gas installed there, and I bought some pine boards and built myself a cozy little research lab. I'd spend hour upon hour in that lab, totally engaged in what was to become my own lifelong quest: I wanted to learn everything there was to know about the fascinating—and somewhat mysterious—process by which the humble juice of grapes is alchemized into the elegance and grandeur of fine wine.

There was so much to learn. Wine making is both an art and a science, but it is not just one science. In order to understand fully the process, you have to learn elements of geography, geology, meteorology, agriculture, botany, biology, and chemistry. A bit of physics can come in handy, too. To master the vineyard, you have to learn about soil qualities, water tables, rain patterns, rootstocks, grape varietals, planting patterns and schedules, insect control, mold and fungus control, trellising and pruning techniques, irrigation, how to measure sugar and acid levels, sun exposure, when to pick the grapes, and how best to pick them. Then to master the wine cellar, you have to learn the intricacies of fermentation, yeast varieties, acid levels, and the composition of grape skins, stems, and pips and how they affect the juice. You have to learn how fermenting juice reacts to its container, be it concrete, stainless steel, or wood. It also pays to know a good deal about engineering, refrigeration, and even welding. If you age your wine in oak barrels, as we do, you have to learn about forests and forest maintenance, about the different varieties of oak coming from different parts of the world, and about how barrels are made and how different kinds of oak and different kinds of barrels impart different qualities to the wine. Even corks are a science unto themselves; imperfect corks or imperfect corking techniques can ruin even the best-made wine. Each different wine you make — red, white, rosé, sweet, or sparkling — uses a different grape variety, and you have to understand the qualities of each variety and learn the specific process for making each different wine. On top of all this, each year in wine making is a new challenge, with different rainfall and temperatures, a different number of sunny days, and different vine conditions, too. Just as each child you raise is different, so it is with wines; with each year and each vintage you have to start anew.

When I started out at Sunny St. Helena, I knew only the rudiments of these various disciplines. But I learned a lot from watching Jack Riorda, who was always tinkering with the way we made wine. For instance, during fermentation, the skins, pulp, and some of the seeds are forced up to the top of the vat by the bubbling action of the carbon dioxide gas. These tend to fuse together and form a thick crust on the top of the wine. We call that crust the cap. The cap can become very dense and make the wine very hot. Inside it, the process of fermentation moves very rapidly—a potential danger to the wine. So at Sunny St. Helena we would regularly punch open the cap and pump liquid from below up over the top to keep the fermenting wine and pomace—the residue of grape skins, seeds, and stems—properly mixed and to extract the quality and flavor from the grapes. We call that procedure punching and pumping over. Now this may be done by machine, but back then we did it by hand, using a heavy metal punch that looked like a big iron fist with six prongs on it. For our fermenting tank, Jack devised a system of gates that we could shut to keep the cap submerged in the fermenting juice, thus eliminating the need to punch and pump over. It was a fairly crude solution, but it worked. Later, I eliminated the gate system and replaced it with a better procedure.

Much of my early experimenting dealt with the chemistry of wine making. For instance, one of the things we measure carefully and try to control is the temperature inside the fermentation vat. At Sunny St. Helena I became very interested in the way the temperature during fermentation affected the quality of our wines. When we bought Krug, Peter and I began experimenting with fermenting some of our white wines at temperatures much lower than the general practice. This was complicated; we had to put refrigeration jackets around our fermentation tanks to control the temperatures. But the results were startling. Cold fermentation helped preserve and bring out the wine's natural fruitiness and delicacy. This is a practice we have developed and refined ever since, and at my winery we cold-ferment many of the wines we make today.

During my years of apprenticeship, I forged a policy that has served me well ever since: I never hesitated to bring in outside consultants and researchers. This often drove my financial officers nuts, but I always wanted the best advice I could get. At Sunny St. Helena, after Jack died, I launched a campaign to upgrade the quality of our wines, and I turned for help to Vic Enriques, my old professor of viticulture at U.C. Berkeley. Vic had been one of my early tutors in wine making. As a consultant, he gave me invaluable advice and I was able to put his advice into practice right away — saving the company time, money, and heartache. To me the lesson was clear: Be flexible. Always pursue your own research and experimentation, but sometimes hiring outside consultants is the smartest and most cost-effective step a manager can take.

This search for the best minds in the wine business led me, inevitably, to one of the true legends of American wine making: André Tchelistcheff. In the late 1800s, the history of the Napa Valley was forged by a number of Europeans, most of them Germans, who emigrated to California and set up their own wineries. Men like Jacob and Fritz Beringer, Gustav Niebaum, Jacob Schram, and Charles Krug. These men were pioneers and visionaries, and their common passion was viticulture and fine wine. Thanks to them, the Napa Valley was making some very fine wines toward the end of the last century—before the terrible infestation of phylloxera, an insatiable root louse, in the 1890s. Our wine industry staggered back in the early 1900s, only to be crippled again, this time by Prohibition. To my mind, by the middle of this century, as our industry struggled back yet again, there were two great wine minds carrying forth in the earlier pioneering tradition: Louis Martini Sr. and André Tchelistcheff. They were both huge in personality and expertise, and I often referred to them as the Mussolini and the Stalin of the wine business. I did so out of affection and admiration; they were both extraordinarily generous with me, always willing to share their time, their passion, and their unparalleled knowledge of wine making.

Tchelistcheff was a man of Old World culture and breeding, and he was a born researcher and innovator. He was a White Russian, born in Moscow in 1901. His father was a prominent intellectual and jurist. The family had an estate southwest of Moscow and André spent his childhood there, amidst the cherry orchards, horses, dairy cows, and other basic elements of gentleman farming in Russia at the time. When the revolution erupted, his family entered a period of turmoil, flight, and eventually exile. André enrolled in officers' school and later joined the White Army. This set him off on several years of varying assignments with an army unit that had no country. He spent time in Bulgaria, Yugoslavia, and Czechoslovakia. In Yugoslavia, now as a civilian, he did a brief apprenticeship in wine making and viticulture. From there he went on to Czechoslovakia, where he enrolled in the Institute of Agricultural Technology, intent on learning animal husbandry and one day owning his own farm. In 1933 André found himself in France, a favorite destination for many White Russian families, and he joined up with an exiled Russian prince in a farming venture outside Paris. André became an expert on chickens, but his farming venture was hurt by bad weather and was forced to close down. Poultry's loss would soon be viticulture's gain. And mine.

At just about the time I joined Sunny St. Helena, André began working at a big winery in France and studying viticulture and fermentation at a branch of the prestigious Institute of National Agronomy. I'm sure André would have been quite content to spend his life doing research in France; he often said so. In 1938, however, one of his professors at the institute introduced him to Georges de Latour, an adventuresome French aristocrat who had emigrated to California and founded Beaulieu Vineyard, one of the premier wineries in our valley. Beaulieu at the time was having some problems with its wines, and de Latour had come to France looking for just the right man to fix them. He chose André. The Russian émigré agreed to come to California, and I believe it is safe to say that their handshake changed the course of wine making in America.

André grew up drinking fine European wines. He was schooled in the art of wine making the French way, and he had what we call a soft palate, meaning he had a taste for wines that were elegant, sophisticated, and subtle in flavor. The big, fruitier, hearty table wines that many vintners in California were making at the time were popular enough, but they were not at all to André's taste. When he arrived in Rutherford, just up the road from where we are now, the situation at Beaulieu was decidedly mixed. On the one hand, the winery had come through Prohibition pretty well. Like Beringer and Christian Brothers, Beaulieu had cleverly secured a special ruling from San Francisco's archbishop, appointing the winery an official supplier of altar wines, which were exempted from the anti-alcohol ban. So Beaulieu was able to keep making wine during Prohibition, and they had plenty on hand when the law was finally rescinded.

Financially, therefore, Beaulieu was in good shape; its wine making was another story. From the vineyards to the cellars in Rutherford, what André found was not impressive. In fact, it was very mediocre. So were the results. Beaulieu's cabernet sauvignon, made in the style of the best Bordeauxs, was quite good. But the rest of the Beaulieu wines were very disappointing, especially to a palate as refined as André's. So André rolled up his sleeves and went to work. Georges de Latour gave him wide latitude (but little money), and André began overhauling almost every aspect of Beaulieu's operation, short of sales and marketing.

What André accomplished was tremendous. He carefully studied soil and climate conditions on the various Beaulieu properties and came up with startling conclusions. In his view, the Napa Valley had three distinct climates, each one corresponding to one of the great wine regions of France. In the south, in the region we call Carneros, the soil quality and the cool, moist conditions created by the area's proximity to the San Francisco Bay reminded André of Burgundy and its rich tradition of pinot noir. The middle of the valley, with its spacious plains and warmer temperatures, reminded André of Bordeaux and the great cabernet sauvignons and sauvignon blancs. The northern portion of the valley, from St. Helena on up to Calistoga, was similar to the Rhône Valley, with its distinctive reds and fine white wines. Once he assessed these similarities, André became convinced that Beaulieu, and other wineries in the valley, had botched up their plantings. Grape varietals best suited to Carneros, say, were planted in areas suited to cabernet. So André ripped out whole vineyards and replanted.

Along with these changes in Beaulieu's viticulture, André pushed forward several important changes in their way of wine making. He took a keen interest, for instance, in malolactic fermentation, a second fermentation that turns the wine's malic acid, which has a tart, green-apple quality, into lactic acid, which is softer and milkier. The result, in some wines, is more roundness and complexity. André also pushed Beaulieu in a direction near to my heart: cold fermentation of their white wines. In all of this, he worked closely with teams of scientists from the University of California who had come to the valley to work with the industry and urge wine makers to take a more scientific approach to their craft. In many ways, André became the Napa Valley's bridge, linking the Old World traditions of European wine making to our young, gung-ho, technology-minded wine industry. With his combination of passion and technical expertise, André and his ideas transformed not only Beaulieu but also many other Napa Valley wineries, and in doing so he earned himself a secure reputation as one of the most influential figures in twentieth-century American wine making.

I got an enormous kick out of André. He was a small man, with an elfish presence and grin, and he spoke with a thick European accent, sort of a hybrid of Russian and French. He was a chain-smoker, and he always held his cigarette in a funny, unusual European way, between his second and third fingers. I liked André and he liked me. I'm sure a part of him, the part that was the sniffy European aristocrat, viewed me as a relentlessly self-promoting novice—born of Italian peasants, no less—a view I'm sure other people in the valley shared. But the world of wine cuts through traditional social hierarchies and establishes its own aristocracy, aficionado to aficionado. And I'm sure that this part of André found in me a kindred spirit.

Thus it was that in my first years at Krug, before the end of World War II, I turned to André for detailed advice about our wine making. With the consent of Beaulieu, I made him a paid consultant. André and I would talk for hours on end, and I always found his ideas very stimulating. During harvest and wine making in the fall, we'd meet at least once a week, from about 7 P.M. on, to discuss each step we were taking in crushing, fermentation, and other procedures. When I set out on my own in 1966, hell-bent on making wines that could compete with the best in the world, I often turned to André for advice and he was always willing to help. For we shared a common goal: making world-class wines and turning California into a model of innovation and achievement in the process.

THE BASICS OF WINE MAKING

So how *is* fine wine made? The question is simple, but I have spent my whole life looking for the right answers. There is no shortage of places to look. Wine-making traditions, methods, equipment, and philosophies vary according to country, region, winery, and, of course, the taste of each individual wine maker. There are at least four hundred different variables involved in the process of making wine; no wonder, then, that so many fine wines have their own discernible character and style. To me, this is a large part of what makes wine making and wine tasting so fascinating; there are so many different kinds and styles of wine to study and taste. I literally have traveled all over the world looking for knowledge, tasting wines, seeing how wine is made in different areas, examining every detail of the different ways to make fine wines — all in the hope of finding some new approach or technique, or even a small tidbit of information, that would help us make our own wines better than they already are.

So it is very difficult to generalize about how wine is made. It is also difficult to be brief on the subject. Huge tomes have been written on wine making and they have to be updated every few years to keep up with technological advances. Amerine's *The Technology of Wine Making* runs nearly eight hundred pages. At our winery, we maintain an in-house wine-making manual, which we constantly update, and it, too, runs several hundred pages. So I will not venture a definitive explanation here. To understand wine in depth, and to learn about the different wines of the world, I would recommend reading any of the books by my friend Hugh Johnson, one of Britain's most distinguished wine writers and connoisseurs.

To help explain my life's quest, though, and the research and innovation we carried forth, let me set forth a general primer on how wine was being made in 1966, when I started the Robert Mondavi Winery. With this as a foundation, I will then be able to explain the various innovations we pioneered right from our beginning. In a later chapter, my son Tim, now our wine maker, will describe how much further we have pushed the art and science since then and the very exciting future we now see on the horizon. First, though, some basics, and please keep in mind that methods, equipment, and philosophy often vary substantially from what I will describe.

Let me start with a simple fact: Nature doesn't need man

to make wine; it can happen spontaneously on the vine. When grapes ripen, they become plump with a mixture of water and a very high level of sugar, about 20 to 25 percent. No one is quite sure where the yeast comes from—it appears to be ubiquitous in the air—but as the fruit ripens, the yeast on the bloom (the waxy coating on the grape skin) stands ready and waiting for the skin to crack open. Once it does, the yeast begins to ferment the sugar into alcohol, and grape juice into wine.

The job of the wine maker, in my view, is to guide this natural process in as gentle and effective manner as possible in order to make the highest possible quality of wine. The quality of the wine depends, first and foremost, on the quality of the grapes. Beyond that, a wine can be made in a simple style (focusing only on the flavor of the grape) or a complex style (having many layers of flavors from malolactic fermentation, barrel aging, yeast contact, etc.). As a general rule, making a fine wine in a more complex style involves the highest quality grapes and labor-intensive winemaking techniques and is, thus, more costly. The techniques for making red, white, and rosé wines are also markedly different.

Most of the fine wines in California are varietal wines, meaning they are made primarily (at least 75 percent) from one grape variety and they carry the name of that grape on the label. For instance, cabernet sauvignon, pinot noir, and merlot are red grape varieties; chardonnay, viognier, Johannisberg, sauvignon blanc are white varieties.

Now here is a greatly simplified introduction to how wines are made. The grapes are harvested when they reach optimum maturity levels. At our winery, we assess the grapes both by tasting for full development of flavors and by measuring the sugar level with an instrument called a refractometer. We prefer to harvest most of our grapes by hand, but there are also increasingly gentle mechanical harvesters that can be suitable alternatives. Ideally, the grapes are picked in the early morning hours when they are still cool from the night fog and then taken immediately to the winery. By pressing or crushing the grapes within hours of being on the vine, more fruit character is captured in the wine.

To make a white wine such as chardonnay, sauvignon blanc, or Johannisberg Riesling, we immediately press the grapes and then ferment only the juice. (I'll tell you about the pressing equipment a little later.) Years ago, we would first destem the grapes and then, after a short time of skin contact, we would press the juice from the skins. Since 1985, however, our white grapes are immediately pressed as whole clusters to bypass destemming and any skin contact time. We have found that the whole cluster pressing yields a more balanced, delicate white wine with less tannin extraction. Tannin is the astringency found in the skins and seeds.

In our wine making, we choose to ferment the juice of white grapes in small oak barrels, stainless steel tanks, or a combination of both. Fermenting in temperature-controlled stainless steel tanks at cool temperatures captures fresh, fruity character in the wine, while fermenting in small oak barrels yields wines with more flavor complexity and depth. The choice depends on the style of wine the wine maker wants to achieve.

Another factor is the choice of yeast. In our wine making, we match the yeast strain to the character of the vineyard. We may use native yeast—occurring naturally on the grapes—or we may select one of dozens of cultured strains that have been isolated for specific characteristics. As the yeast converts the sugar into alcohol, carbon dioxide is released and heat is generated. Fermentation forms chemical compounds that contribute flavors to the wine and the selection of yeast strains is one of many variables that contribute to these flavors. For many of our wines now, we are using the native yeasts because of the layers of complexity they provide.

Temperature of fermentation influences how fast the yeast will convert the sugar into alcohol, in addition to contributing to the style of wine. For example, Johannisberg Riesling is usually fermented cool in temperature-controlled tanks to give the delicate fruit character to the wine. At 50°F, it will take the yeast two to three weeks to convert the sugar into alcohol. Juice fermented in sixty-gallon French oak barrels—chardonnay, for instance—reaches 60–70°F and takes only ten to fourteen days. If we want to leave sweetness in the wine, we stop the yeast by chilling and then filtering out the yeast. Dry wines—those without residual sugar—are allowed to completely finish the fermentation process.

There is also a second fermentation that we employ with chardonnay and the red wines to give them more depth and softness on the palate. This is done by a beneficial bacteria (either native on the skins or added as a culture) that changes the tart malic acid in the wine into softer lactic acid. Again, this is a natural process that we must gently guide to make a high-quality wine. We find a long malo-lactic fermentation in the barrel is most desirable and we often hand-stir the wine (called *batonage*) when this technique is done on chardonnay. This second fermentation is rarely done on fresh, fruity-style white wines but it often contributes to the complexity of dry white and red wines.

Aging is the next step. When I began our winery in 1966, I was convinced that aging in small French oak barrels was imperative if Napa Valley wines were to achieve world-class status. Over the years, we have developed an extensive barrel program. Certain wines are rough and simple in their youth but have the potential to develop great complexity and elegance through oak aging. During aging, the barrel contributes aromatic and flavor compounds that marry with the wine for added dimension and complexity. As an example, our Chardonnay Reserve is first fermented in oak barrels and then aged on the yeast lees, which is called *sur lie*, in sixty-gallon French oak barrels for about a year to achieve a creamy texture with integrated oak nuances.

Now, let me briefly tell you how making red wines differs. After we harvest the grapes, we use a destemmer-crusher to remove the stems. Over the years, our equipment has become more gentle and efficient at removing the grapes from the clusters without mangling the stems or crushing the *berries* (as we call grapes in the trade). For our pinot noir, we have often desired a percentage of whole berries in the fermentation or even whole clusters, including the stems. Our preferences continue to evolve, as we better understand the personality of each vineyard. If we desire the grapes to be lightly crushed, we can bring the roller bars closer together on the destemmer-crusher. The crushed grapes are now called *must*.

The must is transferred to a fermentation tank either by pumps or gravity. We prefer gravity filling, which Tim will cover in more detail in his section. We can either add a yeast culture immediately or let native yeasts propagate slowly, allowing the must a pre-fermentation soaking or *maceration*. Fermentation can be done in a variety of containers, including wood, concrete, and glass-lined steel in some wineries worldwide, but our preference is temperature-controlled stainless steel tanks or small, open-top oak vats. Quite a bit of heat is produced during fermentation, bringing the wine upward to 85°F. The yeast is very active at this temperature and ferments all the sugar into alcohol within several days after the onset of fermentation. During fermentation, the skins rise to the top of the fermenter and we either pump the wine over the cap of skins or gently push them back down into the wine (called *pigeage*). This way, the wine gets full extraction of rich flavors, color, and tannin from the skins. Once the wine has fermented dry, we continue to leave the skins with the wine for additional development of varietal character and softening of tannins. The length of extended maceration depends on the variety and vineyard and is decided on by tasting. On the average, our Napa Valley Pinot Noir has about two weeks and our cabernet sauvignon has about four weeks of skin contact. But there is no set formula; so much depends on the personality of the vineyard.

We experimented with different types of presses as well. For pressing, we prefer a very gentle pneumatic enclosed membrane press or a basket press. The enclosed membrane press consists of a horizontal tank with an inflatable food-grade rubber membrane inside. It works like an air bladder to gently press the wine from the skins, now called pomace. The hydraulic basket press is an updated version of the traditional wood-slatted press that has been used for centuries. We divide the drain and press wines, and may judiciously blend just enough of the press wine back into the drain wine for body, being careful not to get harsh, overly tannic character.

We then transfer the wine to small sixty-gallon oak barrels for aging. As I mentioned before, we like the malolactic fermentation to slowly take place here. As with the yeast fermentation, carbon dioxide is also released during the secondary fermentation. We use loose-fitting glass bungs to allow the CO_2 to escape. The red wines, including cabernet sauvignon, merlot, pinot noir, zinfandel, barbera, and sangiovese, slowly mature and marry with the oak character. The desired length of aging is vintage and variety specific — always dependent on sensory judgment — and lasts up to two years for our cabernet sauvignon.

During aging, the wines may be gently racked, barrel to barrel, to enhance the wine's development and for natural clarification. We may also add egg whites to clarify the red wines and softly sculpt the tannins. In this traditional technique, we add between four and ten egg whites per barrel. The insoluble egg whites bind with some of the harsher tannins and precipitate them out of the wine. We then gently rack off the clear wine from the lees (sediment). These are just a few of the gentle techniques we use to allow us to bottle many of our wines unfiltered since the 1986 vintage. We believe bottling wine without filtration allows us to better capture the wine's full complexity of flavors.

Rosé wines are also made from red grapes but with only very short skin contact. Nearly all red grapes have clear juice, so the color of the wine depends on the length of time the juice is in contact with the skin. To make a rosé wine (or a white wine from a red grape, such as a white zinfandel), we give the juice only several hours of skin contact to achieve the desired light to deep rosé hue. After pressing (or simply draining off the juice), the juice is usually fermented in temperature-controlled stainless steel tanks at cool temperatures to retain the fresh, fruity character of the grape. Generally, rosé wines are not oak aged and are made to be enjoyed when they are young and vibrant.

Since the late 1970s we have made a limited amount of sparkling wine. A grand share of it is enjoyed at our winery celebrations. We have two sparkling wines, Chardonnay Brut and Blanc de Noirs (a blend of pinot noir and chardonnay). To make a sparkling wine we hand-harvest the grapes at slightly lower sugars than for still wines. We press the grapes as whole clusters and then ferment the juice as if we were making a dry white wine, using primarily tank fermentation with a small amount (about 25 percent) barrel fermentation. After the blend is made, we add a specially selected champagne yeast and sugar for the second alcoholic fermentation in the bottle. The bubbles from the second fermentation, which lasts about a month, are captured in the wine. We age the sparkling wine on the yeast for up to five years to add creamy complexity to the flavors. The bottles are then riddled (inverted and turned for a period of several weeks) and the yeast settles into the cap. The yeast is then removed by the process of disgorging (freezing the neck) and we've trapped the bubbles in the bottle.

Although procedures can vary greatly, these are the basics of wine making, the starting point for my winery and my quest. Along with emphasizing research and innovation, and surrounding myself with the finest minds in the business, from day one I was determined to launch the Robert Mondavi Winery with dazzling new equipment and a fresh approach to making fine wines. And in this regard we made quite a splash. If you visit our winery in Oakville today, you can see a small part of the original equipment from 1966 and some of the latest innovations in our approach to making fine wine.

In the early years of our winery, we changed our relationship with our growers. I had concluded that much of a wine's quality comes from the vineyard, as well as from the wine making. So I knew we had to work closely with our growers to help them limit their yields and improve the quality of their grapes. I felt strongly that we had to initiate a system of financial incentives to prod the growers to make the changes and investments necessary to boost the quality of their grapes. The key was price. Up to then, a grower would deliver his grapes by truck, and we'd weigh the truck and his load before and after his delivery. The difference in weight was the weight of the grapes and we'd pay him by weight at a price that was usually pretty standard throughout the valley and the state. I told our growers that if they produced grapes that would make superior wines, I'd pay them more than the going price in the valley. The incentive to the grower was clear: the closer he worked with us to achieve the quality we wanted, the more he earned. And his revenue would be higher than if he sold his grapes at the going price in the valley. It took some convincing, but many growers in the valley came around and joined our plan.

This incentive package led to another innovation: a systematic education program for our growers. Before, come harvest time, the growers would deliver their grapes, check off the tonnage, and say good-bye. Under the new system, we brought our growers back in February so they could taste the early results of the wine we were making from their particular grapes. This enabled them to see the correlation between the quality of the grapes they were producing and the quality of our wine. This was only the first step, though. From here, we would send our vineyard specialists out to the growers' fields to work with their teams, evaluate their procedures, and make the necessary changes to improve quality. The result of this multileveled program was clear: we raised our growers' consciousness and their level of expertise. They came to understand that in their vineyards they were growing wine, not grapes. I think this realization was a major turning point in our quest to make great wines.

Now, the equipment. When it came time for our very first harvest in 1966, we were ready with a system designed to make high-quality wines, yes, but also to make in reasonable quantities for the marketplace. We were going to handcraft high-quality wines but not in tiny quantities like they did in many boutique wineries in Europe and California. In our desire to produce reasonable quantities, one of our primary aims back then, especially with our whites, was to make sure we had the cleanest possible juice before fermentation through the use of new equipment, small doses of sulfur dioxide, and various fining agents and forms of filtration. Only later did we discover that this rigorous cleaning—part of what we call the suppression of fault—stripped the wine of vital essences, flavor, and character. Nonetheless, this was part of our mind-set in those first years.

Our system was quite efficient. When our growers drove their trucks in, they'd off-load their grapes into a large stainless steel hopper. This would then feed the grapes into a crusher-destemmer, as I described before. In today's state-of-the-art wine making, such as our facilities at Opus One, Byron, and Carneros, the destemming process is much gentler and the must slides down into the fermentation and storage tanks by gravity alone. Back in 1966, though, the must was pumped through in-place stainless steel lines into our wine-making facility.

At this stage of the process, we developed two key innovations. By 1966 I was a firm believer in the benefits of cold-fermenting our white wines, right from the moment they were crushed. So we devised a way to chill the must as it left the crusher. From the pipes, the must went into what became one of our major innovations: our fermentation and storage tanks. Instead of using big fermenting vats made of redwood or oak, we brought in brand-new tanks made of sparkling stainless steel. This was a first in the Napa Valley. In my years of experimenting, I had become convinced that stainless steel offered us several advantages. First, cleanliness. Hygiene is essential in a winery; a bout of unwanted bacteria or mold can devastate your wine — and your business. With stainless steel, the tanks were easy to hose down and sterilize. The tanks were also fitted with temperature-controlling metal jackets. This made it much easier to keep fermentation temperatures regulated and stable, thus helping us prevent off flavors from invading the wine. I realized, too, that we could use the stainless steel tanks not just for fermentation but also for storage.

When other wineries in the valley saw the jump in the quality of our wines, they, too, began fermenting in stainless steel.

We experimented with different types of presses as well. One of our most important steps was to pioneer and popularize the use of new French oak barrels for aging our California wines. I realized the importance of aging wine in new or clean barrels when I first visited Bordeaux and Burgundy. The First Growths of Bordeaux used only new barrels and the wines were always clean and well made, whereas the Second, Third, and Fourth Growths reused their barrels over and over. Unfortunately, the results I saw were either spent wines or wines with bacterial deficiencies. Most of these wines had off characters. I knew that we could improve our wine making by using new barrels or very clean used barrels. In California, with the exception of Hanzell Winery in Sonoma County, no one was using new French oak. They were using old casks or redwood tanks. Very few people realized the importance of aging in small barrels. We brought in large shipments of new barrels and sold them to competing wineries. This was the beginning of an important shift in the way we were making wines in the Napa Valley. By aging in proper oak, we were able to make more complex wines, with more layers of flavor, and these wines helped raise the image of the Napa Valley. As a result, many wine growers from regions around the world came to see us to see what we were doing. Barrel aging gave our red wines character, complexity, subtlety, and, when we were really successful, the kind of elegance and polish you find in the best wines of Bordeaux and Burgundy. In those early years, we bought our barrels from Demptos, a French cooperage that also supplied most of the best châteaus in Bordeaux. That was just the kind of company I wanted to keep.

In our first years, we pioneered a host of smaller innovations as well. When it came to bottling, for instance, we went in for the finest equipment and then we adapted it even further. Our main goal was to make sure there was as little oxygen as possible in the finished bottle. So, first we would sparge, or spray, the empty bottles with nitrogen. Then we would fill the bottles with wine. From there, we devised a way to evacuate the air from the neck of the bottle before the cork is inserted. This is to insure that when the cork is pistonned down into the bottle, it does not force any residual oxygen down into the wine. Vacuum bottling, like cold fermentation and barrel aging, soon became standard operating procedure for many wineries in California and beyond.

I cannot claim to be single-handedly responsible for all these innovations. To the contrary, while I was the driving force for innovation and change, the real work in the cellar, experimenting with new techniques, was usually carried out by our wine-making staff, under Michael's direction in the early years and then under Tim's, when he took over as chief wine maker in the 1970s.

In September 1969, however, I was forced back into the cellar in a very hands-on way. Michael came down with hepatitis and went into the hospital for several weeks.

Afterward, he was bedridden at home for several weeks more. Out of the blue, in only our third year in operation, we were without a chief wine maker. So I stepped into the breach. This was a stiff challenge; I had not worked full-time in a wine cellar in nearly two decades. I had done my apprenticeship at Sunny St. Helena and managed our wine making during our early years at Krug, developing many of the fundamentals we are still using today. But then I had turned wine making over to Peter. While we always tasted our wines together and discussed methodology with our wine-making staff, I hadn't done any hands-on wine making since. Even though our philosophy was the same, now we were making our wines in a whole new way, based on our research and new equipment. So I had to learn all the new nuances and equipment right away, almost from scratch.

Talk about a steep learning curve. At Krug, I had worked with excellent cellar masters, Joe Maganini and Bill Bonetti, among others, and a staff of about sixty people. Our goal was to excel in each category of our wines, be it our Premium Charles Krug wines or the CK wines we sold in half-gallon or one-gallon jugs. From day one at the Robert Mondavi Winery, we were determined to make wine the way only a very few of the great European producers do. That meant I was always emphasizing one element above all others: quality. And I established the procedure to do just that.

During my stint as interim wine maker, I had plenty of help. Brad Warner, as meticulous a cellar master as you can find, had left Krug and was between jobs. Michael then brought him aboard to help us run the cellar operations. Brad was someone I could bank on to watch over every detail of our wine making. There are certain key principles that are essential, such as keeping our barrels topped up — a practice often overlooked at many wineries. We also have to monitor our fermentation tanks religiously to maintain the proper temperatures. If they varied by one degree, I'd raise holy hell! Brad maintained strict quality control, so we never had wines that were off character. That's just shoddy wine making and I wouldn't stand for it. Neither would Brad. We were both militant perfectionists.

In several ways, my forced return to the cellar proved to be a blessing in disguise. By working in the cellar myself, training staff, testing equipment, and experimenting with different methods and various kinds of oak, I reconfirmed what was necessary to produce great wines. I could also see firsthand how we needed to modify our cellar and wine-making operation. As a result, we were able to avoid some bad planning and investment decisions, and I'm sure we saved ourselves a lot of time, money, and heartache in the long run. To me, the lesson was clear: It always pays for owners and top-level managers to have hands-on experience at the ground level of their enterprise, especially during the critical start-up years.

During our first years in operation, our commitment to research and innovation soon earned us a reputation as the test-tube winery. I was proud of that label and I still am. What we were doing was generating enormous excitement inside the winery, and it was creating quite a stir in the valley and throughout the wine business. Chuck Daniels, a friend of mine who for many years was a member of our board and our distributor in Northern California, tells a story from our early years that reveals a lot about our spirit and the reputation we were earning.

One day, as Chuck tells it, I was in our cellars with a salesman representing an outfit in Springfield, Missouri. The company was named Paul Mueller and they made big stainless steel tanks for breweries and for dairy farmers to store their milk. The salesman showed me some samples of their work, and, according to Chuck, I came out of the cellar jumping with excitement. "Chuck, you've gotta see this guy's samples! Look at this welding! Have you ever seen such beautiful welding?" Chuck thought I was off on some wacky—and costly—new idea. At that time, we were buying stainless steel fermenting tanks from two companies in California, and they worked well enough. Mueller had never before constructed a single wine fermentation tank, but I was so impressed by that one sample that I decided to give them a try. So we ordered the first Mueller tanks ever to be used in the wine business.

Mueller built the tanks and shipped them out to us by railroad car. They came up the valley on what we used to call the St. Helena rattler, the local freight line. Well, when word got around about those tanks arriving, people up and down the valley flocked to the tracks to have a look. They were huge and gorgeous. What welding! The skeptics, of course, were quick to scoff. Dairy tanks! Another Mondavi folly! Well, what can I say? Mueller tanks are now used throughout the American wine business. One man's folly is another man's fortune.

I am an uncompromising perfectionist. I believe that most people who are successful in business are. In order to get the most from our program of research and innovation—and to justify the investment—I drove everyone extremely hard. Fourteen-hour days and six- or seven-day weeks were common. And I became an absolute fanatic about detail. Many staffers balked, even some of my best people, but I refused to let up. People who knew me complained privately—and even to my face—that I had tunnel vision, that I had put blinders on and could see and talk about nothing but wine, wine, wine. Members of my own family were often the first to become exasperated. "Bobby," my sister Helen used to say, "we know you're in the wine business. Can't you talk about anything else?"

Well, she may have been right—from her perspective. But I felt I was right from mine. To accomplish what I had set out to do, I had to put blinders on. My life's dream was at stake! And I was determined to stop at nothing to turn that dream into a reality. Nothing. Only later, much later, did I come to see how my tunnel vision, my steamrolling personality, and my total commitment to wine, wine, wine ended up inflicting terrible pain on Marge, the children, and some of the people working closest to me. The truth is, I was oblivious to the impact of my ways until it was too late to undo the damage.

There is a lesson in all this, one I learned the hard way. Single-mindedness is a marvelous elixir: it blinds you to the needs and the pain of all the people you're choosing to ignore. It also blinds you to the terrible truth that in life, as in wine, excess and imbalance are no virtues, even in pursuit of a noble goal.

CHAPTER 5

Taste

WHAT DOES IT TAKE to make a truly great wine?

Climate, soil, wonderful vineyards, superb grapes, research, innovation, state-of-the-art equipment—all these are vital. But they only provide part of the foundation. People are key as well. No one makes wine alone; you need dedicated specialists in the vineyards and throughout the entire process of harvest, crush, fermentation, aging, bottling, and corking. These people, too, are vital parts of the foundation. But in themselves, all these people and ingredients are not enough to turn humble grapes into the elegance and grandeur of a Romanée-Conti or a Château Mouton-Rothschild. In the art of making fine wine, the quest for greatness always comes down to this: the artist and his gifts. The wine maker and his skill, his passion, character, sensibility, vision, and, above all else, his powers of taste.

Taste. Some people are born with it. Some people learn to develop it. The best wine makers spend their lives trying to master it. In my view, it takes almost a lifetime of experience and dedication for a wine maker to master all the elements and subtleties of the art of tasting. And he or she had better start early! In my case, I did start early, very early, and I had marvelous teachers: my mother and father.

I have such wonderful memories of my mother. In stature, she was a small woman, but she was very powerful. Momma Rosa is what everyone called her and, believe me, you didn't cross her. Her manner was almost always warm and gentle, but in her domain she was the boss—and everyone knew it. I remember one episode that proved to me what a tough lady she was. This was when I was a little boy in Virginia, Minnesota, during the days of Prohibition. Because families were allowed to have a limited amount of wine for their own consumption, our cellar was full of wine barrels—not just for us; each boarder had his own supply. Well, word got around town. People said, "The Mondavis have all sorts of wine in their cellar." The local authorities heard about it, and one day they showed up at our door, axes in hand. They went down to the cellar and they were just about to swing their axes into all those barrels when Mother appeared on the scene.

"Now you wait just a minute!" she cried. "We have every right to have this wine. It isn't all for us; we have boarders here and we're just housing most of this wine for them!"

The officers, axes in hand, told her to back away, but Mother stood her ground. I remember there was all sorts of yelling and screaming, so loud that I could hear it upstairs, where I had been ordered to go and stay put. I don't know exactly how she managed it, but somehow Mother convinced those men to stop. She then convinced them that we did, in fact, have boarders and that we had every right to have that quantity of wine. To our great relief, the officers soon left, with their tails between their legs. And all those wine barrels were spared the ax, thanks to Momma Rosa.

Also thanks to her, every day of my childhood was an education in taste. We always had at least five or six boarders in our house in Minnesota, and on weekends Mother would cook for fifteen or sixteen people, most of them hungry miners. She'd be up at four or five o'clock in the morning to get started. My sisters would help in the kitchen, and Peter and I would sometimes pitch in, too. Just watching and helping Mother work, we learned about cooking and nutrition and about the care, patience, artistry, and sheer hard work that go into a fine meal. Mother always cooked from scratch and according to the seasons, using what was fresh in the garden or in the market. She was also careful to prepare meals that went well with the weather—both in terms of taste and nutrition.

In those brutally cold Minnesota winters, for instance, when we needed all the strength we could muster to stand up to the subzero temperatures, Mother would prepare huge winter meals. In the morning, for the kids and her boarders going off to the mines, Mother would prepare huge pots of oatmeal or polenta reheated from the night before, and she'd serve them with hot stewed tomatoes. To prepare for lunch, she'd start in the early morning and put a couple of whole chickens in the kettle to make stock. Then with eggs and flour she'd make fresh noodles. From the stock and the noodles would come our first course at lunch or dinner: chicken noodle soup. Then would come one of my favorites: fresh pasta with her special game sauce, made from tomatoes, garlic, herbs, and either robins or some kind of game. Her brother, Nazzareno, whom we called Uncle Neno, was an avid hunter. He'd kill anything and everything, in and out of season, and the game he brought back always found its way onto our table or into a fresh sauce for pasta. As a main course, Mother often made roasts of pork, veal, or beef, or a marvelous roast chicken stuffed with her special dressing.

To go with her roasts, she often made polenta, a favorite among the kids. Making polenta was always a major operation, filled with merriment. We had a big wooden table in the center of the kitchen, and Mother would spread the polenta over the entire table; then we would all gather around and grind the meal and get it ready for cooking. We'd chatter like birds, sing songs, and just bask in the warmth of the kitchen and our mother's love. Mother made her own Italian desserts as well. One of my favorites as a boy was *ciambelle*, a breadlike dough she would fry and then top with honey or powdered sugar. Simple, yet so delicious.

Wine was part of my experience as early as I can remember. At lunch and dinner, my mother or father would
routinely flavor my water with a dollop of wine. I didn't like
water alone, but I loved it that way. So I grew up thinking of
wine as liquid food. It tasted good and everyone thought
even then that it was healthy—good for the circulation and
a general tonic for the system. When I got a little older,
along with the huge breakfasts we had on those cold winter
mornings, I'd get a special treat. Mother would prepare for
me a milder version of the peasant jump starter she made for
the miners: strong coffee, a bit of sugar to taste, and a jigger
of red wine. It's a peculiar taste, but I developed a lifelong
love for this in the morning, whether it's cold or not!

Our family had a very reliable supplier of wine: my father. Every autumn he would bring grapes home and make
wine in our basement. I loved to help him. The process we
used was simple but effective. First, we'd put the grapes in
little tubs, made from barrels cut in half. Then we'd put rubber boots on and stomp the grapes. Some peasant families
stomped the grapes barefoot, but we always wore those rubber boots. Almost all the wine Dad made was red wine. The
grapes he used most were zinfandel, but sometimes he also
used carignane, alicante bouschet, and muscat—the same
varieties he later bought and shipped when we moved to
Lodi. Dad made his wine as pure as possible. He didn't add
yeast or anything else, he just let the grape juice ferment
naturally, right in the barrels, skins and all. He would make

three or four barrels and that would last the family all year long. And he'd make wine for the boarders. So when we finished, we had a cellar well stocked for winter and the year ahead. Were the wines any good? Well, we thought so at the time. They always came out robust and tasting as pure and fruity as the grapes themselves. What they lacked in refinement they made up for in authenticity and richness of character. Just like my father.

After we moved to Lodi and the family began to prosper, Dad still made his own wine. Occasionally he would also buy bottled wines, and so I began learning about different wines and comparing their tastes. I also began to understand the impact of temperature on the taste of wine. Dad liked his wine very cold and I preferred mine at room temperature; I thought it had more flavor. So before mealtimes, I'd go down to the cellar and bring up two bottles. I'd keep his bottle cold and I'd set mine out so it could warm up to room temperature and the wine would properly open. My father not being much of a talker (I talked enough for the whole family, even back then), we rarely discussed wine; we just drank it and enjoyed it. I didn't fully realize it at the time, but by a daily process of osmosis, I was absorbing the basics and the subtleties of food, wine, and the art of tasting.

Watching Mother cook and Dad make wine, I was also absorbing a set of values that would later become the chrysalis of my own philosophy of making fine wine: Use only the best natural ingredients. Don't tamper with nature.

Stay away from chemicals, additives, and anything that weakens or masks the natural flavors. In cooking and in wine making, there are always gimmicks and shortcuts; for true artists, though, purity and simplicity are always the cardinal virtues.

From watching Mother in the kitchen, I also learned something deeper. Cooking to her was hard work, sure, but it was also a joy, a way of expressing the pride she took in her work and the love she had for her family. Her food brought the family together, first in the kitchen and then around the table. As I got older, I came to understand that for Mother, cooking was not work, it was a joy. It was a way for her to bathe us in the warmth of her spirit. Now just imagine if you could distill Mother's values, virtues, love, and generosity into a single bottle — that was exactly the wine I dreamed of making!

Growing up so steeped in the Italian way of life and wine, I didn't fully realize that many American families at that time looked askance at wine. In some quarters, the word *wine* usually signified cheap wine, and it was almost synonymous with winos and derelicts. Sure, some Americans enjoyed champagne on holidays and birthdays, and in big cities some people would order French or Italian wines when they went out for dinner, but few young people had any exposure to wine or any appreciation of its origins and noble tradition. When this really hit me was when I got to Stanford. What a shock I had. We'd go out on what we called beer busts—drinking parties—and what did people bring? They'd bring beer, scotch, bourbon—no wine. And I'd say that over 30 percent of the people, maybe even 40 percent, would get absolutely plastered—and wind up with terrible headaches. I'd say to myself, "My god, I thought Stanford was civilized! These people don't even know how to drink!" Really, I was dumbfounded. They'd get drunk, have headaches the next morning, and still go out and do crazy things like that almost every weekend. Wine was just as fun and so much healthier!

At Sunny St. Helena, I set out in earnest to master the art of tasting. And right away I noticed something funny. In the mornings at the winery, I would often do what my mother had done for me as a child: put a little wine in my morning coffee. But the mixture always seemed weak to me and I found myself putting in more and more of our Sunny St. Helena wine, as I tried to match the taste of what I had at home. Curious about this, I began tasting the wines we were making in the winery against the wines my father made at home, completely naturally. The difference was stark: our Sunny St. Helena wines just didn't have the same body and natural substance as the wines we made at home. Something vital had been stripped out. Because we were making bulk wines in such large quantities, we filtered it and added sulfur to help prevent spoilage. This was common practice; indeed, European wine makers have used sulfur dioxide for centuries to inhibit the growth of bacteria and molds. But while we gained in the cleanliness of our wines, we lost important elements of character and vitality. So right away I learned that wine making was often a trade-off and a delicate balance; the finer the wine you wanted to make, the more delicate the balance.

At Sunny St. Helena I began a ritual that has been my standard operating procedure ever since: I'd ask myself, "OK, who makes the best wines?" Then I'd go buy those wines and taste them carefully in order to discern how they were made and how they compared to our own wines. I'd buy wines from Beaulieu, Inglenook, Beringer Brothers, Larkmead, Wente — I tasted all the best. I didn't get any special budget for this from Jack Riorda — he was too old-fashioned for that — but I just felt that if I was going to learn to make good wines, I had to taste good wines and learn, right in my own mouth, what went into them. As the French would say, I had to "develop my nose" and "educate my palate." But no matter what fancy words you use, I knew that you don't learn the art of tasting from books; you learn it from drinking quality wines. Equally important, you learn it from tasting different foods along with fine wines to see how the flavors marry and harmonize. So in the evening I'd always come home with a new wine to try at dinner. Marge would often taste with me at dinner, though she never drank much at that time, and then I'd take the rest out to my lab in the tank house for a more thorough evaluation and analysis.

The results were often very surprising. I'd buy wines that had the best of reputations, then I'd taste the wines and find they were awful. I'd say, "Now wait a minute: this is for the birds! We're making better wines than that!" In this I learned a lesson that would serve me well later on: always taste the wine, not the label! My regular tastings also led to important changes in our wine-making procedures. For instance, in some of the highly reputed wines I was tasting, and in some of our wines, I often picked up off flavors. One common cause I ferreted out: oxidation. After we ferment and the wine is moved to the storage tanks, if not topped constantly, the wine would become oxidized and show off flavors. The wine loses its vitality. To prevent that, I started insisting that our tanks be regularly "topped up" with more wine to keep the tanks full and keep out excess oxygen. This prevented oxidation — and helped us produce healthy, clean, lively, properly balanced wines.

When I moved over to Krug, I expanded my system of regular tastings. First of all, I invited in people outside our little wine-making circle. I wanted everyone working for us to better understand wine and what we were trying to accomplish. I also expanded the range of wines we were tasting. We no longer tasted just the best wines from California; we branched out and began tasting wines from Bordeaux and Burgundy. I would sit down with Peter; our cellar master, Joe Maganini; our assistant wine maker, Bill Bonetti; Frank Gould, editor of our newsletter *Bottles and Bins*; and some other people involved in wine making, and we would taste those wines and compare them to our own. André Tchelistcheff would also join us. This helped clarify what we needed to do to advance the quality of our wines. It also

Sassoferrato, in the province of central Italy called Le Marche, is a medieval town surrounded by fertile hills and valleys. The landscape is similar in appearance to the Napa Valley. *Paul Chutkow*

My parents, Rosa and Cesare Mondavi, on their wedding day in Sassoferrato, Italy. By birth they were poor Italian sharecroppers, but they had a wealth of knowledge about the value of love, family, hard work, and the daily joys of good food and wine. *Courtesy Robert Mondavi Winery*

My mother's parents,
Lucia and Giovanni Grassi.
Courtesy the Grassi family

My mother's childhood home, outside of town. She had little schooling, but Momma Rosa could work eighteen hours a day and never lose her smile. And what magic she could create in the kitchen! *Paul Chutkow*

My father's brother, Giovanni Mondavi, with his wife and their son Americo. Giovanni came to America at the start of the century and was killed in a mining accident.
Courtesy Robert Mondavi Winery

Mom and Dad with the four of us kids. From left: Peter, Mary, Helen, and me. As you can see from the photo, I was the dreamer in the family!
Courtesy Robert Mondavi Winery

Dad with Peter (right) and me.
My father was a man of few words,
but his word was law.
Courtesy Robert Mondavi Winery

One of my class pictures from St. Anne's Catholic School in Lodi, California. I'm
seated in the second row from the top, the second kid from the right. Marjorie Declusin,
standing in the top row, second from left, was my childhood sweetheart, and later my
wife. *Courtesy Robert Mondavi Winery*

In high school I played football—at 140 pounds. When I got to Stanford, as shown here in 1934, I was too small for football so I took up rugby. Did darn well, too!

Courtesy Robert Mondavi Winery

I graduated from Stanford in 1937. For my immigrant parents and me, this was a very proud day.

Courtesy Robert Mondavi Winery

After graduating, I moved to the Napa Valley to go into the wine business. Six years later, in 1943, my family bought the historic Charles Krug Winery. Dad, shovel in hand, helped us break ground for new construction. *Courtesy St. Helena Wine Library*

Charles Krug was the oldest winery in the Napa Valley. This was probably one of the first wine presses ever used in California.
Courtesy Robert Mondavi Winery

In wine making, quality comes from mastering the details. At Charles Krug, shown here, and later at the Robert Mondavi Winery, I oversaw every step in the process.
Courtesy Robert Mondavi Winery

For generations past and present there is one cardinal virtue in the wine business: Patience!
Courtesy St. Helena Wine Library

At Krug, my brother Peter (right) served as wine maker, and he made some remarkable wines. And, bless him, he always had to do it with me giving him advice!
Courtesy Robert Mondavi Winery

My wife Marge helped me build the Robert Mondavi Winery, and she was a marvelous mother for our three children. She loved to get away, though, for a little skiing at Lake Tahoe.
Courtesy Robert Mondavi Winery

helped us size up the competition. This I did constantly, and still do today.

The more tastings I did, the more I came to understand the importance of climate and proper soil content and drainage. I found that the cooler the climate, the more flavor and character you get in the grapes; this is true with almost every fruit. So I came up with an axiom to guide us: The cooler the climate — but still warm enough to bring the grapes to full maturity — the finer the grapes. And the finer the grapes, the finer the wine. In our tastings, we studied how we could best match different grape varietals to the different microclimates and soil types on our properties and those of the Napa Valley growers who supplied us.

As useful as these regular tastings were at Krug, they took my education only so far. So in 1962, as I said before, I went to Europe and visited the great wineries of France, Italy, and Germany. During that seminal experience, I tasted wines I'd never find in the United States, and I saw firsthand the European way of making fine wines and aging them in oak barrels. I became fascinated by the art of the barrel, and I learned the different qualities that barrels can impart to wine.

I also came to see the role of the wine maker in a much fuller light. Up to then, my focus in wine making had been predominantly on the science side, worrying first and foremost about how to avoid or suppress the negative, such as mold, bacteria, off characters, spoilage, and the like. The approach of the very top European wine maker in many ways was just the opposite: He was trying to find ways to accentuate the positive. He was probing deep into the qualities of his soil and his *terroir*, and then asking himself, "What can I do to bring these innate qualities forth so that they can fully express themselves through the medium of wine?" The approach was similar to that of the chef at La Pyramide: "How do I bring forth the intrinsic goodness and flavors of a given meat, fish, or vegetable? What can I do to make those natural flavors burst forth with grace and harmony and create a symphony in the mouth?" Passion, character, individuality, temperament, and attention to detail — great painters and actors embrace these traits, make them part of their own artistic palette and creations. So do great chefs. And, as I came to understand in Europe, so do great wine makers.

So when I set out to make world-class wines at the Robert Mondavi Winery, I had no intention of trying to copy or imitate the great wines of France, Italy, Germany, Spain, or Portugal. No, I felt strongly that our California wines should have their own style and character; they should reflect our climate, our soil, our grapes, and—yes— our own unique American character and spirit. Our wines would be different from the Europeans', but I hoped that in terms of quality everyone would agree they belonged in the company of the great wines of the world.

With this lofty goal in mind, our tastings in Oakville became more serious and sophisticated. Our tasting room became a blend of science and art. On the one hand, we would have before us a microanalysis of the chemical properties of a given wine in the making. We knew, for instance, that a certain sugar-acid ratio often yielded the flavor we desired. And we'd check our microanalysis: Was this wine within that norm? Then we'd taste—and check our own sensory findings against the scientific findings. This made for very thorough and detailed taste analyses—and passionate discussions! During harvest and crushing, our winemaking team would be tasting constantly, every day, to monitor the progress of our grapes and wines in the making. Later in our cycle, I'd sit down with Michael and later Tim for a crucial step: a progress tasting.

How do these tastings work? We would gather around the table in our makeshift tasting room, with spit buckets at our side. Let's say, for instance, that we were tasting cabernet sauvignon wines. Before us on the table might be fifteen or twenty bottles of fine cabernets, some from California, others from Bordeaux and farther afield. We would definitely include samples of our own best finished cabernets from earlier years to use as guides and reference points in our search for ever-higher quality. Next to these finished wines, we'd have several samples of our own cabernets going into production, each carefully labeled and with its own microanalysis. These might include one barrel sample from To Kalon made from older vines. A second sample might also be from To Kalon, but made from grapes from younger vines. Another sample might be of a cabernet made from grapes we bought from one of our growers in a different part of the valley.

How do we proceed? Each taster has his or her own idiosyncrasies, but as a general rule we'd take a given sample and pour it into a clean wineglass, stopping at just under half full. In tasting a wine, what we learn comes to us via our senses: the sight, smell, taste, touch, and temperature of the wine. I always begin with sight and examine the way the wine looks in the glass. I look for clarity: Is there any sign of cloudiness, impurity, or residue? I look at hue: Is there any browning or off coloring that would indicate problems in the wine making? Then depth of color: Does a given sample from To Kalon, say, have that deep ruby-red quality I like to see in our cabernets? What is the depth of the color? If I tip the wine up to the rim of the glass, what does the color tell me? Does it show richness, or is the wine too thin? And when I twirl the wine in the glass, with a rhythmic roll of the wrist, what can I see in the color of the wine that coats the side of the glass? The eye brings us clear indications of a wine's body, texture, strength, and longevity. Part of wine tasting is subjective, of course, but this visual intake does give an experienced taster vital and objective information about the quality of the wine.

Now the nose. Some of the finest tasters do not even have to put wine in their mouth; their noses are so sensitive and discerning that they actually "taste" the wine in depth. In fact, we all smell tastes more than we realize. The mouth is very good at picking up the basics — sweet, sour, salt, and bitter — but the wider range of tastes that emerge from a cabernet, for instance, are registered by sensing nerves located in the upper nasal cavity and even higher in the head and deeper in the brain. Some tasters make a distinction between a wine's aroma and its bouquet. Aroma pertains to odors coming from the grapes; bouquet refers to odors coming from wine-making practices, such as fermentation, processing, aging, and even bottling and corking. Either way, with nose deep in a glass, a discerning wine maker can determine grape quality, levels of grape maturation, sugar and acid levels, styles of crushing and fermentation, fermentation time, and temperatures — and these are just for starters. With the nose, the taster can also discern flaws such as over-oaking, poor storage or corking, the improper use of sulfites, and the presence of mold or bacteria in the vats or barrels.

Finally, the mouth. Serious tasters don't drink the wine; many don't even take a single swallow. Instead, the taster draws some into the mouth and holds it there for analysis. The warmth of the mouth helps vaporize the wine, exploding its flavors around the palate and up into the nasal cavity. Holding the wine in the mouth, the taster then gently sucks in air between the lips. This, too, helps the flavors blossom forth in the mouth, enabling the taster to better decipher the wine's component flavors and nuances.

How do we communicate to each other the many characteristics we discern in the tasting process? Ah, here's a rub: Wine Speak. As many of you know, wine has inspired a vocabulary all its own. The words vary from country to country, winery to winery, and taster to taster. Some Wine Speak expressions, of course, are pretentious and easy to parody and belittle. But such communication is vital; how else can I convey to my wine makers what I like in any given wine? So we taste the same wines, talk about them, and search for words we both understand to describe the same tastes and sensations. Here, too, though, there is a problem: taste is such an individual matter. What is salty or bitter, for instance, to some people is not to others. So what to do? Work closely with your fellow tasters, understand their palate, talk extensively, and have the patience of Job.

I also like to get opinions from people outside our winemaking staff; their tastes often keep us from veering too far away from our consumers. I also feel it is imperative for my staff outside of the wine cellar, especially in sales and wine making, to taste and understand exactly what I like in wines. This education is vital to our wines and our business. I want everyone at the winery to become learned true believers, imbued with the same passion and commitment I feel.

No matter how serious our tastings were in the early years of the Robert Mondavi Winery, sometimes we succeeded with a given wine and sometimes we did not. But each year we were drawn deeper and deeper into the complexities of making fine wines. And this was always true: Nothing ever turned out to be as simple as it first appeared. For instance, when I visited the great châteaus in France in

1962, I noticed that the top-quality wineries, those producing Premier Cru, or what we call First Growth wines, were using brand-new barrels almost exclusively. And I detected no off-character flavors in their wines. In the wineries producing Second, Third, Fourth, or Fifth Growth wines, though, they were using older barrels, with many years of use behind them, and in most cases I could detect off characters and other signs that the oak was spent. So I became convinced that using new barrels would produce better wines. In fact, I decided we should use only brand-new oak barrels. A good operating principle, seemingly. When we began working with French oak back home, however, I found the advantages of using new oak varied according to the length of time you aged in the barrel. If you have a good year, with good fruit and low yields, you can use 100 percent new barrels and be fine. But if you have a lesser year, then the oak taste becomes too predominant in the wine. So you always need to find the right balance. Sometimes older barrels that have been properly cleaned can be used to advantage. I did not learn this in one year, or two years, or even several years; I've spent most of my life trying to master the variables and subtleties of tasting and making fine wine. And I'm still learning!

One of a wine maker's most valued companions is patience. It took the Europeans many generations to develop great wines; I knew we weren't going to do it overnight. The beauty of it, though, was that we usually learned more from our gaffes and off years than we did from our successes. Take 1967, for example. This was our second year in operation and it was a killer. It rained constantly. Right through harvest. We were picking grapes in the worst mud you ever saw; it was so bad we had to get big boards, two-by-twelves, for our tractors to roll on so they wouldn't sink. Then, in some of our vineyards, we found a strange sight. Many of the grape bunches had skins that were withered and discolored. The culprit: mold. *Botrytis cinerea.*

To an uneducated eye, botrytis looks like a rot, which would have meant that our entire crop was ruined. Botrytis, though, is what we call noble mold. Instead of ruining the flavor of the grape, it draws off a portion of the water inside, leaving behind high concentrations of sugar and other elements that give the grape its flavor. If you taste a grape affected by botrytis, it doesn't taste bad; it tastes wonderfully sweet. In fact, this is the mold that gives sauternes its fabled velvety texture and nectarlike sweetness. Still, botrytis can be difficult to manage in wine making. And its appearance can be disconcerting. In fact, we were afraid the inspectors from the federal Bureau of Alcohol, Tobacco, and Firearms, who regularly came by to check our operations, might raise questions about that ugly-looking mold. So we harvested and transported the grapes in the evening to escape inspection. Then we took those grapes, botrytis and all, and made wine from them. No one, though, was very confident about the outcome, especially me!

How did we come out? With the rain and the mold, the harvest of 1967 had all the makings of a disaster. Indeed, the quantity of wine we produced that year was very disappointing. Along the way, though, we were able to learn firsthand about noble mold and we learned how to exploit its natural virtues. As a result, while our overall quantity was poor, the quality of some of our wines turned out to be absolutely outstanding. God bless that rotten botrytis; it brought forth one of the best chenin blancs we had ever tasted or produced, an irony almost as sweet as the wine itself.

CHAPTER 6

The Extended Family

IN MATTERS OF FOOD AND TASTE, it was my mother who first showed me the way. In matters of running a business, it was my father. And here, too, my schooling began early.

When I was thirteen, Dad wanted to teach my mother how to drive so she could chauffeur the kids around and also do what she needed to do. I'll never forget her first lesson. I climbed into the back of Dad's old Studebaker touring car, Dad got in up front, and Mother got in behind the wheel. She was scared pea green. With my father instructing her, Mother managed to start the car. But the only thing she knew how to do was step on the gas! So we took off like a shot. Poor Mother. There was nothing she could do to stop the car; she was frozen stiff!

Finally, Dad brought us to a halt. Then he said, "OK, Bobby. Now you take over." He taught me how to put the car in first gear, second, third, and then fourth. And from

that point on, I did all the driving. This was typical of my father: Even when I was young, he always gave me as much
responsibility as I could handle and was willing to shoulder.
He always had faith in me and showed me so. The more
faith he showed, the harder I worked to show him that his
faith and confidence in me were justified.

My father was a very fair man. When he hired Peter and
me to help nail grape and produce boxes during the summer, it did not matter that we were his sons. He paid us the
same way he paid his other workers: by the box. He had a
simple and yet very effective system of incentives: the harder
you worked, the more money you made. Good management! My dad and I had a similar bargain when it came to
the car. When I was in grammar school, long before I was old
enough to have a license, Dad let me drive the car to school.
So every day, proud as punch, I'd drive his big Studebaker to
school and park it right in front of St. Anne's Catholic
School. In exchange for this privilege, I had to drive my
mother, sisters, and brother wherever they needed to go.
Through this pact, my father imparted to me valuable lessons
in self-reliance, responsibility, and being a team player.

One time, though, not having a proper license did
cause me some trouble, but it taught me more even about
my father. I had the Studebaker out in Lodi and I made an
illegal U-turn. A police officer pulled me over and asked
me a few questions. Then he said, "By the way, do you have
a license?"

"No," I said. "I don't have a license."

The officer gave me a hard look. "Whose son are you?"

"Cesare Mondavi's," I said.

"Oh," the officer said. "He's a wonderful man. He's as good as gold."

With that, he let me go with a simple admonition: "Now you go and get yourself a proper driver's permit."

I still remember that episode vividly, not just because I got off, but because of what he said about my father: Good as gold. This was something I'd hear over and over about my father in the years to come.

My father was a man of principle. People respected him. He was warm, never harsh, and he was always tolerant of other people. He understood people's failings and accepted them, knowing they were only part of being human. Everyone, after all, has failings of one variety or another. Dad was never dictatorial, but he commanded so much respect that all of us, including my mother, deferred to him anyway. My sister Helen remembers one year at Lodi Union High School, when I was just discovering girls. There was a prom I wanted to go to with a young lady. So one day after school I went into the kitchen and asked my mother for permission to go.

"What!?" Mother exclaimed, in fiery Italian. "You're still wet behind the ears! What kind of nonsense is this? No way!"

To me, there was no point in protesting; Mother had said no and that was that. But after dinner my older sisters, Helen and Mary, took Mother aside and pressed my case. In most ways, Momma Rosa was a very open-minded woman, but not this time. "A prom? Girls? Bobby? No way!"

During this discussion, my father was in his study going over business matters, as he often did at night, and he overheard the ruckus. He came out of his study and with a short wave of his hand, he put an end to the discussion. Then, without so much as a glance at my mother, he called me over. "Here, Bobby," he said, handing me a $5 bill. "Just make sure you take good care of the car."

When the Great Depression hit in 1929, Dad's grape and produce business hit the wall. As with so many families across the country, we were in dire straits. From nailing boxes in the summers, Peter and I had saved up a substantial sum, something like $15,000. One day my father swallowed his pride and came to us. He needed to borrow our savings, he said. In exchange, he made us a solemn promise: Once back on his feet, he would put us both through college — any college we chose. As always, his word was "good as gold." I wound up with two choices for college: U.C. Berkeley and Stanford. Berkeley would have been much cheaper, but I chose to go to Stanford. So did Peter. Dad kept his end of the bargain and paid our way.

By temperament, Mother was warm and outgoing, while my father tended to be shy and solitary. Everyone loved my mother's cooking, and on Sundays we would have five, ten, even fifteen people in for a huge meal. Dad loved company, too, but in his own quiet way. He liked to play cards or bocce, things like that. With both my parents, there was little distinction between family life and business life. Members of our family, including uncles and cousins, worked for my father, and his business associates often came home for dinner at our family table. Everyone pitched in and took care of each other; business and family flowed together into one big extended family. It's the Italian way.

My father was also extremely generous, in ways that I learned about only much later. For instance, once he began prospering in Lodi, he quietly fulfilled the dreams of several families from Sassoferrato by sponsoring their emigration to America. In order to enter this country, immigrants had to show proof they would have a job and the means to live in America. My father provided the necessary guarantees for several families. We often called Lodi Little Sassoferrato, and our house became home to a parade of arriving Italians. Uncle Neno was one. Another was Peter Belardinelli, who had come over from Sassoferrato at the start of the century and somehow wound up living with Mom and Dad in Minnesota. Perhaps he was a boarder; no one now alive seems to know the exact story. Though he was not a direct blood relation, we considered "Uncle Pete" to be a member of the family. Uncle Pete adored my parents, and when we moved out to Lodi, he came with us. In fact, he was indispensable to our family and many of our friends. He'd help Momma Rosa in the kitchen and take us kids to school. Later, when my parents moved into a house on the grounds at Krug,

Uncle Pete came along and for years served as our ranch foreman. He was also a one-man welcome wagon for other immigrants arriving from Italy. He'd help them with their papers and any problems they had getting settled.

My father's generosity was well-known in Lodi and back in Sassoferrato. In part, this was because we had so much family in both places. As I said earlier, my father's older brother, Giovanni, was killed in the mines. Immediately after his death, his widow returned to Italy with their two small children, Americo and Giovanna. When Americo grew up, he decided to emigrate to the United States, and he wound up joining us in Lodi, where he opened up a successful bakery business. With his arrival, the Mondavi family pipeline expanded. In 1954 Americo and his wife heard from Alfredo Santi, a cousin back in Sassoferrato. Alfredo, too, wanted to come to America and find a job and a new life. But he needed someone to vouch for him and guarantee him work. "No problem," Americo assured them. "My uncle Cesare will do this."

Within a month, my father and Americo had everything arranged. But then Alfredo sent back word asking if it would be possible, sooner or later, to bring along his wife, Giulia, and their daughter, Julie. The word back from Lodi was affirmative: "Fine. Uncle Cesare will sponsor all of you." As Julie later told me, my father promised—and delivered— even more. "He sent word that he would even give everyone a place to live," Julie told me. "Whatever it was, Cesare provided." Julie's mother had actually been born in America and was a U.S. citizen. So she and Julie's older sister, Iris, came over first. The following year, Alfredo came over with Julie and her younger sister, Anna. Once they were reunited in the Napa Valley, all the Santis settled in and became members of our extended family. Giulia helped Marge with the kids when they were young. After some years out on her own, Julie joined us at the Robert Mondavi Winery. She has been with us ever since, and I don't know what we'd do without her!

This was my father's way. He was loyal to his family and to the people who worked for him, and he received their loyalty in return. For me this was a tremendous lesson on how to run and build a small family business, and in spirit and practice, I continued the tradition. Julie was one example; Joe Maganini was another. Joe and I are about the same age and we have similar backgrounds. Joe's father was a distant cousin of my father, and Joe's father, too, left Italy and wound up living in Minnesota with his young family. Later, Joe moved out to California. During the first part of World War II, he was working as an industrial engineer down in Los Angeles, and in 1942 he and his wife, Elsie, came up to the Napa Valley for a two-week vacation. They stayed with Marge and me on Charter Oak, and I took him through the operation at Sunny St. Helena. I thought maybe I could entice him to come work for me. But Joe was not impressed. He tells the story better than I do:

"I came away thinking, 'What a miserable way to make a living!' But I fell in love with the town of St. Helena," Joe says.

Still, he was adamant: the wine business was just not for him. Then he and Elsie made the long drive back down to L.A. "We hit Hollywood and Vine at 8 P.M., right in the middle of the worst traffic jam you ever saw," Joe recalls. "Right there we made up our minds to go back to St. Helena."

There remained, however, the issue of money. As Joe tells it, he was making $275 a week in Los Angeles and I was offering him only $200. In the end, he decided to come aboard anyway, even with a pay cut. The allure of the quiet small-town life of St. Helena was one reason. I guess another was that he just wanted me to stop jabbering and trying to convince him to come. As Joe puts it, "Bob talked like a Dutch uncle!" In any event, Joe came aboard, learned how to make wine, and took over the wine making for us at Sunny St. Helena in 1943. Then he moved with us to Krug and worked there for twenty-two years, running our wine making with Peter and later doing a great job of building our sales network and profits.

As I've said, the Charles Krug Winery was not just a family business—it was the Mondavi family compound. And having so many family members close at hand was very helpful in times of need. If someone on my staff fell sick or it was harvesttime, I would not hesitate to press members of the family into service, often with amusing results. My sister Helen, for example, was an accomplished secretary and personal assistant; she had worked for a bank president for nine years. Occasionally, when I needed her, she'd fill in as my personal secretary. As she recalls it, sometimes I would dictate a business letter to her, with my usual quirks of speech, and right in the middle of it she'd just put down her pencil:

"You have to be kidding, Bob. Do you really think I'm going to put that in a letter?" I do have a tendency to be wordy. Helen wouldn't stand for that, either. "Bob," she'd say to me, in the midst of dictation, "try to get to the point!"

At Krug, it was only natural for me to treat our staff as one large extended family; the truth is, it was the only way I knew. As it had been with my parents, in my life there was little or no distinction between wine, business, and family. And it had been like that since I started out in the wine business. When I first came to St. Helena, not only did I go to work for my father's friend and partner, Jack Riorda, I rented a room in a cottage behind the house of Fred and Rina Beroldo, Jack's daughter. All through that period, my meals, too, were always an Italian family affair. For lunch, I'd go over to a little tiny Italian grocery called the Olive Oil Factory and buy myself some Italian salami and slices of Fontina, Gorgonzola, or other Italian cheese, and then some Italian bread. That, plus some red wine, was lunch. For dinner, I'd go to a neighborhood trattoria called Bruni's. It was good, fresh, old-fashioned Italian cooking, like my mother's, and Bruni's was very much a family place with a regular clientele. In St. Helena, we had our own Little Italy and it would remain that way for many years to come. To my delight!

With this background, the Robert Mondavi Winery naturally began as a family affair. Marge and Michael, plus many of the old Krug hands and growers, gave our fledgling

little business a family feeling and spirit. During the summers, Tim and Marcia came back from school and helped
us out. In the early years, our offices also had a warm family
casualness. My desk was two sawhorses with an old door, I
think it was, placed across them. Back then we conducted
our tastings in a makeshift room in the campanile that Cliff
May had designed for us. And while our wine-making
equipment was state of the art, our business tools were very
basic. We kept very accurate logs of the grapes we harvested
and fermented, of vineyard yields, all sorts of things. And we
did it all by hand, on clipboards. Then our secretaries would
type up all the data, using a manual typewriter. To give you
an idea of the sophistication of our operation, the arrival of
our first IBM electric typewriter was a major office event!

But did we have fun. In keeping with our family spirit,
the staff occasionally took turns cooking lunch and they
prepared huge feasts. In those early years, we all worked incredibly hard to get our fledgling venture off the ground, but
we also took time to play. Those staff feasts enabled us to
break up the day and sit at the table, unwind, and be together as friends and family. That, too, is the Italian way. In
wine, I always extol the virtues of harmony and balance. So
it should be in life as well! (Single-minded and hard driving
as I was, though, I did not always heed my own advice.)

I always had a lot of fun in the office with Elaine Clerici,
a Napa Valley native and an experienced accountant who
came to work for us in 1973. While most of our staffers were

my son Michael's age or even younger, Elaine and I were about the same age, in our fifties. So we had a special banter we shared and our own camaraderie. While most of the younger people were rather deferential toward me, Elaine always gave me a devil of a time, kidding me, teasing me, and treating me like anything but the boss. In this, she was just like my sister Helen; neither one would take a moment's guff from me! Because we were such a small team, working in close quarters, Elaine often saw me at my worst, and she'd never let me forget it. I'd misplace my credit cards, and she'd have to telephone every one of the companies and cancel my cards. A few hours later, of course, I'd find them. She'd be nuts with me!

Elaine was especially tough when it came to money. I was the boss but I was also the spender. She was the accountant but also the enforcer. So we had our periodic showdowns. There were, for instance, certain expenses I wanted the company to pay. Restaurant bills, of course. Wine bills, of course. And a bit more. With all the work I was doing, my nerves would get frazzled, and I wanted the company to pay for the weekly massages I'd get at my athletic club down in San Francisco. So I'd try to slip those massage bills by the enforcer. They'd come right back in my face: "No way, Bob! Forget it," she'd say. "The IRS would be down our throat in five minutes!" Elaine was also extremely difficult about giving me cash out of the company till. There is one particular story she loves to tell, just to needle me:

"In the early years," Elaine recalls, "we had good years and not-so-good years. There were times when the winery had no money, literally no money, and Bob would go out and spend $100 on lunch anyway. Everyone else in the winery treated Bob as the boss. 'Yes, sir'; 'no, sir,' that sort of thing. Not me. One day, in 1974 I think it was, Bob was going on a big business trip. The company, of course, always paid for his plane ticket and hotel rooms and meal money. But on this particular day, when he was about to leave, Bob came to me for pocket money. I said, 'Sorry, Bob, we have no money. None.' 'Come on,' he said. 'I can't go on this trip with an empty wallet!' 'No way, Bob. Sorry. We just don't have it . . .'

"Well, Bob Mondavi got down on his hands and knees and begged. Really begged. In the end, I gave him some money, of course; I had to — he was the boss."

Typical Elaine. She never understood what I was up to, spending money. Good lord, it's my business to take people out to a good restaurant for lunch. It was my sales routine to have them taste a few fine wines from France and Italy, and then to have them taste ours. To compare. To see the quality we were able to achieve. But my sales approach was not cheap; somebody had to pay for those expensive French and Italian wines. But try explaining that to Elaine! "Bob," she'd say, "we don't have any money, and you go out and spend money anyway. What am I supposed to do with you!"

She just didn't see the point. Many other people on our

staff didn't see the point, either. So in 1978, after we had a very good year, I decided to take a dozen members of the staff on an educational trip to France and Germany for three weeks. I wanted them to learn, taste wines, and visit châteaus. But I had another purpose as well. I knew that when I talked to my staff about producing wines that belonged in the company of the great wines of the world they didn't really believe me! So I wanted employees from different parts of the company—the cellar, the vineyards, sales, and administration—to see for themselves the kind of wines the Europeans were making and to see our potential to do just as well. We took our people to some of the finest restaurants and compared our wines with some of the finest in the world. I can assure you, by the time they came home, they were all true believers! That gave us all a common cause, we knew what we were working toward, and that made my job easier. And by the end of the trip, Elaine Clerici saw what I was trying to accomplish.

"Until you've actually been to Europe, you can't dream what's going on in the world of wine," Elaine says now. "Bob wanted us to see how our wines fit into the larger picture. We had a great trip, and I'll always be grateful for it. It was after harvest and we were all tired. And we worked for little money, because there wasn't much. But on that trip, everyone became a believer . . .

"Bob and I got along great," Elaine says. "He's not the big, stiff executive type; he's a person you can have fun with.

He's down to earth. And I'll bet I'm the only one who ever made him get down on his hands and knees and beg!"

THERE COMES, OF COURSE, an inevitable crunch point. As the head of this extended family, I never wanted to fire anyone. If someone was not performing up to what I expected, I'd always try to find a different spot for that person within the company. Or if someone was unhappy in a given job, again I'd try to find an accommodation. To me, that was the way to run a family business. Take care of your own. Sometimes, though, that goal clashed directly with my ultimate goal: to become The Best. If, as I believe, becoming The Best demands uncompromising professionalism and perfectionism bordering on the fanatical, what do you do about people who do not share the same ideal and commitment? What do you do about *family* members who are unwilling or unable to join your quest for excellence?

This has been a dilemma that has dogged me for decades. In the beginning, I operated on the assumption that you could change people. I felt that if you could encourage them, ride them, inspire them, offer them the proper incentives, then eventually everyone would fall in line with what you were trying to achieve. And I operated on this assumption for years. Sometimes I succeeded in convincing people to change their ways and improve their performance. Sometimes I failed miserably. Always, though, this approach brought me enormous frustration.

Later in life, however, at the age of about seventy-five, I finally learned to accept the cold, hard truth: You cannot change people. Influence them a little, yes. But truly change them, no — unless they themselves deeply want to change. So after you try and try to work with someone and the effort still doesn't bear the proper fruit, well, then you have to go forward on your own. There is no other way. Being kind and patriarchal, always trying to accommodate all your people under the company umbrella, can end up doing great damage to your company — and to the discontented person as well. Family or not. This was a very difficult lesson for me to learn and accept. But once I understood that you can't change people, that you have to see them as they are and draw the proper conclusions, it is amazing what peace of mind I felt.

This realization gave me a deeper insight into what constitutes effective management and leadership. To inspire people and give them a sense of worth, you have to give them responsibility, like my dad did with me and his Studebaker. You also have to give them freedom and elasticity. You have to let them stretch and grow according to their own abilities and ambitions — not yours. You also have to learn to be open and honest with your people, on every issue, no matter how difficult this proves to be, so that there are no ambiguities, no simmering resentments, and no misplaced insecurities. And as you provide your staff with this sort of elasticity, you as leader must learn how to compromise — without losing your focus.

I learned most of this the hard way — by making mistakes. I had a vision that was clear and firm. And I have a very strong, forceful personality. I am always willing to listen to good, common sense suggestions from other people, but I will not compromise my vision. As a result, sometimes I come across as being too dogmatic, and some may even view me as dictatorial. But those who know me best know that I will always listen to a good idea. And that is one of the reasons that I enjoy the loyalty of so many of the people who work for me.

Nonetheless, I must admit that sometimes I had tunnel vision, and sometimes I was too much of a perfectionist. I was never completely satisfied with what we accomplished; I always knew we could be better. And I pushed others hard to do better — harder than I realized. With some people, this approach can backfire. If you push them too hard, they take it personally. They feel devalued. It undermines their confidence and morale. Sometimes under my pressure, people retreat, they withdraw, they contract. And so does their performance. Which is bad for them and bad for your business. What it took me ages to learn was really very simple: Don't be negative, dogmatic, or judgmental. Be positive and flexible. Instead of constantly trying to impose my way on the people nearest and dearest to me, I should have had the intelligence and the grace to say:

"Here, this is *one way* to do it. If you can find us a better way, great!"

CHAPTER 7

Good as Gold

WHAT MY FATHER TAUGHT ME ran even deeper.

At Stanford I studied economics and business administration, and when I graduated I thought I knew a thing or two about how to sell, build a client base, negotiate deals, and grow a business. After I graduated in 1937, Dad took me with him on a business trip. This was my first business trip, and it was the first time I had ever traveled alone with my father. What a surprise it turned out to be, and what an education!

We left California by train and went to Chicago and Virginia, Minnesota. Then we went on east to New York, New Jersey, and Boston. Everywhere we went, my father would meet with a group of his old cronies, most of them Italian. I'd wait for them to sit down and talk business, but they never did! They'd play cards, they'd play bocce, they'd eat, and they had a wonderful time! And then, just before it would be time for us to get on the train, they'd say to my father, "Now, Cesare, last year we took so many loads of grapes." Then they'd air this or that complaint and place new orders. That was the extent of their business talk! And I'd say to myself, "Now wait a minute. I went to school and learned that you negotiate this; you negotiate that. But they aren't sitting down and doing anything like that. What's going on here?"

There was more. My father hated arguments. He was uncomfortable with any form of direct confrontation. If, during a business discussion, there was ever any problem or harshness, he would simply—*hup!*—get up and leave. I remember one particular time when Dad and I were talking to a grape grower about buying some of his grapes. Some problem arose, and it became clear the grower was doing some double-dealing. I thought my father should pound the table, do something to hold his own. But no. He just stood up politely and walked away. I thought to myself, "My goodness, I'd be arguing like a son of a gun!" I slowly came to understand, though, that my father wanted to do business only with people he considered to be friends, and he always wanted to do business in an atmosphere of openness and mutual trust. If harsh words erupted, he'd just leave. Later, he might seek to restore harmony, and he was often successful. But if he could not, well, he'd just move on, with his integrity and principles intact.

In the beginning, I didn't understand this at all. The Cesare Mondavi way was like nothing I had studied in business administration at Stanford. During that trip, though, I finally came to understand why my father put his name on his business: C. Mondavi. And later: C. Mondavi & Sons. The reason was quite simple. For my father, business was not, first and foremost, about money and negotiations. Nor was it about goods and services. It was about people. It was about family. And it was about trust. For him, a handshake was both a bond and a commitment. He and his business friends understood each other. They played cards and bocce together; they ate and drank together — and along the way this camaraderie deepened their bond, their commitment, and their mutual trust. His customers, like his staff, became like family, with all that implies. You take care of me; I'll take care of you. You win; I win. We're all family. That was the key for my father, not a few dollars and cents this way or that.

The more I thought about this, the more I realized that my father was not selling grapes. He was selling himself. When he went on a sales trip, Dad did not bring along samples of his grapes, his cherries, melons, or lettuce to show to his customers. He didn't need to because that was not what they were buying. No. They were buying my father's word. They were buying his principles of business and his expertise in California grapes and produce. And they were placing their confidence — and money — in his personal integrity and the good name of his company. If the name C. Mondavi was on the label, that was his personal seal of approval, and that was good enough for his customers. For just as that cop back in Lodi had told me when I was a teenager, Cesare Mondavi was "good as gold." And so was his word.

I remember another time when my father's way of operating surprised and dazzled me. This was in 1943, when we set out to buy the Charles Krug Winery. As I mentioned before, some friends had tipped us off in advance. I was so excited I don't think I slept for days. I loved the property and I knew it was a fabulous opportunity for us. My father had visited the Krug ranch and agreed to try to buy it, and Peter and I had agreed to run it together. But the big question remained: Could we convince the owner, James K. Moffitt, to sell us the winery, and to do so at a price we could afford? I was far from certain. I figured the process would demand weeks, or months, of tough negotiations, with a series of proposals and counterproposals, followed by weeks and weeks of working out the details and financing. I did not know Moffitt, though, and I underestimated my father and his business skill.

To make our bid for Krug, we contacted Moffitt and set up a meeting. Peter was on leave from the army at the time, and he and I and Dad drove down to San Francisco to meet with Moffitt at his downtown offices at the Crocker First National Bank. J. K. Moffitt was a very wealthy man. His family had made a fortune in manufacturing paper and had owned the Charles Krug Winery since the early part of the century. Moffitt was now the director of the Crocker Bank, and he served on the Board of Regents of the University of California. He was old-money San Francisco; we were bumpkins from little St. Helena. And when we walked into his office, I figured we had little chance to close the deal. Moffitt's office was big and impressive — and so was Moffitt. Here we were, an Italian immigrant family with peasant roots, knocking on his door. How in the world were we going to convince him to part with a family jewel and entrust it to us?

But here I saw my father at his best. We sat down in Moffitt's office, and for a few minutes Dad and Moffitt chatted about family. Moffitt told Dad that it must be wonderful to have his two sons in business with him. Moffitt said his daughters and their husbands simply weren't interested in Krug or the wine business. He would love to hold on to the Krug property, but what could he do? There was no one to carry on the operation. Just then the phone rang. It was a man from Ohio who wanted to buy Krug. "No. No. I'm sorry, the winery's not available," Moffitt told him. "I've just sold it to Mr. Mondavi and his sons." My father, dumbfounded, said, "What do you mean? We haven't talked about price. We haven't talked about anything!" Moffitt said, "We'll work that out." Over the next few minutes, the two of them covered all the essentials that would take most lawyers weeks to sort through. For the winery, the buildings and the houses on it, and the 160 acres around it, they agreed on a price of $75,000, at $4\frac{1}{8}$ percent interest. My father wanted 4 even, Moffitt wanted $4\frac{1}{4}$. So, amicably, they split the difference and shook hands. Moffitt then called in his secretary, dictated the terms, and took us to lunch at the Old Poodle

Dog restaurant, a San Francisco classic and one of the best in its time. We had lunch, returned to Moffitt's office, and signed the papers. The whole accord took, maybe, a total of three hours! And what an education I had in how to close a deal!

Over the next two decades working at Krug, I came to better understand and to build on my father's teachings, above and beyond treating everyone as extended family. So when I went out on my own and created the Robert Mondavi Winery, I had three clear principles to guide me:

One, always conduct business the Cesare Mondavi way: Be open, thoroughly honest and aboveboard, and strive for an atmosphere of complete integrity and mutual trust. My aim was simple: I wanted the name Robert Mondavi also to be deemed "good as gold."

Two, always remember that business is, first and foremost, about people, not products. To succeed, you have to learn how to communicate with people. And what better way to oil this process than to sit down to a good meal, fine wine, and warm family conversation?

Three, in keeping with these first two points, I knew that to succeed we had to personalize our wines and our company. Just as my father understood that he was really selling himself, not grapes, I wanted to make sure the public was buying flesh and blood and character, not just a fancy bottle and an elegant label. I was not about to name our wines after some town or vineyard or glen. Wine to me is not about real estate, it's about the wine maker's heart and soul and passion, and we had to convey that. So, with a tip of the hat to my father, I chose to name our winery and our wines Robert Mondavi.

Looking back, I think this decision was key to our future success. At Krug, we once named one of our wines Napa Vista, and when it didn't sell very well, Chuck Daniels, our distributor in Northern California, put his finger on what many of us were thinking: "Bob, this sounds like a real estate development, not a wine!" Using the name Robert Mondavi worked in the marketplace almost right away. When Chuck and his salesmen from the House of Daniels went calling on retailers and restaurants, even in those early days when there was little market for fine wines from California, they found our wines got a warm reception, especially from people who already knew our family. Again, Chuck put his finger on the reason: "You weren't buying a bottle; you were buying Bob Mondavi."

Chuck also did me an enormous favor. In 1967, with that botrytis, we had a small harvest and a very difficult year. My two partners, Fred Holmes and Ivan Shoch, started to get a little antsy. They could see that my ambition extended way beyond the initial twenty thousand cases we had set as our first target—and that made them even more nervous. This same year Chuck spoke about me to Alan Ferguson, the head of the Rainier Brewing Co. up in Seattle. Alan was a brewmaster who also loved wine. Rainier had just sold its baseball team in the old Pacific Coast League, and they were looking for a promising new investment. "I was of the opinion that wine was going to be really something and that Bob Mondavi really knew how to put wines together," Chuck says. Chuck organized a meeting, and Alan and I liked each other right away. He believed in what I was doing and in my larger vision for the Napa Valley. So in 1968 he and the Rainier board offered to buy out Holmes and Shoch, at a tidy profit, for their shares of Robert Mondavi Winery. My partners agreed, then turned around and used their profits to buy Howell Mountain Winery. Rainier offered me the same deal, but I said no. Instead, we ended up as partners with one common goal: to grow quickly from 20,000 cases of wine to 125,000 cases.

To help do this, we set up a new company, Robert Mondavi Vineyards & Co. This company, with a fresh injection of capital from Rainier, was set up to help us acquire more land. Done and done: we immediately went out and bought a much larger parcel of the To Kalon Vineyard, 230 acres, in fact. Later we would expand our holdings at To Kalon to 700 acres. We also purchased what would become our Oak Knoll property, over by the Silverado Trail. Over the following eighteen months, much earlier than we expected, we boosted our production to 125,000 cases a year. Rainier was delighted and so was I! Our success sent out a powerful signal: We were making things happen — the market for fine wines was starting to grow.

Rainier was an amazing partner for us. I'd even say it was a deal made in heaven. For one thing, they were a family partnership, so they understood our spirit and approach. Also, they were a company with a deep commitment to the pursuit of excellence. Thanks to my rapport with Alan Ferguson, it was a partnership based on openness and mutual trust. In many ways, our relationship with Rainier would become a prototype for a number of our later joint ventures, almost always with family businesses of a kindred spirit. From the outset, Rainier's intent was clear, and so was mine. Here's what they told me:

"Bob, just make a better bottle of wine. We'll support you. And when you make enough money, come back and buy us out." Now how can you beat that for an ideal partner?

There was one aspect of our partnership with Rainier that became an important part of our later joint ventures. When Rainier came in as a big investor, they of course wanted some control and a large say in how we ran the company. Since I had next to no capital of my own, I was willing to take a minority equity share, 20 percent at the outset, but I insisted on keeping 50 percent of the vote on all substantive issues. I definitely was not going to give away majority voting rights for my own winery!

Now here's another thing. I did not want 51 percent control and I wouldn't take 49 percent. No way. I wanted a fifty-fifty split. Why? If you own 49 percent, you can be right in your decision making and it doesn't matter a bit; you still lose the vote. And if you own 51 percent and you make a fool decision, well, you're still the boss. With a fifty-fifty split, neither side can impose a decision. This way directors and shareholders have to sit down and air their differences and come to a mutual decision, for the good of the company. In my view, a fifty-fifty split builds cooperation and trust. In many ways, this way of thinking traces right back to my father and his insistence on doing business in an atmosphere of mutual trust. In some ways, it also traces back to my own painful experience at Krug, when emotions got out of hand and different members of the family joined forces and voted me out. I was determined: never again. And out of this same thinking came another axiom for my own way of doing things: Keep your emotion in the family and keep your passion in the business.

Looking back, I know I was right not to cede majority control to Rainier. Other Napa Valley wineries took different routes and did not fare as well. As I said, Inglenook was sold to large corporate interests, first to United Vintners. In 1969, Heublein, the giant food conglomerate from Hartford, Connecticut, bought a majority holding from United Vintners. From that point on, only bottom-line concerns ruled at Inglenook, not quality, and on a dime it turned from making prestige wines to jug wines. A terrible loss to our end of the California wine industry. Then Heublein bought Beaulieu, and my heart really plummeted. I figured André Tchelistcheff would probably be out on his ear. But he stayed on, and Beaulieu did not suffer the same fate as Inglenook. In 1970 the Swiss-based Nestlé Company, another huge food and beverage conglomerate, took over Beringer. They actually did a lot of good at Beringer, but now the takeover trend was accelerating. Next to get in the game was Pillsbury, the Minneapolis food empire that spanned from doughboys to Burger King. Confident there was a fortune to be made in the now-expanding fine wine market in America, in 1972 Pillsbury bought Chateau Souverain. And what a success they made with it. Three years later, they were losing $6 million a year and they realized they had made a terrible mistake. They bailed out soon thereafter.

Each of these conglomerates thought wine was just another commodity to be packaged, marketed, and sold. Each thought they could come in, inject some capital, spice up the marketing, and thus boost market share — all within just a few years. In a pig's eye! My family and I had worked for thirty years to learn wine making from the roots up, to develop our sales and distribution network, establish our name and credibility in the marketplace, and earn our stripes by delivering a top-quality product, year in, year out. Show me a conglomerate with that kind of patience and dedication!

Rainier was a marvelous partner in these early years, and so was my wife Marge. I was often on the road two or three weeks at a time, almost every month, and Marge anchored the household and the kids when they were home. When I was home, we did a lot of business-oriented entertaining at our house and Marge always cheerfully carried the load. "Dad would call her at three or four o'clock in the afternoon," Michael recalls, "and say, 'I'm bringing eight people home for dinner at eight o'clock.' My mother would rush around, get what she needed, and prepare dinner for eight o'clock. Then Dad would call and say, 'We'll be late.' Mother always used to say she had an oven like an elevator; she was always turning it up and turning it down."

Marge also helped create a look and style for us, both at Krug and the Robert Mondavi Winery. She helped design dishes with a grape leaf motif. When we put on major tastings, for influential wine writers like Alexis Lichine, we did these at home, and Marge would plan the menus, fuss over the flowers and other arrangements, and then make sure that the entire event came off with grace and elegance. Michael remembers this well: "My mother was a hostess who created a real bond between Dad, the Alexis Lichines of the world, and our company. She was the glue that held everything together."

"My mother did everything," my daughter, Marcia, agrees. "We called her the chief cook and bottle washer. She'd cook for twelve people. She'd plan picnics and events at the winery. She'd arrange everything. Do the flowers, prepare the meal. If Dad invited a large group at the spur of the moment, Mom would get busy and put together huge picnics. And when I say picnics, I'm not talking paper plates and plastic forks. I'm talking silverware and dishes. Then, when everything was organized, she'd welcome the guests and serve them lunch. Literally, she did everything at the winery. Someplace there's even a Polaroid picture of my mother sweeping the driveway in front of the winery. No one told her to do this sort of thing; she just did it."

It's true. In many ways, Marge was more than a wonderful partner; she was as "good as gold." And without her help, I might never have gotten my dreams off the ground. Marcia puts it well about her mother:

"She very quietly, and in a very unassuming way, made the path clear for my father to become a star."

CHAPTER 8

The Touch

HOW DO YOU CREATE AN IMAGE? How do you create a brand name?

They teach that sort of thing in business schools and classes today, I know. But I never had a blueprint to follow. I just did the one thing that has always come naturally to me: talk. Even as a boy, I was the biggest talker in the family, and even then I had the habit of repeating myself quite a bit. It would drive everyone else crazy, as my sister Helen will happily attest! In the late 1960s and early '70s, though, when I was on the road two or three weeks at a time, promoting our wines, what was I doing? Talking and repeating myself over and over, at sales meetings, with customers, with anyone who would listen to what I had to say about fine wines and the Napa Valley.

When I went on the road with our sales reps and distributors, and even when I was alone, I had something else I loved to do. Let's say I'd be in Boston looking for new customers. Boston was a very tough nut for us to crack in the early 1970s. It was just not a wine town, and those restaurants that did carry wine featured only imported wines. You'd rarely see even one California wine on the menu. Well, I'd spend a couple of days in Boston and at night I'd go to one of the best restaurants in town. I'd sit down and order dinner and with it I'd order a bottle of fine Bordeaux, maybe even a First or Second Growth. Then I'd order another fine Bordeaux. When everyone started to get interested, I would invite the owner or the chef or the sommelier over for a taste of these great French wines.

"So what do you think?"

"Lovely," they'd say, or some such. Then I'd open a bottle of our cabernet sauvignon and offer them a taste. Chances are they'd be impressed and often they were downright shocked! Here was a truly fine wine, made in California, and more reasonably priced than a top-quality French château wine. And they could taste the quality! My bit of showmanship opened a lot of eyes, I can tell you. Sometimes the restaurant owner or sommelier would give me an order right on the spot. But even if they didn't, I was never disappointed. I was preaching the gospel as I saw it, introducing them to a new product and a new way of thinking about California wines and the Napa Valley. If they didn't buy now, well, one day they probably would. I knew that what I was really doing, first and foremost, was educating, and I knew that process might take time. Most Americans at that time knew next to nothing about fine wines; so I knew I had to be patient. And work like hell.

From the Krug years on, I was on the road, in spurts, about half the year. I usually traveled alone and met up with sales and distribution people along the way. I preferred residential hotels, where you become a regular and it feels a bit more like family. I hated single rooms; they just made you feel incredibly lonely out on the road, so I always stayed in a double. At lunch and dinner, of course, I was never alone. Even if I went alone to a restaurant, I'd order some fine wines and soon I'd have an entire party going on around me! Wine always inspires sociability.

My life was not very different when I was home. At the winery, we were always having tastings, inside or out on the lawn. We'd bring in restaurant people and wholesalers and friends to taste our wines. Sometimes, too, we had blind tastings with other wines from the Napa Valley. Or we'd have blind tastings versus some of the great Bordeaux châteaus. We really shocked people in those blind tastings; our wines often came out first. The tastings firmly planted our name in the marketplace, and they helped us create an image by word of mouth. We did not have to advertise back then; people in the wine world did it for us.

And I never stopped talking about wine. Even when I was back from my travels, instead of staying at home, I'd take Marge and the kids out for dinner someplace nice in the valley. I'd pick out an interesting couple already drinking wine and I'd go up and introduce myself. "Hi, I'm Bob Mondavi. I'd like to offer you a bottle of wine, as my guest." We generated a lot of excitement like that. And we made a lot of friends, too. Not to mention faithful customers and visitors to the winery. In fact, there are a lot of people who claim I used to go out onto Highway 29 and hail down cars, to invite people into the winery for a sample of our wines! Pure exaggeration, of course.

The winery tours we gave were also central to our efforts to establish our name and our image. We'd had tourists in the Napa Valley ever since the invention of the automobile and the arrival of train service to Napa. Beringer, with its beautiful old Rhine House, had long been a popular tourist destination spot; in the 1940s and '50s it used to attract Clark Gable and other Hollywood stars. At Krug, with our lovely site and historic buildings, we also made tours a prominent part of our approach. Frank Gould was an important part of Krug's success. He created our newsletter *Bottles and Bins*, first suggesting doing tastings out on the lawn, and started our tours as well. In the beginning, we had no idea if they'd prove effective, but Gould was so darn good at giving tours and making them interesting that a year after he started them, he was making enough money to hire several tour guides. So when I started the Robert Mondavi Winery, I was eager to go several steps further with tours. Horace Griswold, whom we all called Griz, came over from Krug and developed our tour program. He would walk visitors through the winery, show them our crushers and gleaming stainless steel tanks, and explain how we made wine. He also ran a little retail room where people could buy our wines. By combining tours and tastings, we made a visit to our winery last most of the morning or afternoon. The experience was delightful, educational, and, at that time, unique in the Napa Valley.

Here I have to thank Cliff May again. With our central location, we were in an enviable spot as a tourist destination. But Cliff's spectacular design made it all the easier for us to charm our visitors. We had an entire wing to use for hospitality, tastings, and festive lunches and dinners. At the end of this wing, looking out onto the vineyards, we built our Vineyard Room, a large, airy space that could accommodate scores of people for a sit-down meal and many more for lectures, tastings, and parties. This was a long way from that whitewashed little corner where we used to hold tastings at Krug and helped change the nature of the tourist experience in the Napa Valley. Other wineries soon followed suit, and the valley started to build itself a reputation as a prime destination for tourists. Before long, this generated new restaurants, hotels, small inns, and bed-and-breakfasts. Our sleepy little farm community started to boom.

There is an important point to make here about the spirit we all shared in the valley at this time. Among the wineries, we all helped each other; there was a spirit of cooperation and sharing. Of course there was some competition, but we were also friends, and we all understood that the more the whole valley succeeded, the better it would be for each of us in it. Let me give you an example or two of how we cooperated. The year was 1965. Jack Davies and his wife, Jamie, had just moved up from Los Angeles and taken over Schramsberg. They were replanting their vineyards, so in order to make wine they had to buy grapes on the open market. Jack wanted to use chardonnay to make a sparkling wine, but he was having a devil of a time finding five tons of chardonnay. Finally, he went to Jerome Draper, a grower in the valley. Draper did not have any chardonnay available, but he offered him five tons of Johannisberg Riesling. Take that, Draper told Jack; maybe you can make a trade. And thus Jack came to me at Krug:

"Bob, I've got this big problem," he said. "We can't get started. We've got to get some chardonnay and I can't find any. Would you somehow be able, if I was to deliver you five tons of Johannisberg, could you possible spare and give me back the equivalent gallons of chardonnay?"

"Sure," I said. "We'll see if we can do that."

Jack wanted chardonnay grapes to make champagne, and we arranged it. Then I left Krug, though, and Jack figured he was going to get screwed. As he tells the story: "I thought to myself, 'Oh my god, there goes our chardonnay! What are we going to do now?' I got in the car and drove down to Charles Krug and I saw Peter." Peter was unaware of the accord Jack and I had worked out, but he very graciously honored it and Jack got his chardonnay. And was able to get his own venture off the ground. For Peter, too, the Mondavi word was as good as gold.

There are dozens of stories such as this one that I could tell, where one winery helped out another in crucial moments. But I have one more, closer to home. In 1966, our first year in operation, our wine-making facility was not yet completed. Well, despite our family feud, guess who stepped up and crushed our very first harvest of chardonnay? My brother, Peter. Sometimes, due to all the bitterness generated later by our fight in court, I forget that gesture of Peter's. But I'm happy to remember it here. And Peter's generosity was very much in keeping with the spirit among almost all the wineries in the Napa Valley. We were a young, struggling industry, we were all in it together, and you never knew when you might need a favor in return. I have countless examples of people helping me out and then of my returning the favor. Out of these experiences, I came to understand one larger thing about life: When you give, you always get more back in return. I'm not talking about material terms; I'm talking about a return in satisfaction and joy. Generosity pays!

So does education. During our harvest in 1968, instead of staying in Oakville and supervising the grape picking and crushing, I went off to Europe, to see firsthand how the French did their harvesting and began their wine making. I believe I was the first wine maker in California to do this. Soon foreign travel became part of my routine. In the ensuing years, I went to wine-growing regions all over western Europe, in Yugoslavia, and as far afield as Australia. And everywhere I went, the world of wine offered me a warm welcome, camaraderie, and more knowledge. I didn't realize it at the time, but by traveling the world over, I was promoting our wines, sure, but I was also generating enormous public relations for the Napa Valley. A lot of people said I was the valley's "ambassador-at-large."

In 1970 my international travel and contacts led to our first venture abroad. That year, in conjunction with Rainier, we began looking at Australia, which was then developing a serious wine industry. Reverty Kent, an Aussie who had worked with us at Krug, took me on a tour of Australia's wine-growing regions, including the Margaret River area of Western Australia. We met a doctor there who was making wines, and we met a man named Denis Horgan who had two thousand acres on which he wanted to build a winery and develop vineyards. He needed help, though; and he ended up joining forces with a company from Washington State and hiring us as consultants and partners. We had only a small share in his company, but to me it seemed like a worthwhile experience, especially since I had always wanted to find ways to develop ventures abroad.

At that time, the Australians were making wines that were strong and had a consistency that I called "jammy."

We helped Denis and his brother John, who worked closely with me, design a winery and plant 225 acres of grapes. Among the grapes we planted were chardonnay, sauvignon blanc, and pinot noir — varietals that up to then had not been planted in Australia. We also introduced them to a new style of wine making, what I call the "international style." By this I mean light, elegant wines like they make in Bordeaux and like we were making at the Robert Mondavi Winery. For the Australians, this was a new approach, and it helped build quite a reputation for the Leeuwin Estate Winery.

We worked with the Australians for almost a decade, with Michael, Tim, and I taking turns shuttling back and forth to Australia. But then the venture ran into problems. The Americans in Washington State wanted to buy out the Australians, and the Australians wanted to buy out the Americans. And we were spending more time as mediators than as partners and consultants. So we ended up pulling out on a friendly basis. But we learned a lot and became convinced there were great opportunities in other parts of the world. In 1971 we also had our first overture from Baron Philippe de Rothschild of Château Mouton. He was interested in some sort of joint venture. But we decided we just weren't ready for that sort of expansion and commitment; we had too much to learn first and too much to do at home.

In 1974 we made a key expansion in a different way: my son Tim and daughter, Marcia, came into the business. I never pressured Mike, Marcia, and Tim to join the winery.

All I told them was that wine was a beautiful way of life, and
if they wanted to come aboard, I'd do everything I could to
groom them to take over when the day came that I stepped
aside. All three kids had worked at the winery during the
summers, first at Krug, then in Oakville. In the beginning, I
was not sure what the three of them would do once they
were out on their own. And they left home young. The high
schools in St. Helena at that time were not very good, so
Marge and I reluctantly agreed to send them off to prep
schools. Michael went down to San Jose, to a Jesuit school
called Bellarmine College Prep, then on to Santa Clara
University. After he graduated, he joined the winery, as I
said earlier. Marcia went off to Santa Catalina for high
school, down near Monterey, and then went to Santa Clara
University. Tim went to U.C. Davis for college, where he
studied in their first-rate wine-making program. In the early
1970s, though, he and Marcia still had their hesitations.

In 1974, I believe it was, my daughter, Marcia, after a
few years working with an airline, decided she wanted to
work for the winery. She was living in New York City and we
decided to make her our East Coast representative. The East
Coast was still a very difficult market for us, and I wanted an
able person there to work with our sales and distribution
people, to try to get our sales really up and running. So we
put Marcia into a training program supervised by Gary Ramona, the head of my sales operation, and then she went
back to New York. She had her work cut out for her! But she
did a great job of promoting our wines.

"The East Coast was very definitely an import-solid area," she recalls now. "There was a sophistication and an attitude that anything west of the Hudson River was the backwash of society. There was also a specific attitude about California. They thought we were all a bunch of poor farmers out here. Those attitudes were what we had to deal with as we went around and tried to sell our wines."

One day, for instance, Marcia went to call on one of the finest French restaurants in New York. She practically had the door slammed in her face! "Madame," the manager told her, "we do not serve any California wines in our restaurant. And we will only do so over my dead body!" Or words to that effect. I won't say what restaurant this was; it's now one of our best clients in New York!

For Marcia, this experience was sometimes discouraging: "Once I went to my father and said, 'Dad, I'm a lousy salesman. I never ask for the order.' 'That's OK,' he said. 'You're there to educate. Just get to know the people. Tell them what we're trying to accomplish. And let them know we're learning.'"

In 1974 my son Tim joined the winery full-time as well, despite his earlier misgivings. Michael was already aboard, and the last thing Tim wanted was to ever see a repeat of the fraternal strife that split the business and the family at Krug. "I was planning a different career," Tim says now. "Growing up, with all the family strife at Krug, I had decided that a family business was something you *don't* want to be in. There was a lot of pride, but little joy." Then Tim and a friend, Steve Taplin, went backpacking around Europe one summer in the early '70s. I gave him a few names of friends of ours in Europe and it opened his eyes. In Bordeaux, he and Steve paid a call on Louis Demptos from the Demptos Cooperage, which supplied us with French oak barrels. The boys ended up staying a week. Louis took them to the great châteaus of Bordeaux. In Burgundy and Portugal they had similar visits with friends of ours in the wine business. It changed Tim's way of thinking:

"This trip had a big impact on me. It helped me realize that wine was family, something you could enjoy doing," Tim says. "And Dad gave me an important perspective: 'Listen,' he said. 'No matter what business you're in, there's always going to be turmoil.'" With that understanding, Tim went on to study wine making at U.C. Davis, which is now the nation's leading center for future viticulturists, wine makers, and wine researchers. Most of what he learned was theory; once he joined us, he got himself a total immersion in the realities of wine making.

Even though I now had all three children working for the company, 1974 was not a good year financially. And 1975 was even worse. By this time, Molson, the big Canadian beer giant based in Toronto, had owned 49 percent of Rainier for many years. They were very leery of the wine business and wanted to restructure or divest many of Rainier's holdings, including us. The timing could not have been worse. Our records were in terrible shape and we had an accountant we weren't happy with. Also, we found ourselves a bit in the red. Then all hell broke loose. Michael and I were summoned to Seattle for a crisis meeting. Part of the Molson contingent even talked about stripping me of the leadership of the company. But Michael and I resisted that. Fortunately, Alan Ferguson of Rainier was brought in to mediate. He reassured Rainier and Molson about our direction and then helped us revamp our systems of accounting and administration. Ironically, this turned out well for me. By 1978, when I got my settlement from the court case with Peter, Rainier and Molson were happy to get out. So, with a lot of support from the Bank of America, I was able to put together a fair package and buy out Rainier.

Despite these headaches, the early to mid-1970s were still positive years for us. Because we were moving so fast on so many fronts, we naturally attracted the attention of wine writers here and abroad. With our reputation as the test-tube winery and our growing sales, plus my own visibility in the wine world, we got all sorts of coverage from newspapers and industry trade publications. More free publicity. In fact, the amount of coverage we received, even early on, was amazing. To help things along, we would invite prominent wine writers to our tastings and, as Michael said of Alexis Lichine, we would have them over for dinner as well. I didn't know beans about public relations agents or media managers; I was just doing what came naturally: talk. And it worked!

I did not confine myself to the American press. Very early on, I recognized that to be taken seriously as a premium wine region, we had to earn the respect of top people in the international wine world, especially in the United Kingdom and London, home of the most knowledgeable and influential wine writers. Therefore, from the outset I solicited the interest of Michael Broadbent, Hugh Johnson, Harry Waugh, Cyril Ray, and other writers based in London. We also began to ship wine to the United Kingdom, via a young distributor, Geoffrey Roberts, who believed in us and the future of the Napa Valley. Our sales did well in the United Kingdom, and as I traveled to other foreign countries, I realized the export potential we had, not just for our wines but for others from California. So from the very beginning, the Robert Mondavi Winery was international in our outlook, our sales, our press relations, and our openness to developing interesting joint ventures beyond our American shores.

"I think Bob's willingness to get out and talk about fine wine in general, and the Napa Valley and his wines in particular, were a big key to his success," Chuck Daniels says now. "He was also tireless in trying to accommodate the press. I remember one day at the winery we were deeply engrossed in a board meeting with Rainier. We had some very serious issues on the table. Some wine writer showed up, and Bob excused himself from the meeting and left to take the guy around!"

There's a famous line I've heard, and it supposedly comes from my friend Ernie Gallo, who is known for his dry wit. Someone once asked Ernie how it was that Bob Mondavi became one of the premier spokespeople for the Napa Valley. "Well," Ernie said, "look at everyone else!" There is some truth in that. Ernie and his brother Julio never spoke to the press. Louis Martini and the Mirassous, for instance, were grape growers at heart, farm people, and they didn't like to speak to reporters, either. Most vintners didn't speak up much at industry meetings, and they did not take major public stands on wine issues. Knowing how much I love to talk, I guess they all figured they'd never shut me up anyway, so they might as well let me speak for all of them!

Talking, educating, spreading the gospel about wine and the Good Life and the many benefits of drinking fine wine in moderation were part of my daily life. I enjoyed every minute of it! And why not? With Rainier backing us, we were expanding our operation and sales. At the winery, we were experimenting all the time, learning new techniques, and improving the quality of our wines. And when I was out on the road, I could feel the excitement we were generating. Just a few years before, at the age of fifty-two, I had hit a dead end, and now my great adventure was really on its way. Moreover, I was coming to see life in a clearer perspective. I realized you have to keep your mind and your heart open. You have to keep reviewing and rekindling what makes life interesting. In business and in life, you have to keep renewing, innovating, creating. To me, that's the real path to business success and personal joy.

Alas, there was a downside; there usually is.

I was spending so much time on the road that I was missing important things back home, both in my business and at home. I should have been riding better herd on that wayward accountant. I should have spent more time and energy grooming my children for their responsibilities in life and within the company. Instead, I just threw them out into the deep end of the pool and expected them to become expert swimmers right away. This was the Italian way. I rode them hard, especially Mike and Tim, and this caused some periodic, damaging rifts. Looking back, I realize I should have given them more encouragement and instruction. Only later did I see clearly that leadership is not dictating but working with others, inspiring them, and helping them do their own thing—within the framework of what you want the company to accomplish.

I also had a worse blind spot: my wife Marge. Without realizing it, I rode Marge awfully hard as well. I didn't see the impact. I was too busy traveling and building the business. I was too busy out in the public eye, promoting our wines and the Napa Valley. Also, I thought people should be strong enough to receive criticism from me, but when the criticism they receive is incessant and constantly negative, instead of positive and reinforcing, it's sometimes hard to stand up to the fire. I never did much to help Marge around the house, either. As my children often remind me, I never helped in the kitchen and I never washed the dishes. A traditional Italian family always looks to the mother to raise the children and handle the kitchen. My father spent next to *no* time with the kids when I was growing up. Now I realize that my own children felt deprived; they wanted my blessing and more of my time. I guess that was true of Marge as well.

In terms of kindness and gentleness, Marge was very much like my mother. She, too, loved the family and didn't have a trace of evil or pretense in her entire being. But she had nowhere near my mother's stamina or strength. Marge was a hard worker, and to please me she had to work beyond her capacity. I didn't see it. I realize now, though, that I wore her out. I was never home enough. I was too overpowering and I asked too much of her. She never complained, and she always worked very hard to satisfy me and the children. This all took a terrible toll on Marge and I didn't see it until later.

Much later.

CHAPTER 9

The Breakthrough

NINETEEN SEVENTY-SIX was a momentous year, both for us and the whole Napa Valley.

By now, several new wineries were opening in the valley each year, almost all of them emphasizing quality over quantity. Everywhere you looked, old vines were being ripped out and being replanted with high-quality varietals, cabernet and chardonnay in particular. There was an influx of high-quality people, too. In 1971 a Frenchman named Bernard Portet founded Clos du Val, determined to make top-quality zinfandels and cabernets and to create one of the leading wineries in America. Bernard had the right credentials. He was from Bordeaux, his father has been technical director at the eminent Château Lafite, and Bernard had studied wine making at the School of Agronomy in Montpellier, one of the best viticulture and enology programs in France.

Four years later, the valley welcomed another newcomer with intriguing credentials: film director Francis Ford Coppola. Francis bought the old Niebaum estate, and he, too, was intent on making fine wines. We figured that if he could make *The Godfather*, he could make some first-rate wines as well. Being Italian by origin wouldn't hurt him; I figured he had red wine and olive oil in his genes. André Tchelistcheff and I gave him some advice and support, and in 1978 Francis brought out his first Rubicon, a lusty, powerhouse red wine blended from cabernet and other Bordeaux grapes. He was off and running.

The big news in 1976, though, came from two brilliant wine makers who had done some of their earlier work with us: Warren Winiarski and Mike Grgich. Warren is a fascinating man; quite, thoughtful, and intense. In the early 1960s, he was lecturing at the University of Chicago and appeared to be headed for a life in academia. University life soon paled, however, and Warren got the itch to come west with his wife, Barbara, and learn how to make wine. He came out here in the mid-1960s and landed himself a job at Chateau Souverain. After two years there, Warren joined our test-tube winery, and we put him right to work in the cellar making wine. But he was a smart young man with a much larger dream, and after two years with us he found what he wanted: a wonderful piece of vineyard property of his own, forty-five acres alongside the Silverado Trail. He purchased it and in 1972 he built the winery known today as

Stag's Leap Wine Cellars. A year later he began turning out some first-rate wines.

Miljenko "Mike" Grgich is an equally interesting story. He was Croatian by birth and Old World by education and culture. Mike also apprenticed at Chateau Souverain and then spent nine years working for André Tchelistcheff at Beaulieu. In 1968 Mike came over and made wine for us for four years, specializing in white wines. Like André, Mike was a purist in his wine making and he was a very hard-working individual. I was happy to have him work for us and I'd do anything to keep a good man like that. At the same time, though, I always told my staff that if they could advance themselves better somewhere else, I would always support them. That happened with Mike. In 1972 Chateau Montelena in Calistoga, a winery with roots tracing back to the 1880s, made him a great offer, including a percentage of the company. He accepted and the following year Mike made a chardonnay for Chateau Montelena that made us all stand up and applaud.

By now, it was clear to us that the revolution in quality was on. For those of us on the inside, there was great excitement: Warren, Mike, Bernard Portet, and many other people in the valley were making excellent wines, as were we. In just ten years, we had seen much of the Napa Valley shift from making jug wines to premium wines. The campaign we were spearheading to turn the valley into one of the world's great wine-producing regions was moving in the right direction. But not fast enough. The public just hadn't caught on yet; we were just not seeing a significant jump in sales of our premium wines. Still, I felt certain that we were on the right track. I felt certain that true quality would, sooner or later, bring us both public recognition and financial success. The only question was when.

In the meantime, though, we had some rough sledding. In 1974 and 1975, with the oil crisis and the nation's economic downturn, the market for bulk wines really plummeted, and that sent shock waves through our industry. For some wineries in the valley, this downturn meant financial disaster. It certainly created plenty of nervousness on our board. I did what I always did to boost sales and keep our ship afloat: talk and promote until I was blue in the face. But we were just not making the kind of impact I wanted. Yes, within the industry we were generating quite a stir, and at wine fairs we were winning our share of gold medals—but as my father used to say, "Bobby, you can't eat gold medals!" On the whole, it was a very, very frustrating time.

Then it happened.

In early 1976 a talented wine connoisseur and entrepreneur named Steven Spurrier decided to do something audacious. Steven is British, like so many of the most knowledgeable people in the world of wine, and he owned and operated a paradise for fine wine lovers: Les Caves de la Madeleine, a small, eclectic wine shop just off the Place de la Madeleine in Paris. Steven stocked the big prestige châteaus, but he also traveled around France and visited the smaller châteaus, tasting, talking with wine makers, and unearthing some excellent wines. Like me, Steven was a big believer in properly educating the public about fine wine, so alongside his shop he created L'Académie du Vin, a school for wine education and appreciation. There he organized wine seminars and tastings and brought in experts to explain the intricacies of wine, wine making, and wine tasting.

Steven was well aware of what we were doing in the Napa Valley, and one day he had an inspiration. Whether to tweak the French, do some clever promotion for his shop, or just have some fun, Steven decided to put on a blind tasting that would pit some of our best California wines against the best of France. Whatever his reasons, it was a brilliant idea. And so was his timing. It coincided with the festivities surrounding the big bicentennial celebration of the American Declaration of Independence. The French gave us invaluable support during the American Revolution; in Steven's view, 1976 was a perfect time to clink glasses in the name of Franco-American friendship, and then have a blind tasting of the elite of French and California wines. He wanted to do this with a blue-ribbon panel of French judges and do it with great style and fanfare.

Steven confined the event to two categories: California chardonnays against their French counterparts—white Burgundies—and California cabernets against their counterparts from Bordeaux. Spurrier selected all the entrants himself. As he has often said since, he chose what he considered to be the very best French wines, whether they were from Grand Cru châteaus or not. For his California selection, Steven made a special trip to the Napa Valley. He was guided by his own palate and by his U.S. representative, Patricia Gallagher. Several Napa Valley vintners gave him a few suggestions as well. He chose some excellent California wines, though ours were not among them. André Tchelistcheff loved Steven's venture, and he agreed to come to Paris hand-carrying the California wines selected for competition.

Thus it was that on May 24, 1976, the unthinkable happened. A few vintners from California gathered together with the elite of the French wine establishment on the patio of the Hotel Intercontinental in Paris, just a few steps from the resplendent Place Vendôme. The selected wines were set out on a table, their labels scrupulously masked. No visible clue revealed a wine's country of origin. Then the tasting began. All nine judges, fortunately, were French—and their credentials were impeccable. They included Michel Dovas, president of the Institut Oenologique de France; Pierre Tari, owner of Château Giscours and the secretary-general of the Association of Grands Crus Classés; Aubert de Villaine, co-owner of the Domaine Romanée-Conti; the great chef Raymond Oliver, owner of Le Grand Véfour in Paris; Odette Kahn, the editorial director of the French wine authority, *La Revue du Vin de France*; Christian Vanneque, the sommelier at La Tour d'Argent; and Jean-Claude Vrinat, the owner of Taillevant. Certainly no one could accuse this panel of eminent French wine experts of even the slightest pro-American bias.

Which made the final results all the more shocking. Among the white Burgundies, the French contenders included some of the most celebrated wines in the world. There was a 1973 Meursault-Charmes from Domain Roulot. A Beaune Clos des Mouches, Joseph Drouhin, 1973. Bâtard-Montrachet, Ramonet-Prudhon, 1973. Puligny-Montrachet Les Pucelles, Domaine Leflaive, 1972. World-class wines! A feast for the senses! The eminent panel of French judges went to work. They sniffed. They tasted. They gargled and spat and ooohed and ahhhed, and after much ponderous tasting and consideration they marked their cards, confident that true quality would emerge the victor.

Here's the first shocker: the panel's top four selections were not all French. Indeed, three of the top four white wines were from the Napa Valley! Their first choice was Mike Grgich's 1973 Chateau Montelena Chardonnay, which edged out the fabled Meursault-Charmes. Third and fourth place went to Chalone Vineyards and Spring Mountain Vineyards. And that was just the beginning.

The red wine competition was just as stiff. The French entries included a 1970 Château Mouton-Rothschild from Pauillac, a 1970 Château Haut-Brion from the Graves region of Bordeaux, a 1970 Château Montrose from Saint-Estèphe, and a 1971 Château Léoville-Las-Cases from Saint-Julien. A preeminent selection if ever there was one! Again that eminent panel of French judges tasted, gargled, spat, ooohed and ahhhed, pondered, and marked their cards. And what wine came out on the very top of their collective rankings? Warren Winiarski's 1973 Cabernet Sauvignon from his Stag's Leap Wine Cellars. It scored just ahead of the Baron Philippe de Rothschild's Château Mouton. The next three wines chosen were French, but the Napa Valley was well represented in the top ten, thanks to Ridge Vineyards, Mayacamas Vineyards, Clos du Val, Heitz Wine Cellars, and Freemark Abbey.

Imagine the shock and amazement on that patio! Imagine how these results rocked the French wine establishment. They had spent more than two hundred years evolving their wine-making techniques and artistry, and here we come, raw upstarts from the backwoods of California, who in just a few short years had produced fine wines of comparable quality. It was a blow to Gallic pride and presumption — and the humiliation did not end there. The French press, to no one's surprise, ignored the results of Spurrier's blind tasting, but a correspondent from the Paris bureau of *Time* magazine, a fluent French speaker, was on hand at the Intercontinental. In a story headlined "Judgment of Paris," he revealed some very startling details. One of the judges, for instance, sipped a 1972 Napa Valley chardonnay and exclaimed, "Ah, back to France!" Mistakenly, of course. According to *Time*, another judge quaffed the Bâtard-Montrachet 1973 and declared: "This is definitely California. It has no nose."

"The judges mistook the best wines for French wines," Winiarski says now. "They thought the most complete wines were French wines. They were mistaken." When the *Time* story came out, making the French defeat public, the results of the Spurrier tasting triggered an enormous controversy in France — complete with claims of rigging and bias. In response, two years later the event was reproduced. With similar results!

Though I did not attend the Paris tasting, I was tickled to death by the outcome. I was happy and proud for Warren and Mike, our alumni, and, in a larger sense, I was even happier. I knew this tasting was going to electrify the wine world, and I was hoping that it would let the general public know, at last, how far we had come. Ten years before, I had made a bold claim and I had staked my future on it: that we in California could make wines that would stand proudly alongside the very best in the world. Now here we were, proving just that. On French soil, no less.

In retrospect, I can say that the Paris tasting was an enormous event in the history of California wine making. It put us squarely on the world map of great wine-producing regions. I saw the impact everywhere I went. Suddenly people had a new respect for what we were doing. They saw that we could make wines as good as the best in France. Moreover, given our commitment to research and development, plus the new methods and technology we were pioneering, people knew we were going to get even better. Marcia saw the impact even among the Europhile enclaves of New

York. Not all the old barriers to California wines crumbled overnight, but we had made a nice dent or two. "The 1976 tasting really made people sit up and take notice," Marcia says now. "For the first time, many traditionalists started to take us seriously."

For Warren, the "Judgment of Paris" was a godsend. "Before the event, I had heard there was some sort of tasting planned, honoring the Bicentennial of the American Revolution, but at that time it did not have a larger shape in my mind," Warren says now. The day after the tasting, though, André Tchelistcheff's wife, Dorothy, called with the news of Stag's Leap's victory. "The phones started to ring right away and gradually the historical significance began to set in," he recalls. "It was a very emotional experience."

The economic significance began to set in as well. At the time of the Paris tasting, Warren's Cabernet Reserve was selling for around $6 or $7 a bottle! Mike Grgich's chardonnay was priced in the same range. Our California wines were terribly undervalued, but we had assumed that was all that the market would bear. I recall that Joseph Heitz had once put one of his wines on the market for $9 a bottle and everyone in the valley thought that was outrageous! The Paris tasting, though, put us on an equal footing, in quality terms, with French wines costing three or four times as much. So why not start charging more?

Back at our winery, the Paris tasting further energized our sense of commitment and calling. I was disappointed we had no wines in the competition, but I was still very happy about the progress of our own wine-making methods and results. After Mike Grgich had come aboard in Oakville, we hired Zelma Long, a promising young woman still in the wine program at U.C. Davis. Zelma helped with the harvest and then Mike brought her on part-time as his assistant. In 1973, after Mike left for Chateau Montelena, my son Michael promoted Zelma to chief enologist and she made wines for us until 1979. All her wines were good and some were fabulous. The 1973 Chardonnay Reserve, for instance, was a memorable achievement. Our Reserve Cabernets of that period were excellent as well, especially in 1974. Still, when I bumped our Reserve Cabernet prices to $25 a bottle, everyone in the valley began buzzing about another Mondavi folly. But I'll tell you this: They were worth every penny!

Zelma loved the work and we loved her. We were in a very exciting and fertile period: experimenting, investing, reinventing, testing centrifuges, using different sorts of tanks and barrels. We were always expanding our tastings, which remained a cornerstone of our operation. Through the tastings, I could convey to Zelma and the others my philosophy, my palate, and my vision. This was not a place for clichés or tired Wine Speak. To emphasize my preference for gentle, well-rounded wines, I'd say things like, "I want a wine as soft as a baby's bottom!" Everyone understood just what I meant.

My son Tim started in the cellar in 1974, and Zelma did a wonderful job of grooming him. From the outset, Tim showed he had the right stuff. He knew the kind of wines I wanted to make, gentle wines with the proper balance of fruit, wines that complemented but never overpowered fine food. Tim had an excellent palate and a deep understanding of wine and the larger culture that nurtures it. He worked hard and learned quickly from Zelma. By the momentous year of 1976, two years into his apprenticeship, Tim had earned the confidence of most everyone in the wine cellar, and I could see that he was rapidly becoming a first-rate wine maker. Tim is an artist at heart, and as such he pours his heart and soul into his work. And there was no one better to learn from than Zelma. Once Tim was firmly in place, Zelma understandably decided to move on. She became vice president and wine maker at the Simi Winery and solidified her reputation as one of the premier wine makers in California. With Tim taking the reins, though, I had every reason to feel confident about the future of our winery.

Despite all this good news, 1976 for me had some terrible downsides. First of all, my long, drawn-out legal battle with Peter, my mother, and the board of directors at Krug had finally come to a head. I could write another book about that legal struggle, with the various suits and counter-suits we filed and later contested in court. Basically, I claimed in court that I had been unlawfully dismissed from Krug, and I asked the court to dissolve the Krug partnership that had been established by my father. My intent was to get out of that partnership all the money I thought I had coming as a 20 percent partner. This raised the issue of what Krug was worth. Peter and his side claimed the business was not worth more than a few million dollars, if that. But it came out in court that the Joseph Schlitz Brewing Co. in Milwaukee had indicated a desire to buy Krug—for a whopping $32 million!

The case was heard by Judge Robert D. Carter of the Superior Court of Napa County. The proceeding lasted 103 days, and I can tell you it was grueling. One of the worst experiences of my life. Peter Ventura, my sister Helen's son, has quite a memory from those dark days. Peter was called to testify, and the night before he stayed overnight at our house. Peter remembers being awakened in the middle of the night by a strange, rhythmic thumping. He says I was roaming the halls in a state of high intensity, pounding my fist against the wall, and saying, over and over, "Only the strong survive! Only the strong survive!"

The court battle took a terrible toll on the family. After the trial was over, but before the final judgment was issued, my mother, stricken by cancer, passed away. Momma Rosa. She died on July 4, 1976, the day of the American Bicentennial. Such an amazing woman. She had come to America as a poor peasant from Sassoferrato, and from our boardinghouse in Minnesota to our grape business in Lodi, she had worked like a slave to help my father build his business and raise a family. She taught me the power of love, and she gave me invaluable lessons in the virtues of hard work, strong family ties, fine home cooking, and the importance of having an open heart and a generous spirit. Even during the worst of the trial we remained close. We had meals together and there was no animosity between us. In the end, after raising her family and accomplishing so much here in America, my mother simply couldn't bear to see her sons battle it out in court. I think it simply broke her big maternal heart.

On August 12, 1976, Judge Carter issued his judgment. There were more than a dozen major points, and on every single one he ruled in my favor. It was a complete victory. In his 159-page verdict and analysis of the case, he ruled that Peter, my mother, and the family partnership had acted improperly in several significant respects. Most damaging, he found that Peter had fraudulently siphoned off $1.5 million from the family partnership to a side partnership he had created for his two sons. The judge also chastised Peter and the family for attempting to conceal the big offer from Schlitz, an offer that gave Krug stock a market value far beyond what Peter had claimed to me. As a result, Judge Carter ordered that Krug be sold and that I be paid compensatory damages totaling $538,885 plus my 20 percent share of Krug, evaluated at fair market value. I ended up with a considerable sum, but the price I paid along the way was terrible—and my mother's death made it even more painful.

Even with the judgment, though, the ordeal was not over. It took two more years to negotiate and settle, but in

1978 we finally worked out an arrangement whereby Peter could hold on to Krug—albeit in heavy debt—and I got my full share. Some people might have taken that money and bought a big house or a yacht or put it away for retirement. Not me. I was then sixty-five years old, but the last thing I was thinking about was yachts or retirement. I did what I'd longed to do ever since I created my company: I bought out Rainier and took over complete ownership of the Robert Mondavi Winery.

At last.

To my mind, this brought to a close the first phase of my great adventure. I had started from scratch in 1966, with no land, no winery, and no money of my own, only a dream and a passion. In many ways, the Napa Valley, too, had started from scratch in 1966. We were a happy little farm community, with no sophistication, little tourism, only a few restaurants and hotels. There were only about twenty wineries, a few of them making pretty good wine, but most others content to make jug wine and sell it by the gallon and half gallon. Now, just a decade later, our industry and the valley were starting to boom. By 1977 there would be fifty-one wineries in the valley, and by 1981 that number would catapult to 110. The price of land was rising, the price of grapes was rising, and so were the quality and price of our wines. The towns of St. Helena and Calistoga were changing as well. The little stores where we used to buy hardware and farm tools were becoming boutiques and cafés. The great old Victorians tucked around the valley, home to the same families for several generations, were being sold and turned into upscale bed-and-breakfasts. Yes, the revolution was on, at many levels, and that Bicentennial year would go down as a landmark one not only for the Mondavi family but for the whole Napa Valley.

Fittingly, exactly twenty years later, the Smithsonian Institution in Washington, the repository of so much American history, held a celebration to commemorate the 1976 Paris tasting and its importance for American wine making and the Napa Valley. The Smithsonian brought to light, for me at least, something interesting about Thomas Jefferson. He had spent much of his life trying to grow high-quality grapes that would produce fine wines. He had no success; he was using the wrong rootstocks and grape varieties. But Jefferson, it turns out, had a dream and a belief, nurtured, no doubt, during his years as ambassador to France. He believed that in this country we could, in time, make great wines, wines that he said would one day be "doubtless as good" as the best in France and the rest of Europe.

It may have taken longer than Jefferson expected, but by 1976 we had truly arrived, and the map of the great wines of the world had been changed forever.

Little did I know, though, that my own adventure was just beginning.

PART TWO

The Flowering

CHAPTER 10

Marrying Wine
and the Arts

AS A LEADER, I am relentless.

By the late 1970s, our little family winery was established and growing. We were turning out some first-rate wines, and for the first time I had full control of the company. The best California wines were now being recognized as among the very best in the world. To my mind, though, we were just getting started. We had many more mountains to climb. So I wasn't letting up a bit, not on myself, nor on my family and staff.

That's how I am — for better and for worse. I always set goals for myself and my company, and when we meet those goals, I immediately set new, higher ones. I always set goals that are just beyond what I think we can actually achieve. This forces us to give our all — then stretch some more. The way I see it, companies, and people, are like grapevines. To grow, they need plenty of sunshine and nourishment. They need constant care and attention. As they mature, they need fresh injections of energy and passion. They need new goals and challenges so that their vitality and their sense of mission do not become blunted and dull. Renew, reinvent, rekindle—these are the constant obligations of any leader who wants to keep his company fresh, creative, and in the forefront of its industry.

This is easy to say but difficult to accomplish. How do you renew and rekindle your company and its sense of mission? In my experience, the key is openness. You have to stay open to new ideas, new people, new technology, and new methods. Too many corporate executives are like bankers, accountants, and Puritans: they're always looking for a reason to say no. To avoid risk. To play it safe. This is the wrong approach. Business *is* risk—constant, unavoidable risk. As a leader, you can't shy away from risk; you have to embrace it. You also have to learn how to trust your instincts. Time and again, people have come to me with new ideas and what sound like crazy ventures. I listen; I try to stay open; I try to trust my instincts. Then I evaluate and decide whether or not to move forward. Sometimes I do this right on the spot, in a matter of seconds. That's why some people over the years have referred to me as Rapid Robert.

This can drive people around me nuts. Remember that salesman from Missouri and his stainless steel tanks? Everybody thought I was crazy to order costly equipment from a company that had worked with dairy farmers and breweries but had never before worked with a winery. What folly! Well, a big corporation would have hired a team of consultants to go to Missouri, inspect the company, and evaluate its history and all of its equipment. Six months later, they would have turned in a written recommendation filled with hemming and hawing and enough hedges to protect their bottoms no matter which way those tanks worked out. Hogwash! I sent my son Michael and Dick Keith, our engineer and architect, to Missouri to see Mueller, and on the basis of their recommendation we decided to move right away. So I say, embrace the risk; trust your instinct. Remember, as my father, Cesare, did, that business is first and foremost about people and trust. I trusted that salesman and I admired the welding on those samples he showed me. So I said, "Fine, let's go!"

Oh, how my way of working used to exasperate André Tchelistcheff. By both training and temperament, André was a scientist: patient, methodical, and rigorous in experimentation and analysis. By training and temperament, I was a wine maker, yes, but I was also a businessman. I needed answers I could implement today, now, this minute; I couldn't afford to wait for every last drop of analysis to come in before I made a decision and put it to work. André once talked about our different mentalities in an interview he gave to my winery, for our archives. He recalled our work together over the years, beginning with our first meeting, back in October 1940, when I was still at Sunny St. Helena:

"Robert Mondavi came to me during the crush in the fermenting room at Beaulieu Vineyard. Young, nice-looking gentleman, exciting, looking around with open eyes, listening to everybody, checking everybody, absorbing everything just as he does now. Quicksilver. And he was quicksilver right from the beginning.

"He was very insistent with his ideas," André went on. "Bob was too speedy for me. I was too logical and too cold in my technical interpretation of what I was thinking was right and what I was thinking was wrong. Even in his interpretation of his first steps here [at the Robert Mondavi Winery], I think he was a little more advanced than I permit myself to be. Because I thought every step in the industry, regardless of how old or young the company was, needed to be proven through cold analysis, rather than being granted approval right from the beginning. So I have always been cautiously critical about Robert Mondavi rapidly changing ideas without sufficient time to prove that the preceding idea was wrong. Bob can change the machinery after two years of experimentation and put in everything new. This is a function of going straight through, not waiting until tomorrow. It's got to be done today."

Yes, André had me pegged. If I saw a new idea I liked, or a new piece of equipment, or a person with a fresh perspective, I grabbed on, right away, and put it to the test. In most cases, my openness and intuition paid off wonderfully; at other times, not. Either way, we learned. And either way we kept pushing, we kept growing, and we kept expanding our horizons. To me, this was absolutely vital; my work was my continuing education. I knew a thing or two about wine, food, and business, but in many other realms, I admit, I was totally ignorant. I had grown up in a family and an environment steeped in grapes, wine, food, and business. That's it. And for thirty years in business, I maintained the same focus. So even by the time I was in my fifties and early sixties, I knew next to nothing about art or music, literature or medicine. Philosophy, spirituality, the inner life; these too were alien to me. I rarely read books; I didn't have the time or inclination. I was too busy building my business and pursuing my quest. That's one price, among many, that I paid for being so single-minded. Still, I knew the company needed to grow. I knew my vision had to grow with it. And I knew that I needed to grow personally as well. So here was the core reason why I wanted my winery to remain a hotbed of creativity, research, and experimentation: to educate me!

Take aesthetics, for instance. Aesthetics were central to my vision right from the first days of the Robert Mondavi Winery. But I made no pretense: I knew absolutely nothing about design or architecture. I did know, though, that they would be key to the kind of showcase winery I wanted to create. I had seen and admired Cliff May's work, and when I met the man, there was an immediate click. So I gave him my full trust and confidence. Likewise, I knew nothing about art or graphics or printing, but I understood full well the role they could play in creating an image for my winery. In the Krug years, I was looking for someone to design our labels, and I met Jimmy Beard, one of Northern California's best printers. And he introduced me to a noted graphic artist named Malette Dean. I liked Dean and his work right away, and so off we went. Malette designed some elegant labels for us at Krug. I remember one especially, done from a woodcut of a farmer harvesting his grapes, with a basket strapped to his back. It was beautiful and captured the feel of the valley and our work. Beard then turned Malette's work into labels. With the team of Malette and Jim, we had a highly acclaimed artist and an outstanding printer, and they were invaluable in helping us create our image at Krug. When Frank Gould began publishing our newsletter, *Bottles and Bins*, we used both of them to give the publication a look that was original and classy.

Naturally, when I started my own winery, I again turned to Malette and Jim to design and print our labels. And what a job they did. They took Cliff May's design, in all its elegance and simplicity, and translated it onto our labels. They were stunning! And they were just what we needed to help us establish our name and image with shopkeepers and consumers. Malette and Jim had that creative flair I so admire, and so did their labels.

So did Margrit Biever. As I mentioned earlier, I first met Margrit when I was still at Krug. She and another woman came to us looking for support for a series of concerts she was putting on for children, under a national program called Young Audiences. Margrit invited me to a press gathering at her home on Atlas Peak, and I could see she was clever and focused. Then she convinced us to hold a few concerts out on the lawn at Krug. We called them August Moon concerts and these were very successful. They were an original, creative way for us to attract people to the winery, do something for a good cause, and promote our wines at the same time. I could see that this young woman was competent, hardworking, and she had that creative flair. Margrit's real love was painting, and she would adorn her invitations and thank-you notes with colorful little sketches and designs. That was about all I knew of Margrit, though, until our second year at the Robert Mondavi Winery.

You may remember I mentioned a wonderful old gentleman who took visitors on guided tours of the winery, both at Krug and later with us. Horace Griswold, or Griz, was a very quiet, thoughtful Yale man who always came to work in a very proper coat and tie and had just the right mix of expertise and humor to make for very effective winery tours. A little while after I left Krug, many of the people closest to me were encouraged to leave. Griz came to see me. Would I take him on? I said yes, of course, and I put him in charge of our tours and our little retail room. Several months later, in the fall of 1967, Griz brought in Margrit to help with our tours and to assist him in the retail room. Smart move. Margrit was Swiss, spoke six or seven languages, and was knowledgeable about wine. Right away she proved to be a tremendous asset to the winery.

Once he had groomed Margrit, Griz decided he wanted to shed some of his responsibilities. He was getting on in years, and though he wanted to continue to lead tours (and he did so into his nineties!), Griz wanted to give the lion's share of his managerial duties to someone else. That someone was Margrit. "Bob," he told me, "she understands your philosophy and she has the heart and soul." "Fine," I said. "I'll talk to her." So I sat down with Margrit and explained what Griz had said about her. I outlined her responsibilities and then we talked a little. I felt she'd be up to the challenge and I offered her the job. But her answer was no! "I'm not qualified," Margrit told me. As she explained it, she came from a very traditional European background, where men dominated everything and women were self-effacing and remained in the background. Moreover, by nature she was shy and lacked self-confidence. As a result, Margrit told me, she would not feel comfortable giving orders to men, either in instructing the tour guides or in managing the retail room. I was flabbergasted! I went back to Griz.

"Griz, she turned me down!"

"Bob," he said, "you know I really think she has the ability. I'd be willing to support her as we go on." So Griz talked with Margrit and together we prevailed upon her and she finally agreed to take the job. That was just the beginning. In the months that followed, Margrit refined and expanded our tours and public outreach programs. She also began planning the menus for our business lunches and dinners. To give them a personal touch, she'd make little menu cards for each place setting and decorate them with her own sketches of flowers or bunches of grapes. Sometimes, too, she would even cook the meals — for upwards of fifty people! Soon she had made herself indispensable. I could see that she had vitality and spirit, and she seemed to love every minute of the work. As I came to understand, the winery was a gift for her: it afforded her opportunities, every day, to express her creative talents.

Margrit has wonderful memories of coming on board and, as she puts it, "getting bit by the wine bug." "We sold only three wines in the retail shop in 1967," she says. "We had the gamay rosé, which sold for $1.49 a bottle; a Riesling at $1.79 a bottle; and our Fumé Blanc, at $1.79. Bob never sold a bottle of wine in his life. He didn't have to. He was too busy convincing people that his wine was as good as any château wine in France and possibly even better. Because Bob was totally convinced himself, he was always very persuasive. He could convince a blind man he could see. He was so charismatic. And when he was around, he had time for everybody. Bob was the catalyst, the attraction."

Margrit brought a wealth of European taste and culture to the winery, and an interesting family background as well. She was a native of the lovely Appenzell region of Switzerland, but she had grown up in the village of Orselina, on the outskirts of Locarno, in the lakes region just north of the Italian border. The way Margrit describes it, her family was strict Calvinist in its thinking and yet her schooling and surroundings were predominantly Italian. Margrit, two sisters, and a brother lived with their parents and grandparents in a rustic little house. Her father had trained as a banker, in a stint in Paris just before World War I. During the war, though, he returned to neutral Switzerland and became an accomplished practitioner of homeopathic medicine. He also made wine, and in her house the family always treated wine with great respect. Good food and good wine were considered vital cornerstones of a healthy, happy life. Margrit's mother was very artistic and she cooked like an angel, two qualities she passed on to her daughter. For Margrit, all this made for a quiet, traditional Swiss childhood, but she did grow up with plenty of exposure to the Italian language, culture, and way of life.

Thanks to a series of high-quality Swiss schools, Margrit received a wonderful education in languages and the arts. She went to grammar school in a little one-room schoolhouse in Orselina, and while that doesn't sound very promising, the kids were blessed with a wonderful teacher. Later, she went to Locarno for high school and then to a finishing school near Lausanne, in the French-speaking part of Switzerland. She emerged, like many Swiss students, speaking fluent French, Italian, and German, and she had learned some English as well. That little bit of English would soon change her life.

One day in 1946, when World War II had just ended and she was twenty years old, Margrit found herself running an errand in a tiny watch shop in Locarno. An American was in the store, a captain from the U.S. Army, and was having a devil of a time. He wanted to buy a music box for his sister back in the States, and he was trying desperately to communicate with the shopkeeper. Margrit, with her smattering of English, wound up interpreting. The officer got his music box and was so delighted he invited Margrit for a coffee. They had coffee and talked, despite the language barrier, and that evening Captain Philip Biever called her at home and invited Margrit to dinner. "My father said no," Margrit recalls. "And so it was no." The next afternoon, though, they met for coffee again and walked a bit through town. Again Captain Biever invited her to dinner, and again her father refused to let her go. So they had coffee again the next afternoon. Then the day came for Margrit to go back to school in Lausanne and Captain Biever escorted her to the train. "I was in love," Margrit says now. "I didn't know with what."

Captain Biever was stationed in Holland, and he wrote to Margrit every single day. "I learned English by corresponding with him," Margrit says. Their relationship deepened via letter and finally, by mail, he asked her to marry him. She accepted, by return mail. Imagine! As Margrit says, "This was Hollywood. This was fantastic!" And scary. He was from North Dakota, where he had been a physics teacher before the war; she was from a village in Switzerland. He was Catholic; she was Protestant. But what mattered? Only that they were in love. For a traditional Calvinist Swiss family, the very idea of this marriage was a shock. But her mother supported her and the family finally agreed. The day before the wedding, Captain Biever arrived in town to take his bride. Margrit's mother had made her a lovely white gown and veil, sewn by hand of course. Margrit had packed all her belongings in a trunk and a few suitcases. She and Captain Biever were married in the local city hall and in the Church Madonna del Sasso, while a U.S. Army Jeep waited outside to whisk them away.

Margrit has an amazing memory. The Jeep took them to a train bound for Germany, where Captain Biever had a new posting, and she recalls almost every detail. "I wore a little blue dress and he was in uniform," Margrit says. "We found our compartment on the train and for about a half hour neither he nor I spoke. We barely knew each other, and up to then we had had no physical contact. For the first time it hit us what an enormity we had done."

From that point on, it was the army life for Margrit, with officers' quarters, wives' clubs, commissaries, and assignments that ranged form Germany to South Dakota, Spokane to Okinawa, and Cincinnati to Puerto Rico. Along the way, they had three children, Annie, Phoebe, and Philip Jr. Finally, Philip and Margrit decided they had had enough of the army life and they chose to settle down in an idyllic little place they had once visited on their way out to the Orient: the Napa Valley. It was not long thereafter that she came to see us at Krug and then came over to the Robert Mondavi Winery.

In addition to running our tours and retail room, Margrit began introducing us to the joys of art, music, and culinary artistry with a European touch. In 1967, under Margrit's influence, we began inviting painters, sculptors, and photographers to display their work at the winery, a tradition we maintain to this day. Thanks to Cliff May's design, that space has a light, airy feel and a spectacular open view onto our To Kalon Vineyard. It is an ideal place to display and appreciate art, and over the years we have been privileged to showcase the work of such eminent artists as Richard Diebenkorn, Wayne Thiebaud, and Nathan Oliveira. The shows have proved immensely popular with the public and the press. To my way of thinking, they have also placed the art of fine wine in exactly the right context and cultural setting.

In 1969, again with Margrit as the driving force, we founded the Robert Mondavi Winery Summer Music Festival. These are amazing events and now an annual highlight of our winery program. We set up a sound stage on the lawn behind the winery and invite people to come on Saturday night. They have picnics on the lawn or at tables we set up in the vineyards, and we all listen to the great artists from the worlds of jazz, R & B, and pop music. We've had Ella Fitzgerald, Dave Brubeck, Harry Belafonte, Sarah Vaughn, Tony Bennett, and dozens of other top music talents. We kick off the festival every year on the Fourth of July, and we run the series for charity, as a benefit for the Napa Valley Symphony. The concerts raise a lot of money and give our winery wonderful exposure as well, just as I had envisioned when I first dreamed of building a showcase winery. Later we developed a winter concert festival, this time featuring classical music, with the proceeds going to local musical organizations such as the Napa Valley Opera.

That was just the beginning. In 1976, the year of the great tasting triumph in Paris, Margrit scored another coup. At her urging, we began sponsoring a wonderful culinary instruction program called the Great Chefs of France, which also became a continuing tradition at our winery. This is a series of weekend seminars and tastings in the spring and fall. Our intent is to provide advanced training for local food professionals and serious amateurs. As always, we have aligned ourselves with The Best, meaning, in this case, three-star chefs from France. They come to the winery and show us how to prepare meals fit for a king or the family table. We emphasize simple, flavorful recipes, using the freshest meats and fish and the seasonal harvest from local producers or the winery's own organic garden. The chefs take us to the local farmers' markets and show us how to select the best produce and ingredients. Then, right in the kitchen, they show us how to use what we bought to prepare a feast for the table. From there, the chefs discuss the best wines to serve with the meal, explaining why this or that wine would best enhance each course. To add the final touch, we provide instruction in the art of presentation, from the china and wineglasses right down to the linens, the fresh-cut flowers, and how to give the meal a festive guiding theme. Our aim is simple: to show people how to turn the simple fruits of our fields and vineyards into the daily pleasures of the table, into a daily harvest of joy for their family and friends.

The Great Chefs series had a very positive impact on the winery and our own arts of the table. I had grown up believing that wine is good for you, that it's liquid food, and that fine wine can turn a good meal into a feast. My mother's healthy, seasonal, delicious cooking had always been a major asset for my father's business, and he always made shared meals a central part of his business dealings and relationships. At Krug and in our start-up years in Oakville, we had followed the same path, and my wife Marge did an admirable job in this regard. Now, though, we were taking my parents' Old World beliefs and traditions to another level. The meals we served amidst the beauty of our Vineyard Room became ideal showcases for our wines, our philosophy, and our commitment to excellence. Here, too, Margrit was the creative force; she gave the right form and substance to what I had envisioned from the very beginning. Thanks in large measure to her, the marriage of fine wine, fine food, and gracious, healthy living has now become an enduring hallmark of the Robert Mondavi Winery.

You can feel my enthusiasm. Margrit grew up in a culture and a household that held fine food and wine in the same esteem that they held art, music, and literature. In my own primitive fashion, I held wine in equal esteem, but I had no idea how to embody this spirit in our winery. Margrit found the ways. From the very beginning, she understood my vision and then added to it dimensions that I hadn't even fathomed. I made sure that we made wines of the highest quality, and I developed the guiding watchwords of my winery: "Making wine is a skill, fine wine an art." But it was Margrit, with her artistry and European flair, who enhanced my vision even further by creating for our wines and business a setting that properly celebrated aesthetics and culture. And it was Margrit who brought us regular infusions of art, music, fine cooking, and all the fresh creative energy that they engender.

What an education it was for me! When I was around Margrit, I realized how limited my horizons were. She pushed me; she opened me; she inspired me. In fundamental ways, she also changed my way of thinking and my approach to life. When it came to embracing new ideas, I may have been faster than André Tchelistcheff, but I was still pretty much 2 + 2 = 4 in my thinking. With Margrit around, I learned to loosen up and give more credence to my instincts and feelings. Reason and analysis have their place, but for wine makers — or captains of industry — to achieve greatness, they have to go beyond facts and logic and instead learn to trust their gut feelings, their root intuitions, their "nose."

So how do you renew and rekindle a company and its sense of mission? By rekindling its leaders, by knocking down their confining inner walls and giving them fresh injections of passion and creative energy. Yes, openness is the key. The proof is plainly visible in where my great adventure went from here!

CHAPTER 11

Bring on the Baron

BARON PHILIPPE DE ROTHSCHILD.

Is there a bigger name in French wine? Probably not. The Rothschilds are, of course, one of Europe's preeminent aristocratic families, and their name is virtually synonymous with banking, high finance, wine, the arts, and philanthropy. Baron Philippe, though, was a breed unto himself. He was a pioneering wine maker, a poet, and a patron of the arts, with a fabulous collection of Eastern and Western paintings, sculpture, and tapestries. All his life he was a free spirit, a bon vivant, a charming rogue with a twinkle in his eye. He was also an incorrigible, irrepressible ladies' man, even well into his eighties!

I loved him.

My first substantive meeting with the Baron was very surprising. During the 1960s, he had been watching the evolution of the California wine industry and was intrigued

by our progress. The Baron was a close personal friend of
Harry Serlis, then president of the Wine Institute, and at
one stage the Baron asked Harry who might make a good
partner for him in California. Harry told him to talk first
with Bob Mondavi. On the strength of that recommendation, in 1970 the Baron invited me to meet him in Hawaii,
during a wine and spirits wholesalers convention. So I
joined him there and right away I was impressed. Because
the Baron came from the celebrated Rothschild family, I expected him to be a bit haughty and standoffish. Not at all.
He was warm, friendly, and very direct. He dressed very ca-
sually but elegantly, and to my shock he addressed me right
away as Bob. The Baron told me he was interested in one
wine: cabernet sauvignon. Could I think of any way we
could work together? I was totally taken aback and said,
"No, I can't. Can you think of any way we could work together?" We spent about forty-five minutes talking together,
and at the end we agreed to try to come up with a way to
enter into some form of partnership.

I must say I came away very impressed with the Baron
and we understood each other perfectly. He had a passion
for fine wine, fine food, and attractive women — and so did
I. We also shared something far deeper: a passion for perfection and an uncompromising commitment to excellence.
With the Baron, I knew that nothing done within his realm
would be less than the best. Ever. The motto he chose to put
on his bottles said it all: "First I am not. I do not deign to be
second. I am Mouton."

Indeed, the Baron's commitment to excellence was part of his legend. In 1855 the official Bordeaux Classification, ranking top wines from the Bordeaux region, failed to place Château Mouton among the Premier Grand Cru Classé wines, the crème de la crème. A century later, the Baron considered this an insult to his wine and the family name. For twenty-five years the Baron fought to have the Bordeaux Classification revised, and it is a testament to both his persistence and the superior quality of his wines that in 1973 he finally won his battle. Château Mouton, from that day forward, entered the pantheon of French and world-class wines as a Premier Grand Cru Classé. With his victory, the Baron solidified his reputation as one of the most respected and influential figures in the world of French wine.

In Hawaii the Baron and I had agreed to stay in touch, and in 1978 he invited me to come see him in Bordeaux. He wanted to talk. I immediately agreed. My daughter, Marcia, came along and we went to Pauillac. Château Mouton is a magnificent place. The architecture, the landscaping, the panorama — everything melds together into a single artistic and philosophic declaration: We're Mouton. We're the best. The Baron gave us a tour of the château and showed us his wine museum, which is filled with paintings, tapestries, and ancient wine vessels, all of them celebrating grapes, vineyards, and bacchanalian feasts. We also visited Mouton's famous Grand Chai, the Baron's sumptuous wine cellar. This is more than a wine cellar; it is a temple to the art of making fine wine. The feel inside is serene and majestic; all is balance and harmony. It's as if you're in a great amphitheater, and spread before you, in theatrical splendor, are perfectly aligned rows of French oak barrels, each cradling a vintage of Château Mouton as it ages and matures.

That night we met the Baron for dinner in the family library. There were a few other guests as well, including Philippe Cottin, the Baron's right-hand man at Mouton. I remember the meal well. We sat around a small table, almost family-style, and we had quail roasted on the spit. During the meal we had the pleasure of drinking three glorious wines. First, a twenty-five-year-old Château Clerc-Milon. This was from a neighboring winery the Baron had purchased and replanted with vines from Mouton. An excellent wine. Then, as the centerpiece of the evening, we enjoyed a hundred-year-old bottle of Château Mouton. Amazing! A wine as smooth and sensuous as velvet. Finally, with dessert, we had a 1945 Château d'Yquem, the fabled sauternes. The Baron liked it served cold—so cold it came to the table with ice in the bottle. It was wonderful.

The Baron, with his bald pate and his robust mutton-chop sideburns, had the look and bearing of a romantic poet, but his manner throughout the dinner was simple and without pretense. I was amazed. Everything surrounding him that night—the magnificent Château Mouton, his art collection, the library lined with leather-bound volumes of the great poets—all this reminded me of the man's wealth and heritage. He was a Rothschild. But inside all this, the Baron was very down-to-earth. He spoke little at the table, and what he said was always mirthful and right to the point. I also noticed that he hated Wine Speak as much as I did. He didn't want to rhapsodize about his hundred-year-old Château Mouton; he wanted to drink it—and do so with gusto! All this made for a delightful evening and it perfectly set the stage for what was to follow.

After dinner, the Baron said, "Bob, we did not speak a word of business tonight. Would you mind meeting me tomorrow morning in my bedroom? That's where I do 90 percent of my business."

So the next morning, at 9:30, Marcia and I met the Baron in his bedroom. Now I was ready to move forward and so was he. In less than two hours, we established both the idea and the framework for a historic joint venture. We agreed to form a fifty-fifty partnership with one guiding ambition: to make a great wine, a wine that would stand alone in spirit and quality. The idea was to take our different cultures and traditions, along with the best materials and know-how from Bordeaux and California, and merge them, fuse them, and see if we could find that touch of magic that produces a wine great enough to be referred to as "bottled poetry." We'd draw our inspiration from Mouton's Premier Grand Cru Classé and the Mondavi Cabernet Reserve, but our aim was to create a wine like no other, a great wine with its own style, character, and breeding. The Baron and I both loved the idea. And we both saw its import and historical dimensions. We had no name yet, and we knew we had enormous obstacles in front of us, but with a simple handshake in his bedroom that morning, the Baron and I gave birth to Opus One.

What an idea, and what an adventure. Over the years that followed, the Baron and I had some tough negotiations but we always worked in harmony. And we always adhered to our principles and to our basic agreement, creating a partnership that could not have been better. Due to a series of unexpected problems, bringing Opus One into the world cost us both a princely sum at the outset. But what's a few million dollars here or there, when you're out to create high art? And what's a few million more when you're building a vibrant business institution designed to last a hundred years and more? Peanuts. The Baron and I knew this. We also believed in each other and we believed totally in what we were doing. Ours was an accord built on shared passions and mutual trust. And not once, during all the hassles that followed, did the Baron ever change one iota of our initial agreement, nor did he waver from our initial goals and spirit. From the outset, we both knew that creating a world-class wine would be a difficult and very costly business. But we also knew that Opus One was a noble venture, a calling really, and the only way to do it justice was to carry forth our endeavor with élan, passion, good humor, and joy.

As heady as this venture was, I also had a well-grounded sense of what it meant for the Robert Mondavi Winery. As soon as the Baron and I shook hands on the deal, I knew this partnership would do wonders for our winery and the whole

Napa Valley. No one in the past fifty years had done more for French wine than the Baron and everyone knew it. The fact that he wanted to have a joint venture with our winery immediately elevated us into a unique position in the California wine industry. The Baron wanted to do business in America, with a Napa Valley winery as a partner, and we were chosen. The prestige value was enormous — and so was the publicity. When we announced the creation of the joint venture, I'd say we got over a million dollars' worth of free advertising. At the same time, this partnership gave us real international standing and it set the stage for a series of other foreign ventures that we developed in the years ahead.

Imagine how proud this all made me feel. My grandparents were poor sharecroppers in Sassoferrato. My parents came to America without a penny in their pockets. Now, thanks to hard work and the ability to turn humble grapes into fine wine, the names Rothschild and Mondavi were going to stand side by side on every case and bottle of Opus One that would travel the world. Now there's a taste of the American dream!

Then came the hard part. Our first challenge was to make a great wine. The Baron had a very good wine maker, Lucien Sionneau. He began to meet regularly with my son Tim, and the following year, 1979, they created the first vintage of Opus One. The joint venture had no vineyards of its own yet, so they used grapes from the best of our vineyards. Like Château Mouton, Opus One is a blend, what people in America call a meritage. Lucien and Tim used a blend dominated by cabernet sauvignon, with much smaller portions of cabernet franc and merlot. We have used these three varietals ever since, with their percentage varying according to the qualities they display at the time of blending.

For both partners, this process was very educational. "We started out with two different wine cultures and two different perspectives," recalls Patrick Léon, who succeeded Lucien Sionneau as Mouton's wine maker in 1985. "I'd say that, in essence, it was science versus nose. The Americans were very strong with testing and analysis, but they were less strong in the art of the *assemblage*, the blending of fine wine. To make a wine like Opus One, you have to be willing to take risks. There's no sure recipe. You can't verify everything in advance."

We taught the Mouton team the ways of American business; they taught us the ways of French wine. Tim and his staff profited from the exchange, picking up ideas we would later integrate into our own operations at the Robert Mondavi Winery. Just as important, Tim and his team were exposed to a different culture and spirit of wine making. In the view of Patrick Léon, for instance, "nose" is what distinguishes a great wine maker, and the true artist also needs something more: *un petit grain de folie*, meaning a touch of whimsy or folly. Now what American wine course or master could ever teach you that?

There was more than a touch of folly in our entire Opus

One venture. And we had some hilarious episodes, one of which centered around another one of our immediate tasks: finding a suitable name. In the early stages, the Baron's only child, Baroness Philippine, was just starting to become involved in the creation of Opus. She was a theater actress by profession, with long experience at the famous Comédie Française, but the Baron was grooming her for the day when she would take over Château Mouton. The way Philippine remembers it now, we began with the idea of using the two names, Rothschild and Mondavi. But whose name would come first? Out of our brainstorming came such names as Duet, Aliage, and Alliance. None had the right ring.

"One day my father announced, 'A Latin name might be good,' and so he went searching through various Latin sources," Philippine says. "He even turned to the horoscope for a bit of inspiration. *Voilà!* There he found it. My father was very excited and eager to share the news. So he chose a convenient hour, for us and for the Mondavis in California, and then he organized a conference call. At the appointed hour, he went to his bedroom and propped himself up in bed. I was there at his side. Then he placed the call. When we had Bob and his team on the line in Oakville, my father said rather proudly:

" 'Well, Bob, I have found the name!'

" 'Really,' Bob said. 'That's great! What is it?'

" 'Gemini.'

" 'Gemini?' I heard Bob say.

" 'Yes, Gemini.'

"Then there was dead silence on the other end of the line.

" 'So what do you think, Bob?'

" 'Well, Baron, that's the name of the biggest gay paper in San Francisco!' "

As Philippine says, we all then had a good laugh, including the Baron, and our search resumed. The Baron then hit upon the Latin word *opus*, and we all immediately decided it had the right feel and stature. In Latin, *opus* means "work," and it is most often applied to art or a piece of music. The Baron then suggested we make it Opus One, to convey the impression that this was the first work of a master composer. That was an essential touch. It was bold and proud, as if our wine was already declaring itself a Premier Grand Cru Classé.

Our logo for Opus One was also the subject of considerable back and forth, in large measure because both sides had the highest standards in this regard. We had Malette Dean and Jim Beard in our heritage; the Baron had commissioned painters like Salvador Dalí, Marc Chagall, Pablo Picasso, Miró, and Andy Warhol to design labels for different vintages of his wine. Susan Pate, a respected San Francisco designer, had the difficult task of finding the right look and feel for our logo and label, but we all contributed suggestions. She presented a label with the two profiles—the Baron facing west and my profile facing east. We finally settled on using our two profiles, Rothschild and Mondavi, back to back. The Baron claimed the idea of using our profiles was his; I remember my son Michael putting two chess pieces, knights, back to back and drawing a rough sketch of the result. Either way, the fused profiles ended up working brilliantly, especially when drafted in deep blue and drawn with Susan's artistic hand.

Names and logos, though, don't mean much without top quality in the bottle. Our 1979 vintage turned out well, but not as well as we had hoped. Lucien Sionneau's French palate, of course, favored elegance and finesse; Tim was more accustomed to making wines with the bold, intense richness of our cabernets. It took them a little time to establish the right balance and harmony. In terms of the marketplace, though, Opus One's prestige and unique pedigree generated incredible demand long before we actually released the first vintages in 1984. At the Napa Valley Wine Auction in 1981, the first case of Opus One ever to be put on sale went for $24,000! In an unusual move, we chose to release the 1979 and 1980 vintages together in 1984, and both sold out immediately, at $50 a bottle.

Then we hit some rough years. Perhaps the novelty wore off a bit or the price was still deemed a bit high. In either event, sales were slower. Top-quality restaurants, one of our prime targets, were not ordering in the kind of quantities we hoped to see. To my mind, we were not properly reaching and educating the consumer, and at $50 a bottle retail and more in restaurants, the price for a lesson in quality was high. So in 1988 we launched a promotion called Vintage Debut. The idea was simple. In the fall, after we released the new vintage, we encouraged restaurants to offer Opus One by the glass. Now, instead of having to pay over $50 for a bottle to try, diners could pay about $10 for a taste, to see if they liked it. This marketing and educational effort worked, our sales bounced up, and the public demand for Opus became so high that the price edged up to $70 and then $80 a bottle, making it the highest-priced wine in the Napa Valley. As a result, Opus One became known as America's first "ultra-premium" wine.

All this constitutes the happy surface of our Opus adventure; the real richness lies below. Opus needed a home. We had envisioned that from the beginning. In 1981 we started purchasing top-quality vineyards. To get us off to a proper start, especially for our cabernet grapes, the Robert Mondavi Winery sold to the Opus partnership a portion of our cherished To Kalon Vineyard. This was a thirty-five-acre parcel of To Kalon we called Q block. In 1983 and 1984, Opus then purchased two vineyards just across Highway 29 from our winery. Together with its To Kalon parcel, this gave Opus One a total of 138 acres of land, about 108 of which were planted vineyards. These new parcels also gave Opus One something more: the site of its future home.

Building the Opus One winery was a very troubled operation, and therein hang several stories, lessons, and cautionary tales. First of all, we envisioned a winery with a small annual production, only about thirty thousand cases. But we wanted the building to make a much larger statement. In 1984, after a lengthy search, we commissioned the noted architect William Pereira and his associate, Scott Johnson, to design for us a building with enough style and impact to become another Napa Valley landmark. We also wanted a structure that would be built to last and look modern for the next hundred years, at the very least.

The architectural plan they created was stunning. It looked like no other winery in the world. The building was not just modern, it was futuristic, blending California boldness with French classical accents. According to the plan, you would enter the site via a long, narrow avenue. At the end of the avenue, surrounded by vineyards, was to be Opus One, its cream-colored Texas limestone dazzling in the sun. In the front of the building was a courtyard in the form of a half-moon, an ideal place for outdoor tastings, or, on very special occasions, candlelight dinners and dancing.

Rising up behind the courtyard would be a kind of rotunda structure three stories tall. On the courtyard level there was a visitor-welcoming area. Below, a grand circular staircase led down to the wine cellar. Above was an open-air pergola and patio, featuring a spectacular wraparound view of the whole Napa Valley. This area was to be set off by a rendition of classical columns, constructed of futuristic polished gray metal. The pergola area, also idea for tastings and parties, would look out onto the valley from under a lattice-work canopy made from redwood.

I loved the design and so did the Baron. Some critics would later say that it looked as though a spaceship from Mars had plopped down in the middle of our vineyard. But we saw the building as bold and distinctive, a modern, yet classically inspired temple to Bacchus, Dionysus, the pleasures of the table, and the art of wine making. But as set forth in the plan, the building was just too big. And way too expensive; the projected cost was something like $30 million. We insisted the building be scaled back without changing the basic look and feel. We put Clifford Adams, my right-hand man at the time, in charge of supervising the entire operation, with an eye to holding our costs down. Well, it took almost a year for us to get the plan down to the size and price we wanted, confirming a lesson I had learned in building my own winery: it always takes longer than you hope or expect. Much longer! And it always costs more. You'd better plan for it.

Then the troubles really set in. In the middle of the project, Bill Pereira passed away. Scott Johnson took over, and while he understood every aspect of what Pereira wanted, the transition still caused us some delays. That was minor in comparison to what happened next. As we prepared to begin the construction, we tested the soil and had engineers inspect the site. We knew the property had a high water table; many of the residents in the area had told us they regularly had flood problems during the storms that come every winter and early spring. But the engineers turned up something far more menacing: under the existing plan, Opus One was positioned directly over some geothermal springs! This was an ideal site for a hot springs or steam bath, and that was a disaster for us. A winery and a wine cellar require cool, even temperatures for making and aging wine. What to do?

Go back to the drawing board. More delays. Escalating costs. We called in the engineers to tell us what, if anything, we could do to make that site work. To make a very long story short, we drained and sealed the site to protect it against water and heat. Then we built a wine cellar that would be waterproof, insulated, and evenly cooled by an elaborate system of pipes. Miles and miles of pipe, embedded in the floor and ceiling of the cellar. Once the cellar was built, we had to install a misting system, a state-of-the-art sprinkler arrangement that used electronic sensors and computers to maintain a constant 87 percent humidity and a constant year-round temperature of 55 degrees Fahrenheit. The cost of all this? Don't ask. Sorting out and fixing these problems cost us at least $8 million and by the time we were done, building Opus One cost us about $29 million.

These delays cost us something far more dear than money. The Baron died in 1988, at the age of eighty-six. He had poured his heart and soul into Opus One; it was the last great adventure of his life. But he died before we even broke ground. His daughter, Philippine, stepped in and took charge of their end of the project, and she has done a marvelous job ever since. But I was so sad that her father, after everything he had put into the project, was not around to see how well the Opus One Winery turned out. He would have been delighted to know, too, that by our fourth year in operation, we had started turning a profit!

"To my father, wine meant both pleasure and art," Philippine says now. "My father loved the design of the building, and I'm sure he would have been delighted with the end result. I am. I think it's a beautiful building. Sure, it cost more than we hoped, but I don't think we could have made it any better."

Like her father, Baroness Philippine has taken on Opus One with a passion. We first met in the 1970s and ever since then she has had quite a soft spot for my family. "The first time I met Bob and Mike, I thought they were mountains," she says. "What extraordinary people! At that stage, I had never even been to California. But what they said about their winery gave me the desire to come to Napa and see for myself." From that point on, during the early years of Opus, Philippine often came to California. And she gave us invaluable help and artistic input. In fact, she and Margrit ended up anchoring what we called our Aesthetic Committee, along with Scott Johnson and Daniel Kiener, Philippine's interior designer in Paris. They made sure that everything in the luxurious, yet homey, hospitality areas was done with style and taste, from the fabrics on the couches to the wine-related antiques and wall hangings. As always, we had only one criterion: The Best.

Once her father died, Philippine took the reins in hand, and she, too, never wavered when the problems and the costs started to escalate. "The first five years were tough," Philippine says now. "But I was always calm inside. And so was Bob. We were convinced we were going to make a great wine. In building the winery, we had only one goal: Aim for perfection. Because we knew it would bring a lot to our two families and to Opus One."

Constructing the building, alas, was not our only headache. In 1990 we were hit with a problem that had already devastated dozens of wineries in Napa and Sonoma counties: phylloxera. This dreaded pest, a voracious little root louse that attacks and destroys the rootstock of grapevines, has long been a nemesis of the wine industry, in Europe and America. Early American settlers in Virginia are believed to have cultivated grapes in the seventeenth century, only to see them savaged by these little pests. In the 1860s, phylloxera ran wild through the vineyards of France and within twenty years had destroyed every vine in France, from the most humble to the most noble. Bordeaux, Burgundy, Champagne—everything was devastated. The almost microscopic insect is native to the Mississippi Valley and may have made its way to France in the 1850s on vines the French imported for research. The savior, ironically enough, was also of American origin. It turned out that some of our native American rootstocks, like St. George, were genetically resistant to phylloxera. These were imported and grafted on to the few remaining European vines not yet affected—making them resistant, too. The procedure worked and the French wine industry bounced back.

The next victim, though, was California. According to

Charles Sullivan in his history *Napa Wine*, phylloxera was detected on some Sonoma County vines in 1873. The pest moved slower here than in Europe, though, which gave some wineries enough time to replant their vineyards with rootstock that was resistant to the louse. But much of the valley's wine industry was afflicted. Inglenook, for one, saw its output slashed from eighty thousand gallons to twenty-five thousand in just four years.

We in the valley thought we had the problem licked. U.C. Davis researchers had developed a rootstock called AxR-1, which we all thought was resistant to phylloxera. Something like 80 percent of the valley's grapes were planted on AxR-1 from the 1960s on. But that damn little louse managed to mutate into a new variety that seemed to love nothing more than munching on our AxR-1! The only solution was to rip out the blighted vineyards and replant them with new rootstock that was resistant to this new generation of the same old root louse. This cost all of us a small fortune. We first detected phylloxera in Q block in 1990. We expected its advance to take about five years, which would have given us time to replant and still maintain our production goals. But two years later, most of the vines were either dead or shriveled to within an inch of their life. In three more years, the whole vineyard was gone. We were shocked at the speed with which it all happened. Here, too, though, the disaster brought us a gift in disguise.

By the time phylloxera began ravaging Q block, we had already changed our operating philosophy in the vineyards, thanks in part to Patrick Léon. At Mouton, they do not plant their vineyards the way we and others throughout the Napa Valley had been doing it for years. They space their vines much closer together. In California, rows of vines were normally planted twelve feet apart, with the vines themselves eight feet apart along the row. At Mouton, the rule of thumb was four by four — four feet between rows and four feet between vines. Tim had long been in agreement.

"Vines need competition," Patrick explains. "It makes the grapes push harder. This way, each vine produces fewer grapes, but the grape quality is far superior. Narrow spacing demands many more vines per acre and much more expensive pruning as well. As a result, the cost of producing Opus One is much higher than the cost of producing many other fine wines. Bob understood this right away, when we explained it to him. To him, narrow spacing made perfect sense. He saw that it was much more expensive, but worth it. Bob doesn't react like a technician. He reacts like a visionary." Hey, I'd better hire this guy!

Patrick also led us in a different direction with our pruning. "We feel that sunlight is more important than temperature," Patrick explains. "Heat makes the grapes more concentrated. But light is what allows the grapes to ripen. Light is what develops tannin and color." In line with this thinking, Patrick instructs his team at Mouton to go through the vineyards three or four times during the growing season. They look at each vine and then cut away a number of branches so that each vine has the optimal number of grape clusters, a number calculated according to each vine's age and individual size. Very precise! Very costly, too. They also periodically thin out the canopy of vine leaves that grows up over the grapes. They don't radically prune, they just open up the canopy to allow more light onto the fruit below. When he first proposed that we do this at Opus One, many of our vineyard hands were shocked. "They told me, 'But the grapes will burn!'" Patrick recalls. "'No,' I said. 'That is one of the beauties of narrow spacing. Because the vines are so close together, they create shade for one another.'"

Working with Patrick, Tim became very excited about these practices, and he has since made them the norm at many of the Mondavi vineyards in the Napa Valley and up and down the state of California. When phylloxera devastated Q block, Tim replanted the whole vineyard, using the narrow four-by-four spacing and improved genetic strains of grapes and rootstock. Tim says the entire experience has elevated his approach to managing our vineyards.

"Our goal is to create wines of soul and expression," he says. "We now have a better appreciation of the importance of site, leaf removal, the display of our vines, and the density of our planting."

Long before we entered into the Opus One partnership, we knew that the more gently we handle the grapes, from the vineyard through the cellar, the gentler and more flavorful the wine is. For Opus One, gentle handling was a primary goal. For instance, at many traditional wineries, the wine is pumped under pressure from the crusher to the fermentation tanks. Not at Opus One. We built the cellar on two levels. At harvesttime, the grapes arrive on the upper level, where they are crushed. Then, thanks to what we call our gravity-flow design, the must streams gently and naturally down into the tanks below. We then leave the must in the big fermentation tanks for a long maceration period—that is, when skins and fruit are in contact. We maintain that contact for four or five weeks so the young wine can absorb as much character as possible from the skins. From the beginning of the wine-making process to the end, there is no pumping, no pressure, no bruising of the fruit. We can see and taste the resulting gentleness and flavor in every bottle of Opus One.

In a bow to the Baron and what he created at Château Mouton, we made sure that Opus One had its own spectacular "Grand Chai." Ours is fifteen thousand square feet and our barrels fan out in a huge semicircle. This houses about a thousand barrels on a single level, so that our staff can move among them easily to conduct the periodic testing, topping up, and "racking"—the transfer every ninety days to a fresh barrel. The young wine stays in these barrels for nine months. Then it is moved to another part of the cellar for another nine months of aging in oak. I'm not sure our "Grand Chai" has quite the theatrical look and feel of the Baron's, but it is breathtaking and I'm sure he'd be proud of what we New World upstarts have managed to create.

As Patrick Léon will tell you, he and his Mouton team learned plenty from our side as well. "First and foremost, we learned a new *méthode de travail*, a new manner of working," Patrick says. "American management, organization, and planning were very different from ours. They use written plans; we use oral. They work in teams; we sometimes barely speak to one another. And they are very conscious of the relationship between the cost of operations and the price of their product. The Mondavis showed us many ways to improve our management practices and our internal communications, and how to be more rigorous in holding down our costs."

Patrick's right about the differences. On the other hand, when it came to promotion and marketing, the Baron and I always saw eye to eye. We always felt confident that if we produced a wine of the highest quality, we would earn the respect of the buying public. It might take longer than we expected, and we might have to do more education than we anticipated. But sooner or later, quality always wins out. We also agreed that marketing wine demanded the personal touch. The Baron embodied Mouton in much the same way as I embodied the Robert Mondavi Winery. People all over the world knew who we were, came to visit us, and became our friends. This gave real flesh and blood to our wines, instead of just fancy names and labels. And the images from our own wines carried over to Opus One.

"Bob and the Baron always had a harmony of vision when it came to marketing," Patrick Léon agrees. "Make a wine of small quantity. The highest quality. The highest beauty. Set it forth in a very personal way. And make it very expensive. With the names Mondavi and Rothschild on it, you have to succeed."

I couldn't have said it better myself!

CHAPTER 12

The Revolution

I LOVE THE FRENCH.

They can be terrible chauvinists, I know, but in terms of inspiration and support, I owe a lot to the Baron, to fine French restaurants like La Pyramide, and to that humble cornerstone of our efforts to revolutionize American wine making: the French oak barrel. But I and the Napa Valley owe someone else a bow as well. Alongside ours in the wine business, there was another revolution brewing in America: the culinary revolution. And in our little corner of the republic, it was a Frenchman who planted some of the first seeds.

The story really begins back in 1968. That year, a shrewd, forward-thinking Frenchman named Robert-Jean de Vogüé came to the Napa Valley on a very serious mission. De Vogüé was the chairman and driving force at Moët Hennessy, producer of two of France's finest champagnes, Moët & Chandon and the celebrated Dom Perignon. At that time, worldwide demand for champagne was very high, and the market in the United States was huge. But de Vogüé had a problem. Under French appellation law, no sparkling wine produced outside the confines of the Champagne district could be labeled champagne. And within Champagne there was next to no additional vineyard acreage to be had — at any price. So with an eye to expanding Moët's production capacity and sales, de Vogüé was doing some serious prospecting in the Napa Valley. He was looking to put together some prime vineyard property and build a winery. Then, using California grapes and traditional French methods, Moët planned to produce a whole new brand of sparkling wine, for sale throughout America and around the globe.

I knew Robert-Jean well. Before I started my winery, I had visited with him at Moët & Chandon and he gave me invaluable advice. For instance, he paid his growers according to the quality of the grapes they produced, as determined by the ultimate retail price he could get per bottle of wine. This to me was a brilliant idea, and I brought it back and put it into effect in my own winery, as I mentioned before. He also urged me to plan my winery with several tasting areas, as they did at Moët & Chandon. Again I followed Robert-Jean's advice, and again he turned out to be absolutely right. He knew his stuff! In return for his advice and kindness, when Robert-Jean came to our valley in 1968, looking for a place to make sparkling wine in America, I suggested a few properties to look at and I gave him my full support.

Robert-Jean liked what he found in the valley. He had a devil of a time pulling his plans together, but four years later de Vogüé and Moët Hennessy formally launched their great American venture. They bought 200 acres of vineyard on Mount Veeder, to the west of Napa, a 550-acre ranch in our Carneros District to the south, and another 350 acres in Yountville, right in the heart of the valley. I thought these were excellent choices. The vineyards had wonderful potential, and the Yountville parcel was centrally located and would make a fine site for a winery and tasting rooms. In 1975 they began construction. As I recall, they deliberated long and hard about what to name their new winery in America. They wanted it to sound French and convey all the class and breeding of a French champagne, but they also wanted the name to work well in English. I think they finally came up with a winner: Domaine Chandon.

Now this guy was smart. I'm only speculating here, but I bet Robert-Jean and his team deliberated long and hard about something else: even by the mid-1970s there was still not a single restaurant in the whole of our valley that I would call first-rate. I'm not proud of this fact, but it's true. I'm afraid that even our best restaurants at that time would merit nothing more than a sniff of disdain from serious Frenchmen and critics like the *Michelin Guide*. I'm sure this was a cause of great consternation to Robert-Jean and his fellow Frenchmen at the helm of Moët Hennessy. Planting a foot in the backwoods of California promised to be a very exciting adventure for them—but where would they eat? Where would they entertain their customers? Where, above all, would they host those glorious champagne lunches that are the hallmark of doing business in the grand French style, both in Paris and in their hometown of Reims, the capital of Champagne? I can imagine their anguish. Back then you could get a pretty good hamburger in nearby Yountville, and maybe a decent plate of spaghetti, but that was about it. What were Robert-Jean and his team to do?

Well, bring real French cuisine to the Napa Valley, of course! The Moët team, in fact, saw a golden opportunity. Creating a high-quality French restaurant at Domaine Chandon perfectly fit their strategy in America. With no high-end competition in the valley, the restaurant could generate substantial revenue—and huge national publicity. It would attract throngs of people to the winery and serve as a wonderful tool for promoting and selling Domaine Chandon wines. And, of course, it would give Robert-Jean and the other Moët executives an ideal place to bring customers in from all over the world—and then wine them and woo them over those big champagne lunches. I'm only guessing, of course, but in Moët's thinking there might also have been just a touch of missionary zeal and noblesse oblige. Having a real French restaurant here would surely teach us natives a thing or two about the arts of living and doing business *à la française!*

In the end, Robert-Jean and his team did a fabulous job with Domaine Chandon. The winery turned out to be exquisite. Their restaurant opened its doors in April 1977, and it proved to be an immediate success. My hat was off to them. The setting was idyllic and the menu, under the guiding hand of chef Udo Nechutnys, featured a cuisine that took the best of French cooking and gave it a light, fresh California twist. The meals were marvelous! And that was good news for all of us. At last, the Napa Valley had a restaurant worthy of the wines we were now making. Domaine Chandon delighted even the most serious food sophisticates. The critics raved, the cream of San Francisco began coming up for lunch or dinner, and more and more tourists started coming into the valley. The public was tasting, learning, and eager for more. I didn't fully realize it yet — few people did — but we were witnessing the first stirrings of what would soon emerge in many cities and towns across America: the culinary revolution.

In many respects, Northern California was the breeding ground for this revolution. For years, our friend Julia Child had been using her cookbooks and television shows to teach Americans how to cook and appreciate fine cuisine. Julia's inspiration was mainly French, and I think she did a marvelous job of raising our national consciousness and inspiring young chefs across the country, whether they were professionals in the trade or cooking meals at home. Then along came Alice Waters. At Chez Panisse, her restaurant in Berkeley, Alice was doing some very exciting things. Alice was creating dishes that were light, healthy, and creative, and always with a special California touch. I ate at Chez Panisse often, and I was very impressed with what she was doing. She offered only a few dishes, and she changed the menu every day, according to what she and her staff had found that morning in the local markets. Alice was using only the freshest locally grown organic fruits and vegetables. And if she couldn't find what she wanted, by golly she went to receptive farmers in Napa and Sonoma Counties and made them grow what she wanted! Alice was amazing, and she became the hub of a small but influential cottage industry in Northern California. With her inspiration and support, many young people were going into business and developing gourmet specialties, from fresh breads and organic lettuces to locally made goat cheese and foie gras. By the late 1970s and early 1980s, Chez Panisse had become a hub of the emerging revolution and Alice was becoming known across America as the creator and godmother of a whole new style and culture of cooking, California cuisine.

The Napa Valley became a hub as well. In the mid-1970s, two very creative young men, Michael James and Billy Cross, approached Margrit with an idea. At the time, they were running a cooking school in conjunction with Hi Tree Farm in Rutherford, but they had lost their lease. So they proposed joining forces with the Robert Mondavi Winery. Margrit introduced Michael and Billy to me and I liked their idea. They wanted to bring three-star chefs from France to America, and I liked the idea of this sort of cultural exchange. I felt confident that if the great chefs tasted our wines, they would be surprised and pleased and would eventually put them on their own menus in France. So we agreed to house the cooking school and it turned into a great success. Michael and Billy eventually moved on to other things, but the program continues today, under the able direction of Margrit.

Thus it was in 1976, through our Great Chefs of France program, that our winery began hosting regular cooking demonstrations and seminars to educate amateur cooks and professional chefs who came to us from many different parts of the country. For these programs, we brought to America such world-renowned French chefs as Pierre Troisgros, Paul Bocuse, Gaston Lenotre, and Michel Guérard. In our local markets and our kitchens, they showed our guest chefs how to plan and prepare meals that were both delicious and nutritious. In the best French tradition, they used only the freshest ingredients, preferably straight from the local farmers' market. These French chefs were always a big hit. Along with their demonstrations, our Great Chefs program also featured seminars on subjects like organic gardening and the health benefits of drinking good wine in moderation. In 1983, as the culinary revolution started to take hold, we expanded our program to include the Great Chefs of America. And we brought in celebrated American chefs like Jeremiah Tower, Paul Prudhomme, Larry Forgione, Wolfgang Puck, Julia Child, and, of course, Alice Waters.

So in the early 1980s, the Robert Mondavi Winery stood at the crossroads of two converging revolutions. One was transforming the quality of the wines we were making in America and awakening the general public to the joys and health benefits of drinking fine wine. The other was revitalizing American cuisine and raising public consciousness about the joys and health benefits of fresh, seasonal cooking, organic gardening, and staying close to nature in what we eat.

I was delighted by both of these trends! America was at last awakening to the arts and pleasures of the table that the French and we Italians had been celebrating for generations. To me, this was a dream come true. My father and Momma Rosa had shown us the virtues of healthy cooking and healthy wine, and the benefits of enjoying them together at the family table. To me, a meal without wine was like a day without sunshine, and a fine bottle of wine could turn even a humble meal into festive banquet. Indeed, enjoying fine food and fine wine at the family table, surrounded by your loved ones and friends, was not just a joy—it was one of the highest forms of the art of living. This was the core belief I had expounded at my winery from the very beginning. And this was a primary element of the gospel I had been preaching all across the country as we tried to educate the public and build, from scratch, a large national market for fine wines. Now, seeing my views finally take hold in America gave me deep satisfaction.

And it was all happening right on our doorstep. By the early 1980s, we were so busy with our tours and tastings that we often had to turn people away unless they had booked in advance. I was amazed. In 1966 I had dreamed of building a showcase winery that would become a magnet and education center for tourists — now we were jammed to capacity!

Soon the entire Napa Valley was swept up in the fervor. With the success of Domaine Chandon, several other very good restaurants opened around the valley. A number of cafés and bistros also appeared, and just a stone's throw from our winery, a few hundred yards up Highway 29, there was another eloquent sign of the times: the Oakville Grocery. In the late '60s and early '70s, when we were still a sleepy little farm community, the Oakville Grocery was a convenient, high-quality, pocket-sized grocery store, with specialty items you couldn't find in the local supermarkets. In 1978, though, the vintner Joseph Phelps purchased the market and brought in some fresh ideas and energy. He spruced the place up, expanded his gourmet product lines, and improved his take-out counter. By the early 1980s, the Oakville Grocery had turned into a "must stop" for the many young, well-heeled professionals who were now driving up from San Francisco for a weekend of relaxation, wine tasting, and gourmet dining.

On Saturday and Sunday mornings in the summer, you couldn't get near the Oakville Grocery. Scores of visitors, young and not so young, would be packed into the place, ordering cappuccinos and croissants and sampling the market's dazzling arrays of cheese, sausage, mustard, mayonnaise, and chutneys. Many of them would put together gourmet picnics for later in the day. Then they would pick a winery for a tour and a tasting. Some local wineries even set out picnic tables to attract the revelers to their tasting rooms.

After lunch, many of the visitors would move on for a coffee or a bit of shopping in the boutiques now springing up in St. Helena. Others would head for an afternoon ride in a hot-air balloon or have a mud bath and a massage at a spa in Calistoga. Come dinnertime, the valley restaurants would be jammed, some of them with lines waiting outside. Soon another phenomenon made its appearance: the stretch limousine. Day and night you'd see them conspicuously zigzagging around the valley. With a limo hired for the weekend, no one had to drink and drive. The snob appeal, apparently, was worth the cost. And our quiet little farm community had been transformed into a burgeoning tourist destination with sex appeal and a glamorous name: the Wine Country. Also, thanks to a brilliant entrepreneur named Marvin Shanken, we even had a new magazine promoting our valley and our products: *Wine Spectator.*

This influx of tourists had a profound impact on our valley. For generations we had been a haven of greenery and calm; what we lacked in big-city wealth and sophistication we made up for in small-town neighborliness and gentility. Now traffic had become a nightmare, especially on weekends, and it made many longtime residents furious. A lot of our friends began refusing to go out on weekends. Land prices started to escalate, too. Instead of real farmers growing grapes, now we had gentleman farmers hiring consultants to hire farmers and field hands to grow grapes for them. Doctors, lawyers, and bankers who had made their bundle in San Francisco were now building million-dollar homes in the valley, to use as weekend getaways or to hold for the day when they would quit their stressful city jobs and "return to the land," in search of a hipper, healthier lifestyle. Other refugees from the big city also came to the valley and settled in, to sell real estate, work in the wineries, set up trendy boutiques, or find an old Victorian to convert into a B & B. I'm sure that before the 1970s, few people in the Napa Valley of old had ever heard the term *B & B*. Now fancy inns and bed-and-breakfasts were sprouting like mushrooms across their landscape. So were new wineries and new restaurants. The twenty or so wineries we had in 1966 had by 1985 grown to 150, with more sprouting up every year!

The resulting transformation in the style and character of our community was stunning. I could see it just walking down Main Street in St. Helena. In what seemed to me like the blink of an eye, we had gone from tractors and farm boots to BMWs and lattés.

I can hear the entire Napa Valley rising up in unison: "Bob, who was always one of the most outspoken advocates of tourism in the valley?" It's true, I am in no position to complain. Nor am I about to: the benefits of the boom far outpaced the negatives. Thanks in part to the tourist influx, by the early 1980s the valley's economy was in high gear.

And as more and more Americans learned to appreciate fine food and wine, sales of California wines, both for premium wines and table wines, started to soar. Our winery was doing very well, and so were many others in the valley.

Not all the innovation was in premium wines. In the late 1970s, one of the biggest phenomena in our business was a little blush wine created by Bob Trinchero over at Sutter Home. In 1975 he made a white zinfandel that was a little sweeter than his usual zin, and the wine really took off. Consumers loved it and Bob's timing was perfect. In 1978 Sutter Home produced ten thousand cases of white zinfandel. By 1982 it was eighty-five thousand cases. And by 1987 the demand had reached 2 million cases! Needless to say, rather than stay the course with high-end wines, which take more time and money to produce, many wineries moved over to zinfandel and tried to catch the same wave.

At the Robert Mondavi Winery, we had built our reputation and prestige on our line of premium wines, and they remained our top priority. But we also made a major move to expand our production of table wines. Back in the 1940s, when my father was selling grapes in Lodi, in California's fertile Central Valley, he took a part interest in a bulk wine facility in the nearby town of Acampo. My brother, Peter, had done part of his training as wine maker there. Also on the outskirts of Lodi was a larger production facility I knew of, located on Woodbridge Road. This winery had changed hands a few times since the war, without achieving much success, but we felt it could be revamped and become the means to boost our production of table wines. Done and done. In 1979 we acquired the winery that we now call Woodbridge, and now it is a pillar of our operation and annual revenues.

In the early years at Woodbridge we made red, white, and rosé table wines, all of them clean, easy to drink, and moderately priced. We called them Robert Mondavi Red, White, Rosé, and White Zinfandel. By the mid-1980s, with demand in the country booming, Woodbridge was turning out over 1 million cases a year. In recent years, we have taken significant steps to further improve the quality of these wines. We started making them with fine varietals and aging them in oak barrels. To reflect their jump in quality, we redesigned the bottles and labeled them according to their predominant varietal. We now call them Woodbridge by Robert Mondavi California Cabernet, Sauvignon Blanc, White Zinfandel, and Zinfandel Rosé.

This was a very exciting period for all of us in the Napa Valley. But in my personal life, I went through some terrible lows. As I intimated earlier, my marriage had run into trouble several years before. I loved the wine business, and I loved all the travel and hoopla that went along with it. Throughout some forty years of marriage, Marge did her share and more, but she never loved the wine life as much as I did. Who could? In the end, it wore her out. I wore her out. I did not do this deliberately; I was simply oblivious to her needs and feelings. To please me and my constant demands, Marge had been forced to work way beyond her capacity and strength—and I just didn't see it. My fight with Peter, the traumatic split in the family, the years of bickering, and then the long, excruciating court case—all these, too, were painful and debilitating. By the mid-1970s, when Michael, Marcia, and Tim had moved out of the house and were off on their own, Marge often found herself home alone. Drained and exhausted. She just didn't have the physical stamina to keep up with our hectic pace.

Looking back now, I can see my own failings. As my children have often reminded me, I never did much around the house—whenever I wanted or needed something, though, Marge came through. I'd bring in guests at the last minute, and with her "elevator oven," Marge always delivered. I asked the world of her, but I rarely helped Marge in the kitchen. And if a roast or a dessert was not done to my view of perfection, I'd give her criticism that, while justified, was often tactless. Often I hurt her far more than I realized. My aim was to be constructive, to push for perfection; I was blind to the reality that relentless criticism, untempered by a positive word of encouragement, almost inevitably becomes damaging and dispiriting.

My way had been the way of Cesare and Rosa, and it was the way of most traditional Italian families, especially those with recent roots in the old country. The example I saw growing up seemed to me ideal: Momma in the kitchen and minding the kids; Papa at work all day and doing his paper-work at home in the evening. It seemed to work well for my parents; why not for us? I took it for granted that Marge would be willing and happy to follow the same pattern, and I was totally oblivious to her deeper needs and growing unhappiness.

When it came to my children, I didn't do much better. As a young family, we lived right on the grounds of the Charles Krug ranch and in some ways that was a problem — after dinner or on weekends it was far too easy to slip back to the winery instead of staying home and spending time with my wife and children. Again, this was how I grew up. My father spent next to *no* time with us kids. So with Michael, Marcia, and Tim, I always figured I was at least doing better than he did. Only later did I come to realize that my children felt deprived; they wanted my unconditional blessing and much more of my time.

Same story at the winery. When Mike and Tim came into the business, I rode them hard year after year. They had big responsibilities at the winery and one day they'd have even more. They had to learn. They had to learn, first and foremost, that there was only one standard to strive for: The Best. And there was only one way to get there: my way. With my unbending passion for perfection, I always set the bar high; if Mike and Tim failed to reach it, I'd let them know in no uncertain terms. Right on the spot. Often I did this in front of other people. Yes, this was callous and uncalled for, I realize that now, but I had my rationale: We were building an empire; they had to learn. People should be strong enough to receive criticism; that's the only way they'll grow. My sons had to toughen up; it's a dog-eat-dog world out there. Only the strong survive. I wanted to teach Mike and Tim how to fly and soar; I had no idea my ways of doing it might be undermining their confidence or clipping their wings.

"My father has not got an ounce of malice in him," Michael says now. "If he did, that might make it much easier for the people closest to him. No, what my father has are terrible blind spots. He focuses so tightly on the goals he has set for himself and his business that he remains totally oblivious to *everything* around him. And to *everyone* around him."

It took me a long time to realize that Michael's right. A long time. And I'm still prone to blindness and total self-absorption. In the mid- and late 1970s, though, about all I could see was that after some forty years of marriage, Marge was unhappy and constantly exhausted. Not me. I was in my midsixties, strong as a goat, full of energy, and despite all I had accomplished, I felt I was just getting started! And, to be frank, a new woman had come into my life. A woman who came to me full of passion, creativity, business savvy, and a wealth of European taste and culture. When I was with her, I felt renewed, revitalized, and rekindled.

Yes, Margrit.

In traditional Italian families from the old country, divorce was out of the question. Men roamed—sometimes women, too—but in one form or another, you stayed together. The Church mandated it; couples obeyed. And for a long time that was my inclination. Finally, though, with some prodding from our children, we decided the best solution was to divorce. We parted as amiably as we could. I told Marge that what we had built, we built together; half of it was hers. We also found a house in Oakville she liked, and we worked out a financial settlement that would leave her comfortable and secure for the rest of her life. Even through all this, Marge was wonderful to me, and thanks to her kindness and forgiveness, we managed to stay close in the years ahead, especially when it came to the kids and the grandchildren.

George Scheppler, one of our guiding hands at Opus One, often says, as a compliment, "Bob Mondavi has no rearview mirror." He's right! And I also have only one speed: fast-forward. Heaven help anyone who gets in my way or tries to slow me down; they'll probably get steamrolled! I think it's in the genes; I've been this way since birth. "Even when he was a little boy, Bobby was not like anyone else in the family," my sister Helen says now. "In fact, he was like *nobody* else we knew. Even as a boy, he was ambitious and hard driving. And even as a boy, everything he did, he wanted to control. And that's never changed."

Now that I'm midway though my eighties, and now that I've handed the reins of the company over to Mike and Tim, I can look back and see all this more clearly. But in the late 1970s, and during the breakup with Marge, I was still blind with ambition and drive. And I was still steamrolling anyone who got in my way or threatened to slow me down. Peter could attest to that. So could Michael and Tim and Marcia. And so could Marge. But my rationale, at that stage anyway, still held firm. We were building an empire, damn it, full speed ahead!

On May 17, 1980, in a quiet ceremony at the Palm Springs home of our friends Harry and Bobbie Serlis, I officially joined hands with Margrit Biever. The speed with which I remarried upset my children, but as usual I was moving full speed ahead and not looking back. With Margrit at my side, I felt confident that we could carry our mission and our winery to far greater heights. And I felt sure we could do so with renewed vigor and style. Yes, I was just about to turn sixty-seven, but I was brimming with vitality and optimism. Life was beginning anew, and I was absolutely positive that the happiest, most productive days of my life were still waiting ahead. And do you know what?

I was right!

CHAPTER 13

Prices to Pay

WITH SUCCESS, there always comes the day of reckoning.

I started out with a vision. I put together a partnership, bought land, and then built a home where my vision could take root and flower. Together with my family and extended family, we created a quality product line, established our image and brand name, educated retailers and consumers, and built a national market for our products. And all along the way we worked hard to raise public consciousness and earn respect and support for our guiding vision.

Then came the hard part: success.

In any business, success inevitably brings growing pains, jealousies, internal rivalries, and power struggles. The Robert Mondavi Winery was no exception. At the start of the 1980s, we were still a small family business, but we were feeling strains in our business and conflicts within the family. We were growing, our industry and market were growing, and I knew that if we wanted to stay in the forefront of the American wine industry, we had to take bold steps. We had to start organizing ourselves and doing business like a much larger corporation.

Being the way I am — fast-forward, no rearview mirror — I was ready to move, but not everyone in my family agreed. We were a family and we were a business. But were we a family first? Or a business? I think my children, to varying degrees, worried that if we always put business considerations first, it might hurt the family, as had happened so painfully at Krug. "Daddy, what have you done to our wonderful little winery?" Marcia asked me at one stage in our expansion. Mike and Tim had some hesitations at various stages, too, but more often they were as swept up in the excitement and challenges as I was. So we started laying the groundwork for the next phases of our development. Our investment in Woodbridge in 1979 was a good step, but I felt we had to move on several other fronts as well.

One was public relations. The culinary revolution was starting to emerge, and we needed to do a better job of promoting our vision and getting the word out about everything we were doing to promote new attitudes toward food and wine. I also needed help in dealing with the press. We were receiving enormous attention in local and national publications, but I felt we needed a professional hand to guide us through the media thicket. I was also eager to speak out on several issues facing the Napa Valley and the wine industry as a whole. What I needed was someone to help me formulate my positions on these issues and then help me articulate them. I can be an effective speaker in public because I speak from the heart and with passion. Frankly, though, I sometimes have trouble formulating what I want to say. Even back in my school days I had that problem, and I developed quite an inferiority complex about it.

So in 1980, in search of help, I turned to my pal Harry Serlis. Harry had hosted my second wedding and was the former president of the Wine Institute, an industry trade organization that had been created back in 1934. The institute monitored key issues in the industry, lobbied in Washington when need be, and mounted campaigns to promote the benefits of wine. My family had long been active in the institute, and so were close friends of mine, like Brother Timothy, the wine maker and driving force for many years at Christian Brothers. When I told Harry Serlis about my growing needs in public relations, he told me he had just the man: Harvey Posert.

I have an unusual way of interviewing and hiring people. I'm not moved by résumés or aptitude tests or anything else of that sort. I sit the person down in front of me and see what I think. I'm looking for ability and experience, sure, but I'm mostly looking for passion and drive. Have they got it in the heart and in the gut? I liked Harvey Posert right away. He's tall, a bit portly, and he has a wit that is dry and often caustic. He's also straight talking and straight to the point. Right away I could see he knew his stuff and knew how to communicate it. Harvey had been running the Wine

Institute's public relations program for many years, so he also knew the key players in the business and the press. Perfect. So in 1980 I brought Harvey aboard with one clear objective: to help me get the word out.

By the time Harvey joined us, we had already established the foundation of our company image. First, through the quality of our wines, namely our cabernet and our sauvignon blanc. Second, through my travels around the country and abroad and through my habit of inviting chefs and restaurateurs to taste our wines side by side with the best of France, meaning such wines as Romanée-Conti, Pétrus, and the Rothschilds of Bordeaux. Third, for years we had been inviting the world's top wine writers to our winery to sit down to meals with us and taste our wines. This had brought us wonderful press coverage and public exposure. But I knew we had to go a lot further and so did Harvey.

"Bob Mondavi was the first person in the California wine business to use classic public relations techniques," Harvey recalls now. "Very early on, he and Margrit would bring press people in; Margrit made nice conversation with everyone, and the journalists were fascinated. First of all, many of the media people knew little about wine, and Bob was the first person to try to explain it to them. Also, the journalists loved the lifestyle and they loved the valley. And Bob Mondavi spoke for the valley. Therefore, he spoke for California, and therefore he spoke for American wine. Bob didn't know from press releases, and he didn't know a publisher's rep from a staff writer. But he was nice to everybody, and the journalists would keep coming back to the winery or they'd send their bosses. So media work early on was key to the creation of the Mondavi image."

That's true, but it was Harvey who built us something no one else in the Napa Valley had at that time: a professional public relations program, with a clear message, strategy, and objectives. This proved key to much of what we were able to accomplish during the 1980s. With Harvey's guidance and the position papers and speeches he wrote for me, I was now able to take articulate stands on the major issues facing the wine business.

"Bob wanted to be an industry leader," Harvey explains now. "He would discuss, publicly, what his dreams were, what was right for the industry, what was right for the premium wine industry. So he rose to the fore. And he had almost no competition. People like Louis Martini and Ed Mirassou, they were nice old guys, but they were more traditional agricultural people and they didn't talk much. The Gallos *never* spoke to the press. They thought they could create an image by advertising alone. But Bob Mondavi loved to talk. So when you went to an industry meeting, he'd be talking. And as the wines being produced in the valley got better, and as the reputation of the valley began to grow, who did the journalists call? And who do they still call thirty years later? Bob Mondavi. He is America's ambassador of wine."

Harvey's right. Few others wanted to speak out. And as he said, there were several very important issues and conflicts that we in the valley and in the wine business had to address, and I insisted on taking a leadership role. For instance, we had constant tussles over the important issue of "appellations of origin," formulations designed to help inform consumers where the wine in a given bottle comes from. For instance, we did not want wineries to truck grapes up from the Central Valley, crush them in Napa, and then claim on their labels that this was Napa Valley wine. Central Valley grapes were rarely as good as ours; we worried that inferior wine might damage our prestige image. In 1977, the federal Bureau of Alcohol, Tobacco, and Firearms (BATF) set down guidelines that established two types of appellations. One type was circumscribed by the official boundaries of a county or state. This posed few problems. A wine labeled Napa County meant the grapes came from Napa County and this carried no implications about quality. The second type of appellation was more troublesome. These could denote specific wine-growing regions, such as Carneros or the Stag's Leap area on the eastern side of the Napa Valley. These did carry implications about the quality of the wine in the bottle. When Warren Winiarski's wine from Stag's Leap Wine Cellars won the 1976 blind tasting in Paris, for instance, many people tried to gobble up a piece of land near to his. Did the name Stag's Leap belong to Warren exclusively? Or was it a wine-growing region, meaning other wineries could find a way to put Stag's Leap on their labels, too? Tim took charge of these very complex issues, and we worked hard to protect our brand names and the image of our valley. We worked no miracles, but I think we helped protect the consumers' confidence in the valley's name and in the quality of our wines.

Another controversial issue was growth in the Napa Valley. As the culinary revolution took hold and tourism in the valley boomed, many people were very concerned that we were going to become overdeveloped. They feared we were going to lose our beautiful landscape and pastoral quiet and wind up as a crowded, noisy tourist site. This came to a head in the late 1980s, when Vincent DeDomenico, a San Francisco businessman with a family fortune from Rice-A-Roni, decided to take an abandoned railroad line and create the Napa Valley Wine Train. The train, using old-fashioned cars restored to perfection, was to be a daily tourist attraction serving gourmet meals to tourists as it made its way up and down our valley and alongside our vineyards. The train touched off a furor in the valley. More tourists! More traffic! The damn train will honk and belch smoke all over our beautiful valley! There were angry public meetings, demonstrations, and sober debates about the future of the valley. Mike and Tim opposed the venture. Vince was a friend of mine, though, and I wouldn't oppose the train, provided it was done with taste and did not disturb either our operation or the environment of the valley. Vince never silenced the train's opponents, and while he ended up getting his project approved, state authorities refused to allow him as many daily runs up and down the valley as he requested.

Much more insidious, to my mind, was the anti-alcohol campaign that gathered force in America during the latter half of the 1980s. Prohibition had virtually destroyed the wine business and our valley once before in this century—I was damned if I was going to see it happen again. Yes, I knew that too many people, including many young people, were reckless in their use of alcoholic beverages and I was all in favor of programs to better educate the public. But I vigorously opposed the suggestion—bandied about by the temperance folks—that wine bottles, like cigarette packs, should carry a warning label about potential health risks. What nonsense! Wine was liquid food! Wine was healthy! We had plenty of medical evidence showing that drinking wine in moderation was good for the heart, the circulatory system, the central nervous system, and more. *That* should be on the wine label! And why should wine be thrown in, helterskelter, with hard liquor? Beer was the main beverage of choice among young people. What college-age kid guzzled fine wine as though it were beer? We had worked so hard, for so many years, to show people the health *benefits* of drinking wine in moderation; to my mind, any warning label would destroy everything we had built. Believing as deeply as I do in all this, I was not about to sit on my hands and see the image of wine savaged by neoprohibitionists or anyone else.

So one of my first steps was to hire a researcher, Nina

Wemyss, to put together for us a history of wine and its relation to culture, civilization, and health. Over the next two years, Nina pored through historical texts and traced the origin of wine back some six thousand or seven thousand years. The Greeks, Romans, and Egyptians all appreciated wine, and in our Western civilization wine has long been an integral part of our heritage, customs, and social and religious rites. Nina drew all this together for us, along with a history of some of the medical research done about the effects of drinking wine in moderation. Louis Pasteur, the great French scientist and researcher, found, for instance, that "Wine is the most healthful and hygienic of beverages." America's Thomas Jefferson was also a believer in wine and its healthful benefits. And many poets, philosophers, and scientists noted wine's positive, uplifting effect on the spirit. As Horace had put it in ancient times, "No poem was ever written by a drinker of water."

Once we were armed with the necessary facts and historical perspective, we at the winery launched a counteroffensive against the anti-alcohol forces. We called this the Robert Mondavi Mission Program. We took Nina's research and turned it into an educational videotape, which we then sent to more than a thousand people in the press, plus wine wholesalers, retailers, and restaurateurs. With Harvey Posert and several other key advisers, we organized a series of symposiums in various parts of the country to examine the history of wine and the latest medical evidence about its impact on the body and mind. We drew together leading figures from the fields of medicine, biology, sociology, religion, and enology. We emerged from the symposiums with a strong consensus from the authorities we consulted that drinking wine in moderation presented no health dangers in most people. "In moderation" was usually defined as two glasses of wine a day. To the contrary, there was evidence it could have a positive impact. As I used to emphasize at these gatherings, wine has been a part of civilized life for some seven thousand years. It is the only beverage that feeds the body, soul, and spirit of man and at the same time stimulates the mind. Of course we invited the press to our symposiums, in the hope of spreading the word to the general public.

I also helped spearhead the creation of an organization called AWARE, the American Wine Alliance for Research and Education. As the name suggests, the group brought together a number of highly respected experts from various fields, including the medical community, to do serious research related to wine. We wanted to generate and collect the absolute best information and research available regarding wine and its effects, short and long term, on the body, mind, and spirit.

Then, under the umbrella of our winery's Mission Program, we took a bold step. We launched a preemptive strike against those forces urging that warning labels be put on each bottle of wine sold in America. We put our own mission statement on every bottle of Mondavi wine. It read:

Wine has been with us since the beginning of civilization. It is the temperate, civilized, romantic mealtime beverage recommended by the Bible. Wine has been praised for centuries by statesmen, philosophers, poets, and scholars. Wine in moderation is an integral part of our culture, heritage, and gracious way of life.

This mission statement received extensive press coverage and helped galvanize our partners in the wine industry. In 1989 the industry was ordered to put warning labels on our wine bottles, but I think the different elements of our campaign helped blunt their impact on the consumer. After a time, the anti-alcohol movement lost some of its fervor. I don't think those forces were subdued forever; they were just turning the bulk of their resources and firepower against the cigarette industry.

Later, though, we received substantial support from new medical findings that highlighted other positive effects of drinking wine in moderation. Some studies suggested that wine, especially red wine, contained a certain element called resveratrol that seemed to be effective in lowering cholesterol. Other studies examined in depth the way the French and Italians eat and drink, and these studies produced some very interesting results. They suggested that wine in the daily diet, combined with meals rich in fresh fish, fruit, vegetables, and olive oil—the so-called Mediterranean diet— could be one of the reasons why many French and Italians had lower weight and lower cholesterol than most Americans. The French in particular, with all the butter, heavy cream sauces, and cheese they consume, plus their tendency to heavy smoking, presented an intriguing question: Why do their cholesterol levels remain generally below those of Americans? Why do even fat Frenchmen, smokers among them, show fewer signs of cardiovascular problems? Is it the wine? Yes, many people in medicine and science told us. Through AWARE and our symposiums, we even heard a term to describe these scientific findings: the French paradox. But few people outside our wine and medical circle paid any attention.

Until it happened.

In the closing months of 1991, CBS's *60 Minutes* and correspondent Morley Safer did a very thorough segment on the French paradox. Through interviews with reputable doctors, cardiovascular specialists, and epidemiologists in France and the United States, *60 Minutes* examined French eating and drinking habits and their collective physical health. The case they set forth was compelling. The French eat like horses. They eat all the "wrong" things, they smoke like chimneys, and yet they suffer far fewer heart attacks and other cardiovascular ailments than Americans of comparable age, weight, and habits. What gives here? Well, *60 Minutes* came away convinced: It was the wine. The show, of course, has tens of millions of viewers, and the very next morning we saw the impact: sales of red wine soared across America! I was elated. This was part of the gospel I had been preaching for decades! At last, people were getting the message!

CBS's French paradox segment, and the impact it had on our image and sales, are now part of the lore of the American wine industry. But there is a twist to the story few people know. Harvey Posert can explain it better than I can: "Experts in medicine and the wine business had been talking about the French paradox for a long time. It was known to us but not the general public," Harvey says. "When he was participating in our Mission Program symposiums, an anthropologist from the University of Pennsylvania named Sol Katz told us about Dr. Curtis Ellison, an epidemiologist who had worked at Harvard's School of Public Health and at the National Institutes of Health. We invited Dr. Ellison to share his knowledge with our Mission Program. Sol Katz and Ellison then made up their minds to approach *60 Minutes*. They convinced Morley Safer to do the story, and Dr. Ellison wound up being one of those interviewed on camera. The rest we know. Looking back now, I think it's fair to say that Bob Mondavi was really the father of that famous *60 Minutes* segment."

Well, the real point is this: I *knew* wine is good for you! I've known it all my life! And I had absolute faith that, sooner or later, I'd be proven right and we'd be able to get that message out across America and the world. And *60 Minutes* helped us do just that. But I can tell you, before that *60 Minutes* broadcast came along, we had quite a battle of it. Even within our own industry. When the anti-alcohol crowd started attacking wine, I believed that we should all stand up—with a strong, united voice—and defend our product and our industry. But few others wanted to join me; most people just wanted to duck their heads in the sand and hope the problem would just go away. Well, not me! Wine was as natural and healthy as grapes and sunshine, and I was proud to stand up and say so! This was an issue that demanded real leadership, and I was happy to carry the torch.

SUCCESS HAS ITS PRICE, and so, inevitably, does divorce.

My children were upset by my decision to divorce their mother, though they agreed that since we were not happy it would be best. They were also upset by the speed with which I went ahead and married Margrit. For a long time afterward, all three of them felt a certain resentment toward Margrit, and I guess that was understandable. On top of that, there had long been some rivalry between Michael and Tim. Mike is eight years older than Tim, and he started at the winery with me eight years before Tim. Their different temperaments — Mike the businessman, Tim the artist — didn't make it any easier. Michael tends to be outward and self-assured. Tim tends to be more inward and sensitive. This, in part, explains why Tim had some hesitations about coming into the family business in the first place. He was worried that he might not be able to express himself fully working alongside his older, more experienced brother. And he certainly did not want to wind up fighting with Michael, the way Peter had with me. So it was only after much reflection that Tim decided to come aboard. And when he did, it was still not easy—for either of them. Working under me and trying to cope with my tunnel vision and merciless demands for excellence, both Mike and Tim chafed from time to time, and on occasion they also clashed among themselves.

As in any company, we had our share of infighting. I wanted all three of my children to have a role in running the winery, but Marcia had married a financial adviser in New York and had decided to stay there. She came out regularly for our quarterly board meetings, but she did not want to be involved in the day-to-day operations and decision making at the winery. So that left Mike and Tim to vie for power and the eventual command of our growing organization. I tried several different leadership formulas. Tim in charge. Mike in charge. Both in charge, together. An executive committee in charge. Nothing really clicked.

I also had some other capable managers in my top management team. Cliff Adams had been at my side since the court case with my brother. Cliff was a young lawyer back then, and he helped prepare the case. Later he decided he was not cut out for the law, and he came aboard at the winery as one of my right-hand men. Cliff was hardworking and nononsense, and I entrusted him with several important tasks, including overseeing the construction of Opus One. Cliff loved power and jockeying for more, and that often put him at odds with Mike and Tim. Then there was Gary Ramona, also one of my right-hand men. Gary did a terrific job of directing our sales force around the country, and he was largely responsible for much of our growth over the years. In his twenty years with us, Gary played a role of great importance, and he earned my lasting respect and gratitude.

In any business, grooming your successors, especially if they are your children, is an essential and very tricky task. And, frankly, I did not do a very good job of it, at least not at the outset. As I said before, I was insistent that *everything* be done my way and only my way. As I learned, with difficulty, this is *not* the way to encourage people to spread their wings and fly. My view of good management was — and is — that you always deal openly and honestly with faults and problems. Put your cards on the table. No back stabbing. That's a fine philosophy — up to a point — but I made a serious mistake with it. In our group meetings, I would highlight faults and then upbraid the person responsible, even if it was Mike or Tim. I was unaware, at the time, of what I now call the humiliation factor. If you're going to give someone a dressing-down, especially your top managers, do it in private. Then they aren't humiliated and don't lose face with their colleagues and the people they are charged with leading. For many years, I was totally blind to all this. And it caused Mike and Tim enormous pain and anguish, sometimes to the point where they were on the verge of leaving the company. What to do?

Finally, at their insistence, we brought in a counselor. A therapist. We had wounds from our family relationships, going back way before the divorce, and we had wounds from the way we worked together inside the company. So Mike and Tim and I, and sometimes Marcia, began meeting regularly with the therapist. Sometimes we went away with him on family retreats, to get away from the constant pressures of the winery and do some really intensive work. Under his guidance, we worked hard to examine our family history and conflicts, and to open up some of those long-festering wounds and rivalries. I'm a pretty stubborn old goat, and it's not easy to make me change my ways, but the therapist did an excellent job. I didn't fully accept all his suggestions at the time, but they did help trigger some serious soul-searching that I carried into the years ahead. Over the past five or six years, several of his suggestions have sprouted up in me again. And now they make perfect sense!

Mike and Tim were able to bring a lot of their individual and mutual issues to the table and bring them into better perspective. We actually used three different counselors at various stages, and the results were so positive that Mike and Tim later hired a counselor to work full-time for the company to help us improve our management skills, decision making, and, above all, our ability to communicate within the company. Through this process, I think Mike and Tim gained a new maturity and a better understanding of how to work side by side with more efficiency and less strain. Together with the counselor, we also worked out a clear division of labor that enabled each of them to operate from his strengths and passions. Michael ran much of the business side, overseeing sales, marketing, and strategic planning. Tim took charge of all of our wine-making operations, from the vineyard to the bottle.

Their dual responsibilities extended from Oakville and Opus One to Woodbridge, Vichon, Byron, and, later, to our new joint ventures abroad in Italy, France, and Chile. Big jobs! Huge responsibilities! They both began to really spread their wings, and I think they both felt they had found, at long last, their rightful roles within the company.

But I still struggled with issues of control. Our work with the counselors had generated significant healing among the three of us, and I handed over the reins to Mike and Tim — with some conditions. If they failed to reach agreement on significant issues, our five-member executive committee would step in to make a final decision. Mike and Tim were not thrilled at that arrangement, of course, and the formula didn't work. Then I named them co-CEOs, and that didn't work, either. So Mike and Tim came to me and said, "Pick one of us and we'll agree to work together." Once I heard this, and I knew I wouldn't lose either one and they were willing to work together, I named Michael president and CEO. In turn Michael appointed Tim director of the winery and the vineyards for the whole global enterprise. This proved to be the ideal formula and both of my sons have responded beautifully.

From episodes such as this, I have learned many invaluable lessons, and I will set these forth in my final chapter. But what have I learned the harder way, through my own mistakes and failings? Even more! Yes, even more. Because mistakes are the best teachers we can have; they show us where and how we need to grow.

CHAPTER 14

The Gamble

WE DIDN'T SEE IT COMING.

In the 1980s, most of America was prospering, and the Napa Valley wasn't just prospering—we were booming. The number of wineries in the valley, the price of grapes, the price of an acre of good vineyard land, the number of tourists who came to visit—all these indicators reflected the strength of the valley's economy. And here's another revealing sign of the times. When a few of us started the Napa Valley Wine Auction in 1981, we managed to raise a total of $324,142 for local hospitals and charities. By 1989 the auction had grown into a weeklong event in the valley and one of the major dates on the calendar of the whole American wine business. Wine makers, wine merchants, and restaurant and hotel owners from all over the country pour in for the festivities and the wine and gourmet food. The take in 1989 was $850,000, and it would keep on growing. In 1997 we raised over $3 million! All for charity.

Margrit and I had a hand in creating the Wine Auction. One day, a friend of ours named Pat Montandon came to us with an idea. She wanted to raise money for the St. Helena Health Center and she asked Margrit and me if we would help her put on a wine tasting for the center. Pat was then married to Al Wilsey, and her plan was to hold the tasting at their beautiful estate in Rutherford. Instead of having only the Robert Mondavi Winery participate, Margrit and I suggested that we start an auction for charity, similar to the one the French hold annually in Beaune, and invite all the Napa Valley vintners to participate. Done and done. We invited the eminent wine connoisseur Michael Broadbent to be our first auctioneer, and we held the first event over three days at Meadowood Resort. Joel Grey came in to provide great entertainment. This first auction was organized mainly by a group of dedicated women in the valley—many of the men were very skeptical at the outset—but they did a great job, and thanks to them what began as a modest local fund-raiser, which I knew would be a great success, has now become a major annual event in the American wine industry, attracting hundreds of wine and food professionals and amateurs from all around the country. Everyone works hard to put up for auction the most outlandish, enticing events. One year Margrit put together a fabulous Roman dinner at our house, complete with a huge feast, fine wines, and everyone dressed in togas. Another year we put up for bids a week-long luxury trip to Italy, including a visit, led by Margrit, to my ancestral home of Sassoferrato.

The Robert Mondavi Winery continued to expand throughout the 1980s, especially on the central coast of California. During the 1980s, we acquired a thousand acres of vineyards down there, and in 1989 we bought the Byron Vineyard & Winery, which included upwards of fifty acres of prime vineyard property in the Santa Maria Valley, in Santa Barbara County. The winery was the creation of Byron "Ken" Brown, and it had earned itself awards and a glowing reputation, mostly on the strength of its Burgundian varietals, pinot noir, and chardonnay. Pinot demands special climate conditions — cool temperatures and sea breezes are ideal — and Byron had just the right mix. Ken stayed on to run our operation. In 1985 we also acquired a young winery that had been through some hard times: Vichon. Located near us in Oakville, in the foothills of the Mayacamas Mountains, Vichon was small, innovative, and committed to making high-quality premium wines, often using varietals that were not in the mainstream of Napa Valley wines.

To me, these were all very important investments. Along with Opus One, they expanded our product lines in strong, interesting ways, and they laid the groundwork for what we would later call the Robert Mondavi Family of Wines. With American demand for fine wines very high and growing, these additions fit nicely into our strategy of growth and diversification — but only within our field of expertise. These acquisitions were important for another reason: we in the Napa Valley were already feeling the impact of a new strain of phylloxera, one that was galloping through the vineyards at an alarming rate. Oakville and Opus One were hit, and so was Vichon. The vineyards at Woodbridge and Santa Maria, though, were seeing no such phylloxera infestation, and we felt that gave us some cushion, both financially and in terms of meeting our production goals.

But these acquisitions were costly, and the financial impact of phylloxera was not paltry, either. In fact, it was staggering. If you flew over a vineyard hit by phylloxera, you could see large pockmarks: whole sections of vines that were being shriveled and killed by those little beasts eating away at their roots. At Opus and some of our other vineyards in the valley, we used the opportunity to replant, using the denser four-by-four-foot vine spacing and better rootstock. After replanting, though, it would still take a vineyard three to four years for the vines to mature enough to begin producing grapes. Imagine the lost revenue! Imagine the cost of ripping out whole vineyards and replanting!

So in the early 1990s, we had serious problems on our hands. Some six hundred acres of prime vineyard that had to be ripped out and replanted, and we already had heavy debt and exorbitant operating costs. To meet our production goals, we still had to buy grapes from outside growers, and prices were very high in the valley: about $1,200 a ton! There was plenty of good news, though. From 1984 in particular, our vintages had been excellent, and our gross sales, from the mid-1980s to the early 1990s, climbed about 50 percent. In 1992 that took us to gross sales of $145 million.

So overall, we were doing very well, but we were facing stiff competition. We were now surrounded by about two hundred wineries in the Napa Valley, many of them making very high-quality premium wines. Worse, many of these wineries were not owned by individual families or single entrepreneurs; they were owned by huge, rich multinational corporations. For them to rip out a few vineyards and replant them was no big deal; it was pocket change. Many of those corporations were foreign-based, making the French, the British, the Canadians, even the Japanese major investors and landowners in our little valley. As the wine and culinary revolutions showed few signs of slackening, especially among upscale Americans, these foreign-based corporations were hungry for more holdings in the valley, and they had the financial muscle to put the squeeze on small wineries fighting for survival against phylloxera. So our competition was going to get even stiffer. The stakes were going to get higher, too. I could see that the world market for fine wines was going to explode. Japan was already a big importer of fine wines, as the Japanese were shifting away from their love of Scotch whiskey. Big market! And just over the horizon we could see China. One billion people! A 1 percent jump in their wine consumption could bring a huge windfall to a forward-thinking California winery!

So we decided to gamble.

Goldman Sachs, the investment firm, had been advising us for years. They wanted to take us public, put us on the stock market. But we had always resisted. We were a small, private family business and wanted to remain that way. So when Goldman Sachs first approached us, in about 1987, we declined. But they kept coming back. Frankly, we were a bit perplexed. "Why are you coming to us?" we asked them. "We're a small company and you're huge!" To me, their answer was very appealing:

"We want the best. We've picked you as the best in the industry, and we want to move forward with you."

I was in favor of the idea, but there was plenty of initial resistance in my family. We already had growing pains; why go public and expand even more? What would it do to the amiable family culture we were trying so hard to maintain in our company? We always put on a company Christmas party. At Easter, we always have a special breakfast for some of our staff. And at Thanksgiving, we always gave all our employees a turkey. If somebody hit a bad patch at home or came down sick, we gave them plenty of leeway. These were little things, perhaps, but they were not little; they were symbols of the same caring "extended family" spirit that I had learned from Cesare. What would going public do to that?

Another issue we worried about was control of the company. This to me was critical. In the Rainier days, I had lived through the hassles of having outsiders on your board. And I had watched those big corporations come into the Napa Valley, thinking that you could market and sell wine as if it were a breakfast cereal. Hire a fancy Madison Avenue ad agency, put together a catchy campaign, spruce up the packaging and labeling, use your clout with the big retail outlets to get your line a prime position on store shelves, and — presto! — you see a bump in sales and revenues. All along the way you do everything possible to cut costs. Trim staff. Hold down travel and expense. And, of course, you start cutting corners on quality. I could envision the little corporate accountant walking with me through our cellar.

"Lot of barrels here, Mr. Mondavi."

"Yup."

"They look new, too."

"Yup."

"What do they run new, Mr. Mondavi?"

"About $600 apiece."

"Really — $600? Wow! You've got thousands here!"

"Yup."

"Why are so many of them brand-new?"

"To produce better-quality wine."

"Yeah, but think of the money we could save if you used each barrel just a few years longer . . ."

The bottom line.

Big corporations often work on cycles of about seven years. They buy a company, bring their people in, and then work like dogs to boost profits. Short term. If they do brilliantly, do they use their profits to work for a higher-quality product? Rarely. More often, they turn around and sell the company as soon as they can, to cash in quick. But if, in those years, the big corporations do not see big profits, they might just throw in the towel and sell the company. Good-bye and good luck. I've seen it happen so many times.

You can't work that way in the wine business. Everything depends, first and foremost, on the quality of your product. Not for one year. Or two. Or even three. To build a reputation that will make people comfortable enough to spend $15 a bottle for a beverage for dinner at home — and double that and more at even a neighborhood restaurant — takes years of putting out a product of consistent excellence. Cut corners on quality? You might as well slit your throat. If one of your pricey bottles of wine comes to the table and tastes mediocre, that consumer will go elsewhere the next time. And maybe never come back. No, the wine business is built on quality first. It's build on personal relationships that take years and years to build. And, perhaps above all, it's built on patience. Patience with the wine, patience in the vineyards, and patience in the marketplace. It's a business built not on the short term but on the medium and long term. You can't think in terms of quarterly profits or even annual reports; you have to think in blocks of five years minimum (to replant a vineyard and bring it back). And to be really successful you have to think in blocks of ten years, twenty, even long enough to embrace the next generation. Now, show me one big corporation whose leaders understand and respect this kind of approach to business — and who have the brains and guts to sell it, long term, to their shareholders.

Show me one.

So maintaining control was key. But were there ways to

go public without our family losing control? With the help of Goldman Sachs, we studied this question for a long time. We looked at companies like Levi-Strauss and the New York Times, companies that were publicly traded but remained family controlled. We carefully looked at Chalone Vineyards, a Napa Valley operation that was already on the stock market. So we were very, very careful. I think we took four or five years to consider from every angle the issue of going public. And this all unfolded at a time when we had considerable turmoil at the top of the company. Cliff Adams was, in essence, running the company, and that did not sit well with either Mike or Tim. And there was dissension in the lower ranks of management as well. So that complicated and slowed our decision making as well.

Finally, we found a formula that we felt would work for us. We found we could issue two tiers of stock, each with different voting rights. Each share of family stock would carry ten votes. Each share of regular public stock would carry only one vote. If we held on to a certain number of family shares, we could always maintain control of the company. This convinced me. Through this formula, I believed we could maintain family control, excel at what we were doing, and still raise the cash we needed from the public offering. Under this formula, Goldman Sachs estimated that we could raise $50 million or $60 million, a sum that I felt would allow for our expansion and take a tremendous debt load off us at the same time.

I pushed my family hard to agree. My argument came down to this: Times were changing, and if we failed to change with them, we'd lose out. We had to find an effective way to raise money to deal with our phylloxera problem, while at the same time expanding up and down the state of California and diversifying our product lines. Michael agreed. Tim and, especially, Marcia took a bit more convincing. Finally, in 1993, though, we weighed all the issues — and the risks — again and then we decided: Let's give it a go.

From there, the whirlwind began. With Goldman Sachs at the helm, working with Hambrecht and Quist, we put together the necessary company profiles and financial history and then we hit the road to drum up interest in our IPO, initial public offering. Mike and Tim carried the biggest load, and along with Cliff Adams and Greg Evans they went to major cities, met the big investors, and explained our company philosophy and our outlook for the future. I joined in a few of these meetings, too. To make our points as clearly as possible, we put together a video explaining our history and guiding philosophy. The darn thing opened with a shot of me in the vineyards saying, "Ever since I was a child I wanted to excel . . ."

Then Tim talked about wine making and our commitment to staying on the leading edge of premium wines. He also emphasized our desire to take the techniques we had learned from making fine wines and use them to make wonderful table wines, available "at appropriate price points," of course. Mike then weighed in with a few words about our unique approach to selling wine:

"We don't sell wines the traditional way," Mike explained.

Constructing the winery was a real labor of love. We started building in 1966; though a lot of people said we couldn't do it, we brought in a harvest and made wine that very same year—before we even had a roof on the winery! *Courtesy Robert Mondavi Winery*

John Daniels, Jr., of Inglenook Winery (center) had long been a mentor to me and a source of inspiration. It was only fitting that Fred Holmes, one of my partners (right), and I offer John the first case of wine we ever produced.
Courtesy Robert Mondavi Winery

Wine to me is friends and family, high spirits and joy. Here, in 1969, we're celebrating the harvest and stomping a first load of grapes. But this is not how we make wine!
Courtesy Robert Mondavi Winery

Momma Rosa was my first mentor in matters of taste. She was always for me a source of strength and maternal wisdom. *Ted Streshinsky/ Photo 20-20*

At the Robert Mondavi Winery we developed a Great Chefs program to help educate people about nutrition and fine cooking. Thanks to Julia Child, shown here, and chefs like Alice Waters, Jeremiah Tower, and dozens of three-star chefs from France, we helped catalyze America's culinary revolution.

Faith Echtermeyer/Courtesy Robert Mondavi Winery

I love to talk. Give me an audience or a tasting (as shown here in my barrelroom with my son Michael [right]) and I'll cajole, proselytize, and spread the gospel about the joys and virtues of wine.

Courtesy Robert Mondavi Winery

Wine and the arts belong together. Along with our Great Chefs program, we created a tradition of holding Saturday night jazz concerts at the winery. Both of these lovely ideas were developed by Margrit Biever, the Swiss-born artist and creator who awakened me to the arts. *Courtesy Robert Mondavi Winery*

I loved the Baron (right), and I love his daughter, Baroness Philippine (center). All his life the Baron was a poet, a wine maker, a rebel, and a charmer. His daughter has the same spirit!
Courtesy Robert Mondavi Winery

In 1979 I joined forces in a noble venture with Baron Philippe de Rothschild of the Chateau Mouton-Rothschild, one of the great wineries of Bordeaux. Our aim: to create a world-class wine that brought together the best of France and California. The result was Opus One, a wine and winery, shown here, of distinction and flair.
Courtesy Opus One

In my travels I've carried the torch for the Napa Valley all over the world. In 1996 I had the honor of doing a bit of the same for the Summer Olympics in Atlanta. *Courtesy Robert Mondavi Winery*

A lovely reunion. In 1997 my sisters Mary and Helen joined Peter and me for a long, nostalgic lunch in our Vineyard Room. *Courtesy Robert Mondavi Winery*

Robert and Margrit in their home, Wappo Hill, in the middle of the Napa Valley. *Courtesy Luc Janssens*

Lucky me. My children, Tim, Michael, and Marcia (left to right), have stayed close to me and now have taken over the leadership of the Robert Mondavi Winery. Our future is secure and dazzling! *Courtesy Robert Gerometto/Photo 20-20*

Today I have a new challenge: the creation of the American Center for Wine, Food & the Arts. A world-class creative center to be headquartered in the town of Napa.
Artist's model courtesy of the American Center for Wine, Food & the Arts

In 1966, I began with only a dream and a vision. Today the Robert Mondavi Winery is a world-renowned institution and creative force. My path was simple: Follow your passion. Pour in your heart and soul. Settle for nothing less than excellence. And with enough hard work and faith in yourself, you can realize your dreams.
Courtesy Robert Mondavi Winery

"We sell wine through education. . . . And we don't sell wine just for wine. We sell it as part of food, wine, and the arts. We believe that people who enjoy fine food, fine art, fine music, also enjoy fine wines. But they also enjoy them more together." I was proud of them; they really had my gospel down pat! When we did the video, I was just about to reach my eightieth birthday, so they let me have the last word: "As I often say, 'Making good wine is a skill, fine wine an art.'"

With that video, and all the PR materials we brought along on these trips, we put on quite a dog and pony show, as the financial boys called it. And I think that video conveyed a very important message. We didn't exactly come right out and say it, but in a subtle way we underlined that while I was the founder and guiding spirit of the Robert Mondavi Winery, Mike and Tim were top flight and already in position to carry my mission forward. And this was accurate. By this time in 1993, I was still doing the world traveling, playing my role as the unofficial ambassador of the Napa Valley, and I had turned over the reins to Mike and Tim.

Well, sort of. I couldn't let go completely!

On June 10, 1993, we introduced our stock on the NASDAQ Exchange. We offered 3.7 million shares, at an opening price of $13.50 per share. We were quoted under the name MOND. An accompanying press release said the sale of shares would be used "to repay bank borrowings, to fund the expansion of the company's business, and for general corporate purposes."

Imagine how I felt the night we launched our public

offering. Proud? Yes. Nervous? A bit. Most of all, I felt amazed. Twenty-seven years before, with a huge vision and barely a nickel in my pocket, I launched the Robert Mondavi Winery. I began with a paid staff of three. I also began with only twelve acres of my beloved To Kalon Vineyard. Now we had vast holdings up and down the state of California. We had a reputation as one of the most innovative wineries in America, if not the world. We were fifty-fifty partners with the great Baron Philippe de Rothschild and his fabled Château Mouton. Our annual sales were approaching $150 million a year and climbing. And now we were making our bow on the NASDAQ Exchange, right beside Microsoft, Intel, and many of the hottest companies in Silicon Valley and the whole of America. Now, I thought, we're really on our way! Twenty-seven years of dreaming and backbreaking work were finally paying off. The son and grandsons of poor peasants from Sassoferrato were helping transform the eating and drinking habits of millions of Americans. We were living and embodying the Good Life, California-style, and we were building an empire in the process! How sweet it is, the American dream!

Yes, just imagine how I felt that night.

And just imagine how I felt only a few mornings later, when I awoke to discover that the price of our star-spangled stock had plummeted to a miserable $8 a share. We had taken an enormous gamble, one of the biggest of my life, and now it appeared to have blown up in my face. And worse was yet to come.

Yes, just imagine how I felt.

PART THREE

The Harvest

CHAPTER 15

To Be a Pioneer

THE CRISIS BIT DEEP.

I was just turning eighty years old. My company was in turmoil. My family was fit to be tied. With my relentless ambition and drive, I had pressed my sons and daughters to embrace the risk, take the gamble. Go public. Now what?

Go fishing, of course! What else would an easygoing, hands-off guy like me do? In truth, I did go fishing, but the trip did not turn out quite as we had planned. Two friends of ours, Bill and Evelyn Hall, had organized a wonderful fishing trip in Alaska, and we had eagerly agreed to go along. Bill was in the music business, with a very successful company he had built in San Francisco, and he and Evelyn also had a home in the Napa Valley. Vintner Clark Swanson and his wife, Elisabeth, other close friends of ours, were also joining us for what promised to be a marvelous getaway. A week of fishing and relaxing along the coast of Alaska, aboard a seventy-five-foot cruiser outfitted with four staterooms, a full crew, and our own chef. The full to-do. If I was headed to the poorhouse, this was going to be a lovely way to make the trip!

"We all met at the Napa Airport and Bob had on a very long face," Bill Hall recalls now. "He didn't seem to want to go. I immediately saw that something was wrong; Bob is usually such an up guy. I think it was Margrit who took me aside. 'The stock's gone down to eight,' she said. And that was all she needed to say."

A part of me didn't want to go; I felt like I was abandoning my own ship in a time of crisis. Well, we flew up to Alaska and for the next six days we were aboard that luxury boat, fishing, eating, exploring the fjords, and putting out crab pots at night. As I recall, we drank a bottle of wine or two as well. But you know what? We fished every single day and I never had a single bite. Not one. We had wonderful guides, and Evelyn Hall hauled in a seventy-pound halibut. And Margrit brought in a forty-four pounder! And me? Nothing. It's a darn good thing I'm not a very competitive guy, or else I'd have been plenty miffed! Anyway, day after day, I sat in the back of the boat, trolling and talking to Bill Hall. Actually, I talked and he listened.

"Bob loves to talk, you know," Bill recalls. "And for six days he never stopped talking. He needed to get it out and I was happy to listen. Here he had built this business and he was finally positioned to really grow, big time, and he went public for an injection of capital. It was a good business decision, I felt, but it wasn't working out as he had planned."

Bill understood the problem. Investors just didn't know what to think about the wine business at that time. After all, we're very capital intensive, and we're always at the mercy of the weather. One morning of frost early in the season or heavy rain at harvest, and—*poff!*—there goes a chunk of your crop—and a chunk of your profits for the year. Worse, there were only a handful of wineries that had gone public—Chalone and Canandaigua most notably—but there was still no solid industry track record to calm investors.

"I think this was more than a business crisis for Bob," Bill recalls now. "So much of Bob's life and family were wrapped into the business that this was clearly a personal crisis, too."

Day after day the investors on Wall Street remained skittish, and day after day more nervous tremors rattled through our company. Mike and Tim were on pins and needles, while Cliff Adams was in the hot seat, trying to anchor day-to-day operations. Questions and worries buzzed through our corridors. How were we managing the crisis? What could we do to reassure Wall Street? And who was really in charge and calling the shots? Legitimate questions, demanding clear, substantive answers. And where was I? Plunked in a chair in the back of a damn fishing boat off the coast of Alaska—and not even a bite to show for it!

Then one day, during a stop on shore, I got more bad news: our stock price had fallen even further, to a pathetic

$6.50 a share. Down to half its original value. I knew I had to move and move quickly, but I wasn't sure which way to go.

"As we trolled, Bob let everything out, business and personal," Bill Hall recalls now. "He felt that he hadn't spent enough time with his children when they were growing up, and now he was worried that he wasn't spending enough time with his grandchildren. And he was worried that he wasn't giving enough trust and responsibility to Mike and Tim. Cliff was running the company; was that fair to Mike and Tim? He also worried about how Mike and Tim were getting along between themselves. This brought his own problems with his brother, Peter, right back up in his face. Every day in the back of the boat, Bob went over and over all this, for hours on end, until finally he was talked out. Then, at night, he would sit by himself and write in a booklet he carried. He'd write page after page every night. It was very emotional for all of us, watching what he was going through. You could feel the emotion drifting all through the ship."

Yes, Bill's right; I did a lot of soul-searching that trip. I had one ultimate goal: find a way out of the crisis. I knew the company was as good as gold, but I had to take a hard look at what, if anything, we had done wrong in the company or in our decision to go public. At the same time, I had to look long and hard at my own strengths and failings, to see where I had slipped up and what steps I could take to set matters right. My life and my company, everything I had set out to accomplish, were now on the line, and I was determined to pour myself, heart and soul, into finding the right solutions. All I can say is, Thank god those damn fish had the good sense not to distract me!

I THINK THIS IS an appropriate place to talk about fear.

When I was a boy back in Minnesota, I used to love to roller-skate. The skates we had back then were nothing like the fancy in-line skates kids have today. They were metal contraptions that you strapped over your shoes and clamped onto your soles. You had a skate key you always carried with you, to tighten the skates to your soles and/or adjust them once you got out on the road. We used to tear up and down the street on our skates and I just loved it. The speed, the wind in your face, the feeling of total freedom you had when you built up a big head of steam.

I loved to swim, too. As I mentioned before, on Sundays in the summer, many of the Italian families in our little town of Virginia, Minnesota, would get together for huge family picnics at one of the many lakes outside town. I loved those picnics. The weather would finally be warm, there were always wonderful things to eat, and we kids would play hide-and-seek, organize marble tournaments, and, of course, we'd spend a lot of time swimming and horsing around in the water. The water was always very cold, but we didn't mind. Near the quarries outside town there were deep pits that stayed filled with water, and a group of us used to go swimming there as well. The water was cold and clear, and you could dive down and see amazing rocks—and you never knew what else you might find down there, too.

Here's my point: Momma Rosa and my father never said to me, "Don't roller-skate, Bobby; you'll hurt yourself." Or, "Bobby, don't go swimming by the quarry; it's too dangerous." They knew I was a good swimmer and they knew I'd be prudent. They had faith in me—and they communicated it. They did not communicate fear.

Looking back now, I realize how privileged I was to have a childhood like that, filled with adventure, a lot of freedom—and very little fear. In this, and in so many other ways, my parents, in their own earthy, knowing way, gave us a very strong foundation. I look back now and see five important life lessons that my parents communicated to me and my brother and sisters. Mother taught us, first and foremost, the power of love. Love, to her, was the most important ingredient—in life and in raising a family. Then she taught us the importance of nutrition, of eating a natural diet, meaning fresh, nourishing foods that were naturally prepared and well seasoned. Third, she and my father taught us the importance of hard work. We watched Dad work day and night at his business, and we watched Mother run the boardinghouse, cook marvelous meals, take care of her four children—and do it all joyfully and without complaint. Seeing them work so hard I know left a deep imprint on me. The fourth lesson they taught us was generosity. Both my parents were very giving people, with us and with the rest of our family, friends, and community. "Give freely; you always receive more in return"—this was an ethic that was never formally articulated to us because it never had to be; we saw it in action in our house every single day.

To these four lessons that they instilled in us, Mother and Dad added a fifth: Love without fear. They believed that the way to raise strong, confident children is with love and sharing—fear should have nothing to do with it. Yes, I was disciplined by my parents, when it was warranted, but never to the extent that it threw me off base or filled me with fear. When I went to church, and later when I went to school with the nuns, fear was used as a prod and a means of keeping you in line. And I realized that using fear they could break the spirit of even a strong-willed kid like me. Luckily, though, I came through all right. Nevertheless, I did come away from my Catholic training with a better understanding of the power of fear. And my long experience in life and business has been deepening that understanding ever since. So now let me say it loud and clear:

Fear can cripple you.

Unchecked, it can eat away your self-confidence. It can drain away your initiative. It can sow paralyzing doubt deep in your psyche. To succeed in life, no matter what your field, I believe you have to start with complete faith in yourself. You have to have the confidence to set yourself a goal and know that with hard work you will achieve it. You also have to have the confidence to properly handle failure. We all fail from time to time. People who succeed accept their failures, learn from them, and then move forward all the stronger. There's more. To succeed in business or in life, you have to have the strength to deal openly and honestly with other people, and not wring your hands, duck responsibility, or retreat at the slightest sign of incoming criticism. These are some of the basic qualities that anyone needs to succeed — and fear can cripple all of them. Fear of failure. Fear of criticism. Fear of risk. These are like those lousy little phylloxera mites that gnaw away at the roots of our grapevines. In a year or two, those little buggers can take a strong, healthy vineyard and reduce it to ruin; fear can do the same thing to men and women.

Fortunately, there are men and women who, like some of our rootstocks, seem naturally resistant to being eaten at by fear. They feel fear, of course, but the fear doesn't knock them off balance or eat into their core. During my eighty-five years and in all my travels around the world, I have met a lot of very successful people who seem to be naturally fear resistant. I think many of them share a common trait: by nature, they're very *positive* in their outlook. And they have an uncanny ability to stay focused on the positive. They've also learned how to roll with adversity, how to turn a negative into a positive. I think they do it by sheer force of will. It's as though they refuse to accept a setback; they take it as a challenge that stimulates them even further. And they *know,* deep inside themselves, that they can do whatever it takes to succeed, to turn that negative into a triumph. Joe Montana, for instance. Watching Montana play quarterback for the San Francisco 49ers, I always had the feeling that he had total faith in himself and his ability. Here was a guy who was *sure* he was going to lead his team to victory in the big game. He might not know exactly how, or on what play, but he knew, deep down, he would succeed. No doubt. And no fear. That's what it takes to be a leader. That's what it takes to be a pioneer.

I'm not Joe Montana. But at the age of eighty, when our stock plummeted, I had already been through my share of trials by fire. The breakup with Peter. The ensuing court battle. The lean years we had at the Robert Mondavi Winery. And that's just for starters. So even when our share price hit its low of $6.50, I was not consumed by fear. I was worried, sure. But I'd been seeing this all my life. At every stage, when I moved out front with some new innovation, people always said I was crazy. It'll never work. Another Mondavi folly. I'd heard it all before! And I had always confounded the doubters. Even in years of recession, we were always able to sell our wine. Yes, our stock price was down. But I knew that what we were doing was good. What we had was gilt edge, better than all our competitors. And quality always wins in the end. I was sure of that! I knew we'd emerge!

Still, I knew we had to make some serious changes in what we were doing. I knew we had to be bold and innovative. Doing nothing would be a ticket to disaster. So on the boat I talked and talked and wrote and wrote and tried to get down to the core truths, the ones that would point the way out of the crisis. One answer, as always, was more education. The wine industry was not highly regarded by the investment community. So I knew we had to educate them, show them we had the knowledge and know-how to build a strong, enduring business, based on a product line of the highest-quality wines, plus quality table wines we could sell in very high volumes. And we had to explain to them what we were doing globally. Opus One was a huge success; it had cemented our international prestige. Well, we had to make investors understand that Opus was only the beginning. We had to explain that we were going to establish other joint ventures of similar quality, in many parts of the world—something no other winery had ever done. I also realized that to get our message across we had to put on major presentations for the top stock analysts around America. We had to send a team to New York, Boston, and Chicago to put on first-class presentations, receptions, and tastings—all to show them, in the most visceral, penetrating way possible, what we were doing. I could see that these analysts were prima donnas. But they control huge blocks of stock, so they control what's going on. Well, we had to mount an effective campaign and take it right to them, and not just explain our approach but put our wines right in their hands! Let them taste, in their own mouths, our expertise and commitment to excellence.

"By the time Bob got finished talking and writing, I could see that he was fired up and ready to go," Bill recalls. "And his humor improved. It was as if he had made up his mind: 'I'm going to solve this sucker. And I'm not going to let it get me down!' And he didn't. In fact, what he wrote down was what he went back and did."

When I got back to Oakville, we moved aggressively on several fronts. Michael, Cliff, and Greg Evans went around the country and met with the leading financial analysts. And I went around and talked, one on one, with all sorts of people inside the company. Managers, personal secretaries, cellar staff, you name it. I wanted to find out, at the ground level and with my own ears, how the company was working, what we were doing well and what we weren't doing well. And I'll tell you, I got an earful. This proved to be one of the healthiest, most productive things I ever did. People needed to talk—and I needed to hear.

There was more. As I realized through talking to Bill on the boat, I also needed to set things right with Mike and Tim. I had not spent enough time with them when they were kids. And I had not done a great job of grooming them inside the company. Now was the time to do better. To make amends. Michael at this stage, in 1993, was fifty years old, and he had earned his stripes, in production, sales, marketing, and administration and finance. Tim was forty-two, and he had done a wonderful job improving the quality of our wines and overseeing our vineyards and wine-making operations—at Oakville, Opus, Woodbridge, and Byron. He, too, had earned his stripes. So the time had come—in fact, it was long overdue—for me to give them all the trust, power, and responsibilities they clearly deserved. I had to cut the cord; I had to let them fly on their own and see if they would soar.

Done and done. It grieved me to do it, because he had been so competent and loyal to me over the years, but we

finally asked Cliff Adams to step aside as chief operating officer. But I was not about to let Cliff go. I made him the first director of a new project, the American Center for Wine, Food
& the Arts, which I will discuss later on. Now it was up to
Mike and Tim to carry forth the multiple missions I had established for the Robert Mondavi Winery. I also made clear
that I hoped they would take us in new directions as well.

The move turned out to be just what the doctor ordered.
It took Mike and Tim a little time to get their bearings and
spread their wings. And, of course, when they slipped up or
slowed down, there I was to give them a prod. But the
change quickly proved to be very healthy. As hard as it was
for a while, the crisis triggered by the plummet in our share
price ended up giving us a wonderful opportunity to grow
stronger, both as a family and as a company. Out of this period of turmoil and introspection came a new confidence
and, I think, a welcome sense of healing.

Oh, yes. And another thing. The changes we initiated
inside the company also did wonders for our share price.
From that low of $6.50, we started to really climb. Into the
teens, the twenties, the thirties. By 1997 our share price was
firmly in the forties, and in early 1998 we moved up to over
$50 a share! With that, we were able to move aggressively to
expand our operations and landholdings in California and
to launch several exciting joint ventures abroad. As impor-
tantly, we've learned some vital lessons. Thanks to this trial
by fire, we all know now that we'll have our occasional ups

and downs. Rain in August 1997, for instance, hurt our chardonnay production and the market took our share price down for a while. But did that shake our confidence, our core faith in ourselves and our mission?

Ask Joe Montana.

TIMES OF CRISIS can give leaders and managers invaluable information — if they know what to look for and learn how to use what they see. A crisis tends to bring out the best in some people — and the worst in others. Mike and Tim handled themselves with great aplomb as we reformulated and implemented our response to the fall in share price. Marcia gave us sound input as well, and I think the whole episode brought wonderful experience and insight to our senior leadership team, consisting of Mike, Tim, Greg Evans, Martin Johnson, Mitch Clark, Mike Beyer, Steven Soderbergh, Pete Mattei and Alan Schnur. I'm sure I often sound as though I built this company single-handedly, and if I've left that impression, let me apologize and set the record straight. In truth, we may have started out in 1966 with a staff of three, but our fabulous growth since then has been the result of the hard work of the hundreds of people who have joined our extended family. Hell, I'm just a cheerleader now; they do the real work, day in and day out, and they do it with dedication and, yes, an unbending commitment to excellence. The Robert Mondavi Winery now counts more than nine hundred employees, and I can tell you this: it makes putting on our annual Christmas party one helluva night-mare! We have to do it in five different venues!

No, I haven't done this single-handedly, not by a long shot. And I can tell you this: that crisis over the fall in our share price brought out the best in someone very near and dear to me: Margrit Biever Mondavi. Bill Hall was there; he'll tell you:

"Throughout our week on the boat, Margrit was amaz-ing to see. Every day she'd be busy with some sort of activity and every night she would make pasta for all of us, from scratch," Bill recalls. "As I said, it was a very emotional time for everyone on the boat. But Margrit always kept her spirits high—and ours, too. And her faith in Bob never wavered. The more that people are around her, the more you see how much she's given to Bob."

Yes, Margrit is amazing. And she's been a godsend for me. By nature, she is a very generous person. At holiday times, I'll go out and buy for five people. She goes out and buys for a hundred! She knows all my faults—better than I do!—and yet she's always very generous and supportive in her love for me. Our offices at the winery are side by side. During the day, she'll slip me affectionate little notes, and she tells me she loves me at least five or six times a day! In response, I've become much more open and giving. I like what she likes. Ninety percent of the time, Margrit instigates what we do and where we travel. And I always end up lov-ing what she plans! I want to satisfy her, and I'll bend over backward to do so. And you know what? I enjoy it!

In the spring of 1980, when we got married, I felt my life was beginning anew. But I had no idea how profound the changes were going to be. In her shy, deft European way, Margrit removed my blinders, alleviated my tunnel vision, and opened me up to art, music, movies, and the spiritual side of life. In terms of wine, I created the style of wine making and built the business. But it was Margrit who turned our winery into a showplace for painters, sculptors, photographers, jazz and classical musicians, and the great chefs and wine makers of the world.

She was also a tremendous asset during my travels around the world. In Europe, everyone marveled at her. She was Swiss by birth, Italian and French by education, she had lived in Germany with Captain Biever, and she spoke perfect English to boot! Almost everywhere we went around Europe, Margrit spoke the language and felt perfectly at home. She's so genuine, so giving—everyone feels it. Cesare had taught me that business was first and foremost about people, and I had always tried to personalize my winery and our wines. Margrit brought whole new dimensions to this sort of personalization, and everyone in the world of wine loved her. That's why for me she's been a godsend. And often a shock: plenty of times now, I'm second fiddle!

My home life changed dramatically, too. Like me, Margrit is a doer. A high-energy, nonstop doer. And we're both early risers. If we have company coming for lunch, she'll be up at five to prepare and boil the chicken for the soup she wants to serve as a first course. Or she'll have me out on the tennis court at the crack of dawn. And she loves to ski. She loves to take a break from her work at the winery — and get me away from the place — and whisk us up to Tahoe for the weekend. Or before I know it, she has me packed off to Zermatt for a week in the mountains of Switzerland. I tell you, I thought I knew France and Italy — until I went there with Margrit. She'd take me to places I never even knew existed. And with her as my guide, orchestrating everything, it was like being in seventh heaven!

To celebrate our new life together, Margrit and I decided to build a house for ourselves. We found a superb piece of property, commanding the top of a hill above some of our vineyards along the Silverado Trail. Naturally, we called in Cliff May and asked him to design us something really special. He did. He came up with a vision that embodied the spirits of California, the Napa Valley, and our own conception of gracious living. It was ideal for living and entertaining, and it was like no other house we had ever seen. I love to swim and so does Margrit. So Cliff came up with an ingenious idea. He designed the house around one huge, open-feeling living space in the middle. With two levels. On one, there was an entryway and a relatively traditional living room, but spacious and airy and very California. A few steps down, there was an even larger open space with a rather unusual item in the center: a swimming pool. In clusters around the pool were different little enclaves, some with elegant lounge chairs, for swimmers to relax; others had small sofas and tables, ideal for intimate business conversation. Of course the house — and the money we put into it — were the talk of the valley for many years to come. Wags said that "the king and queen of the Napa Valley" had built themselves a castle, but I couldn't care less; I was ecstatically happy. And the best part is this: Margrit and I are learning from each other. And to do that, you really have to open your mind and your heart to the other person. The result? I'm happier today than I was the day I married her!

MARGRIT

When I first joined the winery, back on November 3, 1967, we were a very small staff. Often, at night, I was the last one working in our little retail shop. Bob would come by and ask for a bottle of wine. And I'd see how sweet he was. He was not sexy, really, but he was really very sweet. There were times when he spoke that he was endlessly repetitious. His view is that most people don't really listen, so you have to repeat yourself to make yourself understood. In the beginning, I found this annoying, but then I realized it was just his way. It was part of his eagerness to communicate and share. And I did admire him. He was a sharp dresser, always. He looked good; he took care of himself. And he was always very generous, with me and everyone else. He was not a big man, but he had this amazing presence and charisma.

Bob had a curtailed childhood. He never read. He never really played. Not golf. Or tennis. He doesn't know how to play cards. And he's totally helpless in the kitchen. We've been living together for seventeen years now and he still doesn't know where the coffee is. But this doesn't matter. None of it. Bob has class. So did his parents. Rosa and Cesare Mondavi came from the poorest of the poor — sharecroppers in rural Italy. But it didn't matter. They had about them a great nobility.

To really understand Bob Mondavi, to understand how special he is, you have to go to the movies with him. He's like a little kid. He gets so excited and swept up into what's happening in the movie that he actually talks to the screen. I'm not exaggerating. We'll be sitting in a crowded theater and he'll cry out, "No! Don't do that!" Or, "Look out behind you; he's coming! Oops. Well, I told you so!"

Bob is very disarming in his naïveté. He doesn't understand the theater. He doesn't understand art. He buys books and never reads them. I scan the newspaper for him. And when Bob does read, he moves his lips. With Bob, though, none of this is a liability. In fact, it is one of the keys to his success:

Because he is so naive and childlike, Bob is interested in everything. And he is totally open to everything. Like a child. So he's always free in himself to respond to new ideas and people. And this is one of the things that gives Bob his most important and most remarkable quality:

He's a man who can make dreams come true.

CHAPTER 16

The Future of Wine Making

THE OTHER DAY I had a real treat. I went back to visit what used to be the Sunny St. Helena Winery. That, of course, is where I first went to work making wine in the Napa Valley, way back in 1937. Six decades ago! Sunny St. Helena is long gone, but the shell of the old winery still stands, right on Highway 29 just before you reach the town of St. Helena. It's now the home of the Merryvale Vineyard, and it's been completely transformed. Inside that old shell is a bright, lively, modern winery. I was impressed!

Frankly, I was also a bit shocked. I went through the winery remembering where we had our old presses and fermentation tanks, where we had our little antique lab, and where we kept those old iron claws we used to use to punch and break up the cap that formed on the top of the wine. All I could think of was, "My god, how far we've come!" In sixty years, we have totally transformed American wine making. We've transformed our philosophy. Our equipment. Our

methods in the cellar. Our methods in the bottling line.
Our methods in the vineyard. And we've totally transformed
our approach to sales, marketing, and finance. Before my
very eyes, we've gone from the Model T to the Mercedes-
Benz and the Ferrari, and we're only now beginning to
understand the subtleties and mysteries that go into the
complex art by which we turn humble grapes into great
wine. Amazing!

And in the art of modern wine making, Tim Mondavi is
among the very best in the world. Since 1974 I have
watched Tim pour his heart and soul into learning how to
make great wine. He's gone all over the world in pursuit of
ideas, knowledge, and inspiration. And now he is taking us
in some very exciting new directions. Along the way, Tim
has created wines that have earned him a sparkling reputation, here and abroad. Most recently, in 1997, at a blue-
ribbon blind tasting in France, a group of distinguished
judges from England, France, Germany, and Italy set themselves down before an array of the finest white wines in
the world. Montrachet Marquis de la Guiche. Meursault-
Charmes. Chevalier-Montrachet. Nuits Saint Georges Clos
de l'Arlot. And more. Fabulous wines! And of all these great
wines of the world, Tim's Chardonnay Reserve came out on
top. We beat out the next two choices, Meursault-Charmes
and Montrachet Marquis de la Guiche, by more than a hundred points! Now I call that a triumph. And an outstanding
achievement for Tim and his team. To me, it was also an-

other indication, again on French soil, that we in California have not only joined the ranks of the best wines in the world, we're leading the parade! And as Tim will now tell you, we're just getting started. Am I proud of him? Nah!

TIM

I have some wonderful childhood memories.

I grew up on the Charles Krug ranch, with Mike and Marcia. And some of my earliest memories are of great meals around the family table. My mother was an excellent cook, and Dad was always there, tasting wines and having us taste them, too. One day we decided to turn the tables on him. We organized a blind tasting of our own, to see how Dad would do. We blindfolded him, and then set before him carefully measured samples of some excellent labels and vintages: Coke, Pepsi, Fanta, Royal Cola, and I forget what else. Actually, Dad did pretty well. He has a good palate. And we had a wonderful time putting him to the test.

I had great admiration for my grandparents, Rosa and Cesare. "Nonna" was warm, loving, always joyful with us, and, of course, she was a fabulous cook. My grandfather died when I was only nine or ten but he was unforgettable. He was a very short man. So short that when he drove his car, you couldn't see him; his head was below the steering wheel. So we called him the Phantom of the Vineyards. And I don't think I ever saw him without his stogie. By any standard, my grandfather was a man of honor and distinction. He was very quiet; in fact, he rarely said a word. But there was wisdom and something gracious in that. He didn't force people; he allowed them to come to his side. He was a man who conveyed confidence and inner strength. He was never petty. And though I was just a young boy, his manner with people conveyed to me an important lesson: Don't be judgmental. Be forgiving. Even to back stabbers.

In terms of our family's philosophy toward wine and business, I think my grandfather set out three wise and enduring guideposts for us all to follow. One, remember that wine is an integral part of any good meal. Two, always conduct your business in the most honorable way with respect for yourself and others. And three, always keep in mind the long perspective. My father followed those guideposts and then staked out many more as he built our winery and made it into the industry leader that it is today. With those to guide our path, Mike and I are now pressing forward with a whole new phase of development. We have two primary objectives, and they go hand in hand. One, to improve even further the quality of all of our wines. And two, to take what we've learned from our grandfather and father and use it as a foundation for developing more top-quality joint ventures in various wine-growing regions around the world.

WE ARE ALREADY transforming, yet again, the way we grow grapes and make wine. When I started working full-time at the winery in 1974, our reputation and methods had already been established by a series of superb wine makers, men and women who helped put the Napa Valley on the world map of great wines. Warren Winiarski. Mike Grgich. Zelma Long. Still, our main preoccupation in those early years was what I call "suppression of fault." We were processing the wines a lot with centrifuges and filters and correcting vineyard deficiencies by adding acid. We treated wine as though it were a frail damsel, and we had to rush to her aid. Same thing out in the vineyard. There our main preoccupation was also to suppress potential problems, be it mold, parasites, or rodents. The main thrust of our approach in both realms was scientific and technical; we felt science held the keys to making great wine. In my view, we were like doctors eager to administer antibiotics. These are strong medicines that do suppress illness, but they're harsh on the system, and, in the longer run, they don't do anything to invigorate the body or address the root cause of the illness.

Today we've embraced a profound philosophical shift. We no longer view grapes and wine as weak and vulnerable; we see them as intrinsically strong and healthy, as products of nature. Our main aim is no longer to suppress fault; it's to enhance the natural virtues of our vineyards, our grapes, and our wines. Our aim now is to work closely with nature, not fight against it. We treat our vineyards as complex ecosystems, with their own unique balances of soil, sunshine, rainfall, and varieties of plant and animal life. We work to nurture that ecosystem, not upset it. That means, wherever possible, we use no pesticides, no insecticides, no herbicides, no chemical fertilizers. In essence, we're saying: No more antibiotics. Let's look at our vineyards and wine making in a different way, a deeper way, a "holistic" way.

We call our new philosophy and methods natural farming. To understand what natural farming means in practical, on-the-ground ways, the man to see is Mitchell Klug. Mitchell manages To Kalon and all our vineyards in the Napa Valley. And he's a specialist in both resource management and nature conservancy. When you see him in action out in the vineyards, you realize that Mitchell is on a first-name basis with each of our vines and the people who care for them.

"We treat each block of vineyard individually,"

Mitchell explains. "Every block has its own manager and we try keep the same team of pruners on that block year after year. We do this for continuity and to give the team a sense of pride and ownership. And every vineyard has its own experiments going on, experiments that are specific to that vineyard."

Mitchell works like a holistic doctor. On an almost daily basis, he is busy out in the vineyards, examining the condition of their soil, their vines, and in growing season, the quality of their fruit production. After harvest, sometimes a given block will be tired or out of balance. "The vines themselves, through their output, will tell you how they're feeling—provided you know how to listen," Mitchell says. If a block is tired out, Mitchell will have the block team plant an appropriate "cover crop" around the base of the vines, to rejuvenate the soil. Cover crops, properly used, can provide much-needed nitrogen and other nutrients. Using this natural approach, we have no need to use chemical fertilizers.

Likewise, if Mitchell spots a potential infestation of insects that might attack the vines, he'll counter by introducing predatory insects that will eradicate the problem—naturally. Without insecticides. Mice and gophers are always a problem in the vineyards. The natural farming solution? We have erected hawk purchases and owl houses at various positions throughout our vineyards, to build up our hawk and owl populations. Then, instead of resorting to potentially harmful pesticides, we let the hawks and owls take care of the mice and gophers. Weeds? The quickest fix would be chemicals, but that is against all my principles and those of natural farming. So instead we plow between the rows of vines with a mechanical cultivator, using the fingers of the machine to tear out the weeds. This way we don't upset the balance of the soil nutrients that are nourishing our vines.

My exposure to France's rich wine-making tradition, through our Opus One joint venture, has also improved our practices in the vineyards. Now, in many of our properties, we use the close four-by-four-foot planting technique, so we "stress" the vines and force them to produce higher-quality grapes. Like Château Mouton, we also do summer pruning, to achieve the optimum number of grape clusters per vine. We are also more sophisticated in our weak-shoot removal and "canopy management," to make sure the fruit gets its full share of light, which enhances the berry character and balance of our fruit and wines.

We're also going many steps further to protect the ecology and the wildlife in our vineyard properties. For instance, to protect against soil erosion around our streams and reservoirs, we now plant appropriate shrubs and trees. We work closely with state and federal wildlife scientists to make sure we protect the fish and plant life in those streams as well. And we do our best to recycle natural waste materials back into our ecosystem. When my fellow wine makers and I have finished in the cellar with the seeds, stems, and skins from our grapes, we take their residue and scatter it back through our vineyards. It serves as an excellent natural fertilizer. And we have another nice touch as well in our natural recycling. To help control the spread of weeds and wild grasses, we maintain a herd of Nubian goats. They eat all day long, and from the milk they produce we make goat cheese that our chefs at the winery, in turn, use to crown our gourmet salads. Salads created, of course, from our own organic vegetable gardens.

"Ours is a natural approach, a holistic approach," Mitchell Klug explains. "No other winery is doing this level of research and experimentation. The layers of complexity we have added to our farming are exponential. And so are the costs. But in the long term, this will pay off handsomely in terms of the quality of grapes we'll be able to harvest, year after year."

This same guiding philosophy is transforming the way we make our wines. Again, we are working with nature, not against it. To see how this works, I need only take you to our Carneros vineyards, on the southern rim of the valley. As my father explained earlier, we believe in cold-fermenting our white wines. And he developed jacketed stainless steel fermenting tanks to do just that. He also pioneered a cooling system that chilled the white juice as it made its way to the fermenting tanks inside the winery. At Carneros, we use a very different system. Right next to the vineyard, we have built a very simple open-air shed. Inside the shed, we have installed our fermenting tanks. Instead of artificially cooling the juice after crushing, we do our harvesting late at night, when the temperatures in the valley are cool. Our crews in the vineyards hand-harvest the grapes from the vines into small bins, being careful not to burst or bruise the fruit. Tractors then deliver the bins to our fermenting shed. There, forklifts hoist the bins up and tip the freshly picked grapes into our presses, avoiding the crusher-destemmers of the past. Our current system is guided by gentleness. Our reds are destemmed directly atop our fermenting tanks. This way, the juice and skins gently drop, by gravity alone, down into the fermenting tanks. So at every stage, we are treating the grapes and juice as gently and naturally as we possibly can, to improve the ultimate quality of the wine.

Thanks to our years of investment and research, we have also developed effective ways to lower the use of sulfur in making our wines. Gone, too, are the days when we systematically used centrifuges and filters to cleanse the wine. Now we have ways to achieve the purity and clarity we want — without resorting to those sorts of treatments that often strip a wine of its character and vitality. In wine making, the balance between sugar and acid is critical. Twenty-five years ago, it was common practice to adjust that balance in the wine cellar by adding acid. Adding sugar is illegal, and adding acid is against my philosophy. So we work hard to get that balance right in the vineyard, by using rootstocks, varietals, and low enough crop yields that are properly matched to the vineyard's soil and climate. If we work carefully and harvest at the optimum moment, nature will give us the exact sugar-acid balance we want. That way, in the cellar we don't have to intervene much with the wine, only give it a gentle nudge or two and let the natural process of fermentation take its course.

With nature as our guide, in the wine cellar I have steered us away from relying too heavily on technology. What we learned in Burgundy and from pinot noir in the Napa Valley was this: respect for *terroir*, meaning soil and climate. This is the real key to making great wine. The art of wine today is a blend of science and technology, as well as the art and intuition of the wine maker. But the essence of great wine remains *terroir*.

Over the years I've learned that you have to learn to trust your own gut, your own judgment and intuition. For a long time, the American public — and many prestigious wine publications — seemed to favor big, bold cabernets. They also favored chardonnays that were heavy in oak flavor. Not me. I've always preferred wines that were more refined, wines of elegance, character, and finesse. And I always stayed the course and followed my own palate, which reflects that of my family. Now, to my delight, we're finding that American tastes have evolved, and our wines are now scoring well in international competitions — and enjoying popularity as well.

My father did a beautiful job of laying the groundwork for where we are going today. The stainless steel fermenting tanks he pioneered help us maintain even temperature control and avoid off flavors, and they're easy to clean. We still follow his lead in our maceration periods, leaving the juice in longer contact with grape skins to improve the richness and character of our wines and to add layers of flavor and complexity. I think these longer maceration periods have been particularly important in the progress we've made with our pinot noir.

In fact, our experience with pinot noir is the bridge to our future. It has had more impact on me than any other variety because of its sensitivity. It's a tender taskmaster that displays differences in soil better than any other variety. It demands low-vigor soils, a cool climate, proper clones and rootstock, low yield in the vineyards, proper balance of canopy with a precision and sensitivity that few other varieties demand. In the cellar, pinot noir demands gentleness in handling the fruit, minimal handling as a young wine, as few rackings as possible, and absolutely no filtration. It is also a variety that, when done right, can please the most sophisticated connoisseur and tantalize the novice wine drinker as well.

The lessons we have learned from pinot noir and its many demands only benefit how we handle each of our other varieties. The stoicism of cabernet has not demanded as tender a handling, as scrupulous a selection of site, as low a yield, or as gentle a finishing as pinot noir. But cabernet loves this kind of scrupulous treatment and, with it, displays its true character even more magnificently than ever before. So I'm sure pinot noir has inspired an improvement in all of our wine growing and has pushed our evolution from grape grower and wine maker to wine grower. This has given me a greater understanding of the importance of the land and appellations. If the site has such an incredible impact on character potential, then we have to capture these differences in *terroir* in a way that allows the grower, vintner, and consumer alike to understand through the wine what God has given us in our land. This appreciation of the land has led us to try to develop a logical overview for the evolution of appellations within the Napa Valley. Looking at each appellation within the valley and its specific characteristics adds interest and complexity in a way that makes sense and contributes to the rising interest in the Napa Valley. Here again we should learn from the lessons of Europe and, with a true American spirit, develop an appellation system that is better for the grower, the vintner, and the consumer.

There has never been a better time for wine in the world than now. We are learning from each other and I'm sure that trend will continue. One of the trends in Europe, which they have drawn from us, is to embrace technology. At the same time, we in America are embracing the reverence for the land that has long been one of the greatest characteristics of Burgundy. All over the world, wineries are improving their wine growing to the benefit of the consumer. Now, not only is the appellation, the vintner, and the vintage important, now the varietal is being expressed more frequently on European labels as well. So the consumer is receiving much more information and learning more than ever before.

In a similar way, we continue to learn from our experiences with Opus One and Byron and from our various joint ventures around the world. With the Rothschilds in Bordeaux, the Frescobaldis in Italy, and the Chadwicks in Chile, we learn from each other, we share information, and the result is better wines and a deeper understanding of the art and spirit of wine. Yes, the Robert Mondavi Winery has grown far beyond the little winery my sister used to worry about protecting. Today we are a large, multi-faceted operation, joining together to make different wines that enhance different meals and occasions. The result is a very dynamic and exciting synergy. In quality terms, we can reach for the stars in Oakville and at Opus One, and we can take a broader approach at Woodbridge, where we are producing nearly six million cases of wine a year. But our experience with one enhances our performance with the other. And as I've said for twenty years, I'm glad for every drop of wine we touch, because it's a learning experience that allows us to better understand the essence of wine. And with every new year and harvest, and every region we work in, we gain new knowledge and expertise. So we remain a small family business, but we have much more ability than ever before.

The Austrian philosopher and educator Rudolph Steiner had a lovely saying. "If you hear, you forget.

If you see, you remember. If you do, you understand." I think that applies to what we are doing with wine. Here in California, and through our many joint ventures, we are doing and understanding more and more about the subtleties and mysteries of wine. And I think we are really learning how to allow the soil and climate of a particular region to express themselves naturally through the medium of wine. That is our goal for the future, that is our vision. And I think many people who understand wine are coming to understand our approach. Recently, in London, I heard the finest compliment I think we've ever received. A journalist from Britain spoke to me during the launch of Luce. He said he had tasted our pinot noirs from Carneros, our Byron wines from Santa Barbara County, and our wines from Italy, Chile, and the Languedoc. And he said, "You know, your wines really do reflect great things of their origin. They reflect the best that their land has to offer. They reflect their origins and they do so with strength, finesse, and balance. And these are the virtues I've come to associate with Robert Mondavi wines." I thought that was a lovely compliment and perfectly in line with our guiding spirit.

Luce embodies this spirit. Italy, of course, has a special meaning for our family, and in the early 1980s my father was already thinking about going to Italy to make a great wine. In the ensuing years, I went to Italy frequently, to visit different regions, taste their wines, and get to know the leading wineries. Others from our winery made the same sort of exploratory trips. The more I traveled and the more I discovered what I liked in Italian wines, the more my passion grew for one region: Tuscany. Florence, of course, is perhaps the highest expression of Italian art and culture, and the soil, climate, and grape varietals of Tuscany seemed to me ideal for the kind of wine I wanted to create in Italy. What really clinched it for me, though, was a day I spent in the vineyards with a remarkable man: Vittorio Frescobaldi.

Vittorio is the patriarch of the Frescobaldis, one of the most respected noble families in Italy, with a 700-year history in the wine business. The Frescobaldis own several wine estates in different parts of Tuscany, but their crown jewel is Castel Giocondo, in the region of Brunello. Vittorio took me to Castel Giocondo one day, and as we walked around the property, he talked about his family heritage, his philosophy of wine making, and about the estate's marvelous soil, climate, and exposure to the sun. I could see and feel his passion for the land, and I could see that passion expressed through their wine. I must say this all really swept me off my feet. Talking with Vittorio; his brothers, Leonardo and Fernando; and his son Lamberto, I could see many synergies between our two families. I felt certain we each had a lot to offer, in terms of lineage and experience, to a joint venture. Then there was the wine they were making there in Montalcino. It's just incredible wine. So my mind was made up, and from then on, I went back and forth to Italy frequently, to move the project forward.

The result was Luce, an ultra-premium wine that Lamberto and I created to express both the richness of the Montalcino soil and the elegance and refinement that our two families bring to the art of wine making. Luce della Vite, which means "light of the vines" in Italian, is a subtle blend of sangiovese and merlot grapes. And it was Margrit who came up with that wonderful name. We age it in French oak for one year and in *botte* (large Italian casks) for six months. We launched Luce in the fall of 1997 and it was an immediate success. Our initial production was a modest two thousand cases a year, and the retail per bottle price was about $55. We sold out right away. Now we plan to bring out a more modestly priced version called Lucente, and in the coming years we intend to join with the Frescobaldis and build another estate in Montalcino. As with Opus One, both families entered this fifty-fifty joint venture with the same objectives: make a wine that will stand with the best in the world, and have a great time and make money in the process. We're doing that and, as with Opus One, both families are teaching each other a lot about the art and business of wine.

"We understood the Mondavis right away," says Leonardo Frescobaldi, who handles international marketing for Frescobaldi wines. "And I think they understood us. We teach them about our vineyards and our style and process of vinification. They're teaching us about American production techniques and marketing. They're brilliant marketers."

I only wish my grandfather Cesare were alive to see what we're doing in Tuscany today. When he left his peasant roots in Sassoferrato and set sail for America, I'm sure he never dreamed that one day his son and grandsons would be in a wine-making partnership with one of the most distinguished aristocratic families in all of Italy. But I know he'd be absolutely delighted. Absolutely. If you were to apply the context of his day, he might at first say, "Good gosh, what are you doing? I wanted to come to the land of opportunity. So why are you going back to Italy and its closed situation?" But a lot has changed in Italy, and I'm sure that if he saw Italy now and what we are trying to do, my grandfather would say, "Absolutely right. You're carrying on the spirit of discovery that Rosa and I had when we left for America in the first place!"

The way I see it, Michael and I now have the

good fortune to build on what our grandfather and father did before us. My grandfather came to America and infused us all with his spirit of discovery. And he made us keep in mind that wine was a natural part of any good meal, bringing people together in a spirit of sharing, and that in growing grapes we should stay as close to nature as possible. My father built on that philosophy and added to it his own drive and virtues: his unbending passion for perfection, his commitment to be The Best, and his insistence on always searching beyond America's borders for ideas and inspiration. On top of these two layers of foundation, Michael and I now have the responsibility and joy of building on the past and taking the best of the past and refining it for the future.

You know, sometimes people ask me what it's like to grow up in the shadow of a giant like Robert Mondavi. I never looked at it that way. From my vantage point, I wasn't growing up in the shadow of a giant. I was growing up on the shoulders of a giant. I could feel Dad's strength beneath me, and from that lofty perch, I could look out on the world and feel free to follow my passions and embark on my own adventures and dreams.

What more could I ask for?

CHAPTER 17

Globalization

MICHAEL

Now that my brother, Tim, has explained the future of wine making, it's my turn to discuss how we intend to build on my father's business success. I can almost hear Dad saying, "Michael, talk about our commitment to passion, perfection, and common sense!"

With Tim and Marcia, I grew up on the Charles Krug ranch. And from junior high through college, I spent every holiday and every vacation working at the winery. Before I was eighteen, I would work in the shop or in the laboratory, and when I turned eighteen it was legal for me to work in the cellars. So over a period of about nine summers, I did everything, from vineyards to maintenance, to the lab, and then to the cellars and wine making. My senior year in college, in 1965, I worked the harvest at

Krug. Santa Clara University was on the quarter system, and I had no classes on Wednesday. So during the harvest I commuted back up to the Napa Valley on weekends and on Tuesday afternoons. Then on Tuesday night and all day Wednesday and again on the weekends, I was in the cellar learning how to make wine. I had no idea that the following year, after graduation, my father would be starting his own winery and I'd be helping him make the wines.

Growing up, I had few doubts about my direction in life: after my schooling I was going to work at the Charles Krug Winery. That, in fact, was the plan. After graduation, Dad was going to make arrangements for me to work at one of the top châteaus in Europe. And for six months to a year, I'd learn their methods of wine making. Afterward I was to go to London and work for Harvey's, the great wine merchants. At the end of anywhere from a year or two in London, I was supposed to come back and go to graduate school, to get an MBA. By 1969 or 1970, I'd be ready to begin working at Krug. Needless to say, come November 1965, when my father and my uncle Peter had their fight, all that was thrown out the window.

So instead of apprenticing in Europe and going on to business school, I went straight into the wine business, right at the start-up of the Robert Mondavi

Winery. And what an education this turned out to be. In the beginning, we had only three paid employees: Dad, Bill Hart, and me. Bill was great. He had loaned my father some money to get him started, and he insisted on being paid only minimum wage. And Bill told us he had only one other condition on his loan: "That I can help you sweep out the joint."

In many ways, Bill became my mentor. He loved fine wines. And he had a great wine cellar. He had a lot of half-bottles of wonderful Bordeaux wines. First and Second Growths. And he had one of those traditional black lunch boxes. Bill and his wife, Ina, did a tremendous amount of entertaining. They'd hold a dinner party and the next morning Bill would come to the winery with some of the leftovers: fabulous cheeses and pâtés, and he'd bring along a wonderful bread. He'd also bring along a half-bottle of a fine Bordeaux, such as Château Lynch-Bages. The half-bottle always fit perfectly in his lunch box, where the thermos usually went. So a fine wine like Château Lynch-Bages constituted part of what we called our "brown bag lunch." Bill would open one of these great bottles of wine, and then with our brown bag lunches—Dad was usually off doing something else—Bill would teach me about some of the great wines from Bordeaux.

Not all the lessons I learned, though, were as easy and pleasurable to absorb. My father always set the standards incredibly high; perfection was always his goal. We all worked incredibly hard to meet his standards, but we often fell a bit short. And then my father would nitpick. The leg of lamb my mother would prepare for dinner. "Gee, Marge," he'd say, "it was great but . . ." And then he'd go on for twenty minutes. "Gee, Peter, this wine is wonderful but . . ." It took me probably eight or ten years of working with him to understand: he wasn't picking on you; he was measuring everything against the image of perfection that he carried in his mind — but had never experienced. Once you understood that, you could relax. Because instead of arguing with Dad about something, I could say to him, "Have you ever tasted a wine yet that is as good as this one?" And he'd say, "No." I'd say, "Great. Let's be happy about that. And *now* let's attack the perfection. But let's not tear everybody up without, first, conveying what's *positive*."

At Krug and then at our winery, my father was always the leader. He drove it. There's no question about that. He has an enormous energy and capacity to work, and he instilled in us his relentless drive. But just as perfectionism has an unhappy underside, when carried to extremes, so does that relentless drive. Year in, year out, Dad would spend months on the road, doing business and promoting our wines. Often he'd be on the road for two, three, sometimes even four weeks at a time. This was very hard on my mother. She always had her hands more than full with the house, the kids, and the various things she'd be doing at the winery. It was exhausting for her. I remember when I married Isabel, my mother gave me some very good advice, and I knew it came straight from her heart: Take time off. Make time for your wife and children. There's more to life than work.

Over the past few years, since Dad passed the baton to me, in terms of the CEO position, a very strange thing has taken place in our relationship. He went from being my boss — and not my father — to being my father and mentor. And this has been wonderful. I can have discussions with him now that would have created a huge fight before. We can have a good, positive dialogue, and if he starts to balk at something, I can point out this and this and this, and he'll say, "You know, you're right." Or he'll say, "I don't agree with you." But it is in a dialogue, not an argument. That's new. For years, he didn't listen. I probably didn't, either. There was no malice; he was just oblivious. He had blinders on so he could focus totally on what he was doing. Ironically, that was one of the reasons he was so successful. It's different now.

We meet regularly, usually for early-morning breakfasts, and we can talk easily and openly about specific
decisions and the larger directions Tim and I want to
pursue. And Dad gives me guidance and the benefit
of his own experience. It took a long while, and all of
us went through some very painful times, but I think
we're really maturing now, both as a family and as a
company.

Our globalization started, I believe, from my father's
quest to learn how to make wines better. All the time
we were growing up, he was always tasting wines.
Not just the wines of Charles Krug, the Napa Valley,
or of California, but wines from around the world.
And he wasn't tasting them to say which is better. He
would taste these wines to study them, to say, "What
in this wine is the soil? What is the climate? What is
the grape variety, or the clone of that grape variety?
What is the pruning technique? What is the art of
the wine maker?" In essence, he was asking, "What
do we have to learn from the way this wine is made?
And how can we improve on it?"

Through these tastings, he made me and all of us
aware of the global aspect of wine. I had the pleasure
and luxury of going to Europe in 1961, the year before my father did; and Bill Hart, who had traveled
there extensively, outlined an itinerary for my friend

Peter Stern and me to follow in Europe for three months. At, literally, $3 a day. Peter is now a wine maker and consultant for the Golan Heights Winery in Israel, as well as for wineries here in California. On our trip, we were able to visit the top growths and top wine producers in Burgundy, Bordeaux, the Loire, Germany, and Italy. We were very enthused about all this — and, of course, about being kids going through Europe and being independent, at the age of eighteen.

I came back and kept telling my father, "You gotta go. You gotta go." And the next year, 1962, he did go. Because what they did there — the way they made wine and the way they planted their vineyards — was *totally* different from anything I had ever seen growing up at the Krug ranch. And when I grew up there, and the same with my brother and sister, the winery and the cellar was our jungle gym. The cellar master, Mike Bertolucci, was our baby-sitter. We'd have a baby-sitter at home, but we'd say, "Bye. We're going to the winery." Which was all of seventy-five yards from our house. Mike would make sure we didn't get hurt, but he would also teach us about the winery. So through our formative years, just by osmosis, you do pick up a lot. That, plus what I saw from working at the winery during the summers, made what I saw in Europe all the more surprising.

There was another seed for our later globalization. My father at one stage hired a fellow named Henri Conch. Needless to say, he was a Frenchman. My father used to say that red wine ran in this man's veins. Red French wine. Henri represented Krug wines in the eastern part of the United States, to teach people about the wines and get them to buy the wines. But the other part of his job was to help teach my father about the great wines of the world. And at lunch or dinner Henri Conch would order very good French, German, and Italian wines, and my father would order Krug and other California wines. Then they would taste and compare. They usually did this on the East Coast, but periodically Henri would come back to California and he'd bring some wines with him. That's when I'd get a chance, periodically, to be in one of those tastings. When I was a ten-, twelve-, or fourteen-year-old kid.

My father, Henri Conch, and others would always be talking about wines in other parts of the world. Then in about 1970, a financier in Seattle, Washington, contacted us because of our association with Rainier. He was putting together a financial group to invest in Australia. My father had visited Australia with a man named Reverty Kent, a former employee of ours at Krug who had decided to return to Australia and become a wine consultant.

As my father explained earlier, Reverty took Dad through the wine-growing areas to teach him what the Australians were doing. They went to most of the traditional wine areas, but there was this new, unexplored area for wine in western Australia, about a hundred miles south of Perth, and Reverty took him there as well. The region was called Margaret River. As Dad said, there was a retired doctor there who had planted a small vineyard, and Dad tasted some of his wines. He said, "Well, the wine making isn't great, but I can tell there's good opportunity here because of the character of the grapes." Later, for a different project, we agreed to be wine consultants. Tim and I went back and forth to Australia to help the joint effort to improve the wines, plant the vineyards, and set up the business plan. But the partners in the project started to battle. We ended up being Henry Kissingers, trying to mediate between them, rather than being wine makers. The Australians finally bought out the Washington State investors and for us, that was that.

But we came away with some very important lessons. One, there were great opportunities in other parts of the world. Especially in the Southern Hemisphere since you can do twice the research because of the growing cycle difference. In addition, we learned something very important: The most valuable thing we had was our human resources. And our time. We didn't have the time to take three or four weeks a year and focus on developing an Australian business. We were going through very dramatic and formative growth at Robert Mondavi, and we had to devote 100 percent of our attention to developing and growing it. So we said, "Let's slow down." A couple of years later, when Baron Philippe contacted my father and asked if he would do a partnership, my father's response was—and I think very wisely—"No, we're too small. We're just a baby. We're just getting started. Thank you, it's a real honor that you would even consider us. Could you wait awhile?" The Baron essentially waited almost ten years before both sides finally decided to join together in a full partnership and create Opus One. And so through all this, we learned another valuable lesson: patience.

During this period, Dad and Tim and I talked about expansion. Our first expansion was outside the Napa Valley in 1979, when we acquired what is now our Woodbridge Winery in Lodi. A few years later, we acquired the Santa Maria Vineyard, to supply grapes to Woodbridge. But in doing the viticultural research, we realized the vineyard could not only supply Woodbridge—it could also produce world-class Burgundy-style wines. The more we would expand in other regions, the more we would learn. We knew a little bit about growing grapes and making wine in Napa, but over in Lodi it was different, so we had to learn more. In Santa Maria it was quite different, so we had to learn even more.

We felt that within California and on the West Coast, we could probably expand and do everything internally. But then when Dad, Tim, and I talked about getting involved in other wine-growing areas, we really embraced the Baron's philosophy. Which was: Work with a local partner. Let's face it: the Rothschilds didn't need additional money to do something here in Napa. They also had the expertise; their team, after all, had done Château Mouton, Mouton Cadet, and their other petit châteaus. So they had the money. They had the human resources. There's no reason why they couldn't have done what every other winery had done historically up to that time: just buy a winery or a vineyard wherever you want and own it 100 percent. Or as much as the local country will allow you to own. Baron Philippe, on the other hand, said, "I want a fifty-fifty partnership. Because I don't know the local culture. I don't know the local history. I don't know the local people. And those three will make the difference between producing wine and producing great wine."

So Tim and I have, essentially, adopted Dad's zest for learning about things around the world and the Baron's philosophy of fifty-fifty and working with local, talented, passionate people who share the same philosophy and values. It's not as easy to do a partnership. It would be a lot easier to appoint one or two of our key people and say, "Go over to Chile. Or go to Italy. Or go to France. And we think this is the best area, so research all that and then we'll buy this and we'll develop a winery there. Or we'll buy a château and we'll develop it." That would be, from a management standpoint, less risky. Because you have total control. And it's less time-consuming, because you don't have to negotiate and develop rapport and relationships with partners. But we think this approach would be qualitatively demeaning, and it would take you thirty to forty years of the learning process to begin producing truly great wines, if you do it independently. If, however, you do it as a partnership, especially with families who have a good long history and who are passionate and active families, then you can do something in a very short time that will, from a quality standpoint, shock people. Luce, with our partners the Frescobaldis, and Seña, the ultra-premium wine we're producing in Chile with the Eduardo Chadwick family, I think are perfect examples of doing thirty to forty years' worth of independent growth and quality in three to four years.

When we started selling our wines all over the world, sometimes we would talk about the Napa Valley being in the global wine business. To me, that was a misnomer. Robert Mondavi was a local winery that thought locally, grew locally, produced locally, and sold globally. We weren't a global company — we were a global *marketing* company. To be a truly global company, I believe it's imperative to grow and produce great wines of the world in the best wine-growing regions of the world, regardless of the country or the borders. There are wonderful wine-growing areas in the Southern Hemisphere as well as the Northern, and in the eastern-bloc countries there are going to be some phenomenal opportunities, once the political situation settles. In China, the opportunities are also going to be amazing in the future for growing world-class wine.

In terms of globalization, our experience in Italy and Chile has taught us that you can go way beyond cabernet and chardonnay and pinot noir and sauvignon blanc. In Italy, for example, the sangiovese, the nebbiola, and the pinot grigios — the grapes that are more traditional and typical of that country — all make for very interesting wines. In Chile, as in the United States, what you find is essentially European varieties, and these make up most of the wines we call Caliterra. But Chile has one unique variety that

I think will become the signature wine of that country, and that is a wine called carmenera. In the early 1850s when many of the traditional French cuttings were brought to Chile from Bordeaux and Burgundy, just a few years before phylloxera ravaged Europe, they planted these traditional Bordeaux varieties together. Then phylloxera wiped out Europe. In the replanting of Bordeaux, they decided not to replant carmenera, because in the cooler Bordeaux climate they couldn't get the grapes to grow productively. In Chile, where it was a little warmer, the vines thrived. Up until about 1993, everyone thought their merlot and carmenera were all merlot. It wasn't until my father and others were looking at the vineyards and saying, "Wait a minute. These aren't clones of merlot; these are different varieties." So they brought in experts and discovered this was that old grape variety from Bordeaux that no longer exists there. It produces a wine of a different character and style from either cabernet or merlot. Now it's one of the key ingredients in our new wine, Seña. The largest single variety in the new vineyards we're planting with the Chadwicks in Chile is carmenera. We'll have probably the largest plantings in the world of this variety.

This is a tangent, I know, but I think it illustrates this point: Each country or wine-growing region should have a variety that excels there and is some-what or totally unique. The sangiovese of Italy, the cabernet of France, the red zinfandel of California, and the carmenera of Chile—and the eastern-bloc countries, too, have many fine varieties that are not traditional French varieties but will make great wines. I think part of the globalization is not to give the public just more of the same, but to give them wines that reflect the culture of the country, reflect the soil and the unique grape varieties of the country. We could be just like the Mars candy company if we wanted to be, and in forty or fifty countries around the world produce exactly the same style and character of cabernet. And call it Cabernet, all under the same label, like M&M's or Snickers. We'd rather celebrate individuality and diversity.

There's another element in this approach, too. Every time we've dealt with the Frescobaldis, for ex-ample, I've learned a dramatic amount. In working and spending time with Philippine de Rothschild, it's the same thing: you learn. And you don't have a negotiation with them; you have a *dialogue*. What is so beautiful about a fifty-fifty partnership, even if it takes more time and care and feeding than a majority-control situation, is that it forces you to sit down and have a dialogue. And you'll never have a situation where one is the bully and the other is the beggar. And that's far healthier, because through that dialogue there usually emerges a far better solution for both partners.

In the Languedoc region of southern France, where we're producing Mediterranean-style wines under our Vichon label, we don't yet have a local partner. But the key word is "yet." We'll find the partner, and it will be a family with the same values and passion that we have. It will be a family that will enrich us with their own history and expertise in grapes and wine making. In the Napa Valley, we've been making wine for 150 years. The Frescobaldi family is thirty generations in the wine business. In Chile, they've been making wine for four hundred years, and the Chadwick family started in the wine business in about 1858, when our forefathers in the Napa Valley were just getting started. The Chadwicks have five generations in the wine business. So the Robert Mondavi guys are the babies in these partnerships, and you know what's neat? We'll probably *continue* to be the babies. I stress this with our management team. Because if we admit that we are the younger partner, we'll keep our eyes open, our ears open, our noses open—and our mouths *shut*. And we'll learn more.

And this makes for a better partnership. Too often the gringo comes in on the big white horse and says, "I know better than you. Make it." Our attitude is we know a little bit about growing grapes and making wine in the Napa Valley. We know a little bit about marketing, mainly in the United States but also a bit globally. We want to work with the local partner and learn from the local partner. I like to say that we become schizophrenic partners, in the best sense. One minute we're the teacher, and the next minute we're the student. If only one is the teacher, it's no good. There's no winning. But if you keep going back and forth between being student, teacher, student, teacher, that gives you a great learning— and winning—partnership.

Our relationship with the Frescobaldis is a perfect illustration. They've survived for thirty generations. Now I'll guarantee you that not all thirty of them have been milk and honey. There's undoubtedly been turmoil and all. But they are surviving as a family, and each member of the family now does his own thing but each is involved in the business and *supporting* the business. We need to learn from our partners not just how to grow grapes and make wine and sell wine. We can also learn from them how to manage our family, on one side, and then, totally separate, how to manage our business successfully for the very long term.

This is the real wealth we've gained from working with our wonderful partners around the world. We're always enriching our understanding of other peoples and other cultures. When we sit down with Vittorio Frescobaldi, we don't talk about just grapes and wine. We talk about life. Love. Communication. Philosophy. Together we're not just cultivating the soil and cultivating a business venture. Through the medium of wine, we're cultivating something much deeper, much richer. As my father likes to say, "Wine is something larger than we might imagine. Wine is passion. It's family and friends. It's warmth of heart and generosity of spirit. Wine is culture and refinement. And wine is the very essence of civilization and what we mean by the Art of Living."

Yes, what a marvelous education we've all had. The Mondavis and the Frescobaldis and the Chadwicks and the Rothschilds have all learned so much from each other. And what greater legacy could our families leave to our children and their children and all their children to come?

CHAPTER 18

The Feast

HOW FAR WE'VE COME.

Listening to my sons, Mike and Tim, talk about their plans and aspirations, seeing their confidence and maturity, I realize how far we've come. And I know that the future of the Robert Mondavi Winery is in strong, capable hands. They are taking my dream, building on it, and adding their own layers of heart and soul, expertise and vision. We're making wonderful wines, wines that stand proudly next to the very best in the world, and by golly we're just getting started!

Now that Mike and Tim are in command—and doing a great job—I'm free to spend more time immersed in my next great adventure: the American Center for Wine, Food & the Arts. This is an idea I've been brewing for quite a long time. It started back in the late 1980s, when I began thinking about creating a small wine museum on the grounds of the Robert Mondavi Winery. I envisioned a place where we could display wine-related art and artifacts from the Napa Valley and other wine-growing regions around the world. At the same time, I wanted to have a few educational exhibits that would show people how the history of wine goes all the way back to ancient Egypt, Greece, Rome, and the Bible.

From this modest idea, a larger vision started to take shape. To help people better understand and appreciate fine wine, we decided to develop interactive displays to show the general public how we make wine and what we do in the different seasons of grape growing. We also began developing some creative exhibits to help teach people the basics of the art of tasting. This led us, of course, into the realm of food. We have our Great Chefs program, and we work closely with the famous hotel school of Cornell University and the esteemed Culinary Institute of America. So we began thinking about creating a demonstration kitchen for our cooking classes and our seminars with Cornell. We also do some joint research with the enology department of U.C. Davis. So why not include in our center a state-of-the-art research lab?

From the beginning, I had always envisioned the Robert Mondavi Winery becoming a creative haven for wine makers, chefs, food lovers, and artists from many different fields. Margrit had taught me the importance of marrying wine and the arts, and this new center, I realized, could help us do just that. So we started thinking about including the arts. Margrit and I are big supporters of the Napa Valley Symphony, our local opera group, and various art programs in our community. So with a group of experts we had brought in as consultants, we began exploring plans to include in our center a small hall for concerts, lectures, and large wine tastings. And there was more. Margrit holds art appreciation classes at the winery for local schoolchildren. What could we do along those lines? Then there's another one of our favorite local institutions, the local farmers' market. The town of Napa, too, could use a helping hand; it has never prospered in our boom times the way St. Helena and Calistoga have. Was there some bold, innovative way to draw all these noble causes together under the same umbrella?

My response was an enthusiastic "Yes." Out of these differing ideas — and out of my own commitment to give something important back to our community — came the idea of creating the American Center for Wine, Food & the Arts. The idea, in a nutshell, was this: Build a world-class center for the arts in the town of Napa. The center would turn the Napa Valley into an international crossroads not just for wine and food, but for painting, sculpture, music, dance, photography, graphic design, and arts education for children. The hub, the magnet, for all this creative activity would be an architectural landmark as stunning as Opus One, to be located in the town of Napa. The building would house artistic activities and, at the same time, become a popular tourist venue that would stimulate economic renewal in the town of Napa. To give the center added dimensions, we planned to surround it with lovely gardens, an experimental farm, and a small, very exciting school for the arts.

To get this burgeoning, multifaceted dream off the ground, we created a board of directors, with my daughter, Marcia, as a member. Then we went out and enlisted the support of many prominent valley residents, including Judge Thomas Konsgard, Julia Child, Alice Waters, Francis Ford Coppola, and the distinguished film producer David Wolper. To get the ball rolling, I contributed some start-up funding and began an intensive fund-raising campaign, with the aim of opening the center within the first year of the new millennium.

Creating a vision is one thing, though; turning it into a reality is quite another. When we first unveiled the project, we met with plenty of skepticism and resistance up and down the Napa Valley. Another Bob Mondavi folly, some people were quick to say. The valley's biggest ego trip, others chimed in. Ah, the naysayers, always nipping at my heels! We've persisted, though, and slowly, patiently, we've earned broad public support for the American Center for Wine, Food & the Arts. So now we're moving forward full steam. Peggy Loar, the director of the project, has put together a strong team, and we're working hard to convince some of the top vintners in the state to join us as founding members. Education, as always, is the key. Now people are finally starting to realize that this center — unique in the world — will be good for the valley, good for our children, and it can turn the Napa Valley into a world-renowned gathering place for wine makers, chefs, food lovers, and prominent artists from around the globe. It's a noble idea and vision, and I'm pouring my heart and soul into making this center a reality. And I'm sure the result will be another enriching step in the evolution of the Napa Valley and in the quality of life and culture in America.

YES, HOW FAR WE'VE COME.

On a recent morning, I did something I rarely do. I got up very early, as always, and after a swim and a light breakfast with Margrit, I went for a long walk in the vineyards. When I set out, the air was fresh, the sky was a stunning blue, and as the sun peeked up over the mountains, the To Kalon Vineyard was spread before me in a blaze of majesty and color no painter could achieve. I've lived and worked among the vineyards of the Napa Valley for sixty years, and yet every single day I remain awed by the beauty of this landscape and by the power and rhythms of nature, by the way vines that are bare in February will bring forth grapes that we can harvest in September and turn into fine wine — wine that I know will mature with age and for years to come brighten our meals, nourish our health, and enliven our spirits.

By nature, I am not an introspective man. All my life I've been a doer, a builder, a creator. Even now, I still charge forward and rarely look back. And yet there are some days, like this one, when I do slow down and pause to reflect. And then I'm just amazed by all we've accomplished. In 1965, when I first came to To Kalon at the age of fifty-two, there was no winery here. There was no Opus One across the way. There was no one in California making wine that could rival the very best of France. There was very little market in America for fine wine. There was very little tourism in the Napa Valley. And across most of America, there was next to no awareness of the joys and nutritional benefits of fresh, natural cooking or the benefits of drinking wine in moderation. Yes, how far we've come. How much we've learned along the way.

People often ask me, "Bob, what are the secrets to your success? What are the biggest lessons you have to share with people who are starting out or trying to remake their lives?" Well, as I've tried to illustrate in the preceding chapters, in my philosophy of life there are some basic tenets that I believe lead to success in business — and in almost every other life endeavor. To succeed in business or in life I don't think you need fancy schooling or highly technical expertise. What you need is common sense, a commitment to hard work, and the courage to go your own way. This is the necessary foundation. On top of this foundation, there are fifteen other qualities that have served me well, and I think of them now as the basic components of my philosophy for success:

- First and foremost, you must have confidence and faith in yourself.
- Second, whatever you choose to do, make a commitment to excel, and then pour yourself into it with your heart and soul and complete dedication.

- Third, interest is not enough—you must be passionate about what you do if you want to succeed and have a happy life. Find a job you love and you'll never have to work a day in your life.
- Fourth, establish a goal just beyond what you think you can do. When you achieve that, establish another and another. This will teach you to embrace risk.
- Fifth, be completely honest and open. I never had secrets. I would share my knowledge and experience with others if they would share with me. I always had confidence that there was enough room for all of us.
- Sixth, generosity pays. So learn to initiate giving. What you give will enrich your life and come back to you many times over.
- Seventh, only make promises and commitments you know you can keep. A broken promise can damage your credibility and reputation beyond repair.
- Eighth, you must understand that you cannot change people. You might be able to influence them a little, but you can't change anyone but yourself. So accept people the way they are. Accept their differences and try to work with them as they are. I learned this late in life, and it is amazing what peace of mind I found when I finally understood it.
- Ninth, to live and work in harmony with others, don't be judgmental. Instead, cultivate tolerance, empathy, and compassion. And never berate people, especially your children, in front of their cohorts. This can be dispiriting and

damaging to them, and it's counterproductive for you. As I've learned, if you want to teach someone to fly, you don't start by clipping his wings.

- Tenth, human beings experience the same thing in very different ways. Two people can live through the exact same experience and come away with totally different understandings of what happened. So between people there is always a large space for misunderstanding. Always be alert for misunderstandings and tread lightly, especially when it comes to politics, religion, or moral standards.

- Eleventh, it is very important that we understand one another. We need to learn how to bridge those spaces of misunderstanding. To do this, listen carefully, and when you talk, be sure people understand you. On important issues, have people repeat back to you what you've said, to make sure there are no areas of confusion or conflict.

- Twelfth, rarely will you find complete harmony between two human beings. But if you find it, maintaining this harmony requires individuals or soul mates to have complete confidence in one another. Make time to be alone, to share experiences and appreciate together precious moments and the beauty of life. Open all of yourself to that person—emotionally, physically, spiritually, and intellectually. And always, always leave time for playfulness and laughter. There is no better tonic for keeping love alive and vibrant than laughter and good cheer.

- Thirteenth, in both life and work, stay flexible. Whether

in a country, a company, or a family, the same holds true: Dictatorship and rigidity rarely work. Freedom and elasticity do.

- Fourteenth, always stay positive. Use your common sense. And remember this: America was built on the can-do spirit and will continue to thrive on the can-do spirit.
- Fifteenth, out of all the rigidities and mistakes of my past, I've learned one final lesson, and I'd like to see it engraved on the desk of every business leader, teacher, and parent in America:

The greatest leaders don't rule. They inspire.

ALL OF THESE LESSONS I learned from my own experience, and on the morning I walked through To Kalon I realized that many of these lessons came directly from what I've learned from growing grapes and from my lifelong probings into the mysteries of making fine wine. As I often say, "Making good wine is a skill; making fine wine is an art." I believe the same is true of life. Living a fine life is an art form. And learning this art requires time and patience and passion, and I believe that learning the art of life also requires a heart that is not constricted by fears or prejudices but is open and accepting and filled with compassion.

Yes, what Petronius told us two thousand years ago is absolutely right: "Wine is Life." Wine has certainly been the core of my life, and it has been a brilliant teacher and mentor; the deeper I probe into its nature, the more I find I have to learn. We have made enormous progress in our understand-ing of wine, but we are only now beginning to understand its inner workings and inner beauty. Perhaps the same is true of life. After sixty years in the vineyards, I know I still have a lot more to learn. But this much I know for sure: Wine holds up to our eyes light and color that no man could create. In its essence, I believe that wine holds out to us all the order and wisdom of nature and of God himself, if only we have the patience and faith to pursue all the mysteries and truths waiting inside.

And this I also know for sure: Wine has in it a touch of magic. The simple, pleasing sound of the pop of a cork is enough to announce the beginning of the happiest moment of daily life: the gathering of family and friends around the communal table. To share the fruits of our labor. To share our heartaches and our joys. To put aside our worries and our fears for a while so that we can celebrate the bounty of nature and the greatest riches of being alive.

A *tavola!*

What warmth and joy I feel when I hear those two little Italian words. A *tavola!* To the table! Even now when I hear them I can hear Momma Rosa calling the family together; I can see her emerging from the kitchen with a steaming bowl of fresh pasta or one of those wonderful homemade soups she used to make. A *tavola!* and I can see my father pouring wine, and I can see Mary, Helen, Peter, and me taking our seats at the family table, ready for the best moment of the day. A *tavola!* and I can see Mike and Tim and Marcia when they were little, rushing in and taking their seats around Marge and me at the family table. A *tavola!* In those two magical words I hear tradition, I hear sharing, I hear generosity of spirit, and I hear all the warmth and conviviality of a big, boisterous Italian family.

And so it remains right to this day. This morning I was up long before the sun, and after an early breakfast I headed to the winery. As usual, Mary Azevedo — my personal assistant, trusted adviser, and traffic cop — had my day beautifully organized, and I put in a full morning's work, part of it with Paul Chutkow, the writer who has been helping me bring this book into being. At the stroke of noon, though, it was time for "A *tavola!*" and Paul and I joined Margrit and Tim in our Vineyard Room for some rest, relaxation, and the high spirits that great food and wine inspire.

As usual, lunch was a true family affair. All the wines we drank were, of course, Mondavi. Some of the vegetables came straight out of our own organic gardens. And our master chef was Annie Roberts, Margrit's gifted daughter. Even the elegant little menus showing the day's fare had the family touch: they were designed and decorated by Margrit's own artistic hand. This was the Good Life, Mondavi style, in the idyllic setting of the little family winery we had built from scratch thirty-two years before. Now, at the age of eighty-five, what more could I ask for — beyond, of course, my ritual afternoon massage? As I often say: Everything in moderation—with a few glorious exceptions!

Lunch today was wonderful. We started with a generous slice of salmon, served with baby asparagus on a bed of frisée and flavored, ever so delicately, with a champagne shallot vinaigrette. To complement the salmon, we had a 1996 Robert Mondavi Napa Valley Fumé Blanc, served chilled by Hubert Verdeille, the resident Frenchman who for years has run our Vineyard Room. As usual, Tim and I swirled the wine in our glasses, tasted, and then began appraising.

"I think we've made a lot of progress with Fumé Blanc," Tim said, holding his glass up to the light. "In the beginning, we wanted to create a sauvignon blanc that reflected the Napa Valley, as opposed to, say, Sancerre or Bordeaux. Fumé Blanc is a little bit richer than Sancerre. The Napa Valley is an area of sunlight, it's an area of good soil, and we have the ability to mature the fruit. So Fumé Blanc should be a richer wine, with the brightness of sauvignon blanc, and this wine does that. But it does so in a way that is more refined and elegant than ever before. It's not a poor man's chardonnay. It is its own very proud wine, with a natural acidity that is very vibrant and that whets your appetite for a meal. I think this is the best Fumé Blanc we've ever made."

Margrit agreed. "Fumé Blanc, to me, is the wine for which the Dungeness crab was invented. It's a wine that has kept its promise all these years, and I think this 1996 vintage is an especially wonderful example of all its great qualities.

The fruit speaks very strongly. This wine is totally balanced, and it has this aroma that makes it wonderful to drink. It's an invitation for more. Frankly, Bob and I drink much more Fumé Blanc than we do chardonnay, because we find it is the epitome of the best."

Tim and Margrit wondered why so many American wine drinkers overlook Fumé Blanc in favor of chardonnay. "People like what they're accustomed to," I suggested. "It's like the farmer who kisses the cow. If that's all he's had, God bless him. But we know there are other avenues to explore."

This is my life. This is what I've worked so hard for all these years. Fine food and fine wine bringing everyone together around the table, joined in happy celebration of two pleasures that are so universal that any barriers of personality, language, or culture just naturally melt away.

As a main course, we had grilled flank steak, served with a slightly piquant green salsa. With it, arranged lovingly around the plate, were garlic-roasted baby red potatoes, a roasted red pepper, and baby green beans. The steak was tender and flavorful, and it called out for our 1994 Napa Valley Cabernet Sauvignon Reserve. The marriage was magnificent! And tasting them together recalled to me one of the happiest memories of my life.

"Both these wines," I said, "remind me of that day when I had lunch at La Pyramide in Vienne back in 1962. Now, after all our years of effort, we are finally getting the gentleness and harmony in our wines that I had first encountered at La Pyramide. And here I have to compliment you, Tim. For twenty-four years I've watched you nurture your passion for wine and evolve as a wine maker. And all I can say is, thank God we were able to keep you and Mike in the family together. Because with you in charge of wine making and Michael as president and CEO, we have a marvelous future. Now you've worked things through and you're helping one another. That is called maturity. That is called wisdom."

"Bob," Paul said, "I think I've finally come to understand your philosophy of raising children and grooming them to take over the winery."

"Really?" I said. "What's that?"

"It's called 'stressing the vines'!"

We all had a good laugh at that. Including me!

During the course of the meal, Paul couldn't help but wonder: What would Cesare think of the Robert Mondavi Winery today? He had been the son of a poor sharecropper and now, just a generation later, his son was in a partnership with the family of the Baron Philippe de Rothschild and the Frescobaldis, one of the oldest and most respected noble families in Italy. And there was more. Cesare had made his own wine in little wooden tubs; now the Robert Mondavi Winery was one of the most sophisticated winemaking operations in the world. And it was pioneering new techniques for growing grapes and making premium wines on a large scale, with an annual production of six million cases a year.

What would Cesare think if he could see this all today? My father would be very proud of what we're doing and of how far we've come. He'd be amazed, I'm sure, at the progress we've made with our wines and our business. Much of it would be unbelievable to him. Yet he knew that in America we as a family had a wonderful opportunity; that's why he came here. Dad always had great faith in America. And he had great faith in the power of hard work. So I know he'd be very pleased to see that we're taking advantage of all the opportunities America has to offer. I hope one day my grandchildren will say the very same thing!

For dessert, we had a lovely crowning touch: a home-made blood orange sorbet, served with fresh strawberries and a sugar cookie. With it, we had one of my favorite dessert wines: the 1996 La Famiglia di Robert Mondavi Moscato Bianco. This is from our new series of California-grown Italian varietals, and it was wonderful—light and fruity, with a touch of bubbliness. It was a combination I think even La Pyramide would be proud to serve. Afterward, Annie came out of the kitchen and took her bow. Deservedly so; I imagine even Momma Rosa would be proud of her!

Yes, this is my life. It's a daily feast. With Margrit at my side and with our children and their children around us, life is a continuous Harvest of Joy. It's been a true pleasure for me to share my life and passions through the course of these pages, and all I can add is this: The next time you come to the Napa Valley, come see us; our doors are open. In the meantime, I hope the Mondavi spirit has proved infectious, and that now when you gather around your own family table, you will feel everything that we do when we hear those two magical words:

A tavola!

Acknowledgments

I want to acknowledge here the great contributions of people in the wine media who, through their support, have helped us and the California wine industry. First must come Marvin Shanken of the *Wine Spectator*. Marvin has been quite interested in us over the years, and his tireless work for wine in America has moved our industry years ahead. He is truly a standard-bearer. When we were starting out, Robert Balzer played an important role, as did Hank Rubin, Frank Schoonmaker, Alexis Bespaloff, and many others.

The support we received from English wine writers and authorities helped us get recognition in this country and even more overseas. Hugh Johnson, primarily, and Michael Broadbent, Cyril Ray, and Jancis Robinson come to mind. Others—I'm going to miss some, unfortunately—are Jim Laube, Frank Prial, Gerald Asher, Dan Berger, Andy Blue, Robert Parker, Terry Robards with the *Wine Enthusiast*, and Pierce Carson.

To all of them, mentioned and unmentioned, I salute you!

—R.M.

Index

ROBERT MONDAVI

1995

Coastal

CABERNET SAUVIGNON

NORTH COAST

ALC. 12.5% BY VOL.

LUCE

1995

B Y R O N

1 9 9 4

RESERVE

1994

NAPA VALLEY

CABERNET SAUVIGNON

RESERVE

UNFILTERED

1 9 9 5

RM

1979

OPUS ONE

A NAPA VALLEY
RED TABLE WINE

PRODUCED AND
BOTTLED BY

Robert Mondavi

ROBERT MONDAVI

Baron Philippe

BARON PHILIPPE DE ROTHSCHILD

CALITERRA

RESERVA

1995 VALLE CENTRAL
CABERNET SAUVIGNON

LAFITE

LUCENTE

Carneros

1995

ROBERT MONDAVI

CARNEROS

CHARDONNAY